SHAKESPEARE SURVEY

SHAKESPEARE SURVEY

AN ANNUAL SURVEY OF
SHAKESPEARIAN STUDY & PRODUCTION

10

EDITED BY
ALLARDYCE NICOLL

Issued under the Sponsorship of

THE UNIVERSITY OF BIRMINGHAM
THE UNIVERSITY OF MANCHESTER
THE SHAKESPEARE MEMORIAL THEATRE
THE SHAKESPEARE BIRTHPLACE TRUST

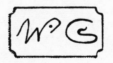

CAMBRIDGE
AT THE UNIVERSITY PRESS
1969

PUBLISHED BY

THE SYNDICS OF THE CAMBRIDGE UNIVERSITY PRESS

Bentley House, 200 Euston Road, London, N.W. 1.
American Branch: 32 East 57th Street, New York, N.Y. 10022

Shakespeare Survey was first published in 1948. For
the first eighteen volumes it was edited by Allardyce
Nicoll under the sponsorship of the University of
Birmingham, the University of Manchester, the Royal
Shakespeare Theatre and the Shakespeare Birthplace
Trust.

Standard Book Number: 521 06423 6

First published 1957
Reissued 1969

*First printed in Great Britain at the University Press, Cambridge
Reprinted in Great Britain by Stephen Austin & Sons Ltd., Hertford*

EDITOR'S NOTE

For the next, the eleventh, volume of *Shakespeare Survey*, the central theme will be the 'Last Plays'. The twelfth volume will be concerned particularly with 'The Elizabethan Theatre, Past and Present'. The latest date for consideration of articles for vol. 12 is the end of August 1957.

Contributions offered for publication in *Shakespeare Survey* should be addressed to: The Editor, *Shakespeare Survey*, The Shakespeare Institute (University of Birmingham), Stratford-upon-Avon.

CONTENTS

[Notes are placed at the end of each contribution. All line references are to the 'Globe' edition, and, unless for special reasons, quotations are from this text]

vii

LIST OF PLATES

SHAKESPEARE'S ROMAN PLAYS: 1900-1956

BY

J. C. MAXWELL

The Stratford International Shakespeare Conference of 1955, which was centred on the Roman Plays, not only furnished a happy example of critical co-operation, but showed how deeply these plays engage the interest of present-day Shakespearians. It is evident that the concern of critics has, over the past half-century, tended to concentrate on a rather later period of Shakespeare's career than had previously been customary, and it is not entirely a result of the chronological basis of arrangement that the plays linked with *King Lear* by L. C. Knights under the title '*King Lear* and the Great Tragedies' in the Pelican *Age of Shakespeare* (1955) are not the other three of Bradley's 'great four', but *Macbeth*, *Antony and Cleopatra* and *Coriolanus*.

The early years of the century saw a number of substantial studies along later-nineteenth-century lines, culminating in M. W. MacCallum's *Shakespeare's Roman Plays* (1910). After a less fruitful interlude, a second notable period begins with the publication of Harley Granville-Barker's first series of *Prefaces* (1927), soon followed by G. Wilson Knight's *The Wheel of Fire* (1930). It is not yet possible to distinguish any more recent date of cardinal importance, but perhaps the last few years have seen a heightened concern for an eclectic approach to the plays, with a certain bias towards stressing, in L. C. Knights' phrase, Shakespeare's "political wisdom".

This attitude towards the plays involves recognition of their affinities with the history plays, but it has not meant treating them as necessarily prevented by those affinities from being fully tragic. The present-day approach thus differs from that of A. C. Bradley, who, in excluding them, along with *Richard II* and *Richard III*, from *Shakespearean Tragedy* as "tragic histories or historical tragedies", conjectured that Shakespeare would have met criticism of their sometimes "undramatic material...by appealing to their historical character, and by denying that such works are to be judged by the standard of pure tragedy" (p. 3).

I propose to survey the main critical work of the century under the three periods noted above, but there are certain more technical subjects—Canon, Text and Chronology, and Sources—that are more conveniently dealt with separately and without subdivisions, and there is one other play that calls for some comment before the 'Roman Plays', as commonly understood, are examined at all.

TITUS ANDRONICUS

The three Plutarch plays are obviously very different from the early work that was, none the less, described on the title-page of the 1594 Quarto as *The Most Lamentable Romaine Tragedie of Titus Andronicus*. The context in which this play could seem much less un-Roman than it does to us has been admirably studied by Terence Spencer in this volume.

At the beginning of the century, British (though not German) scholars were generally inclined to reject Shakespeare's authorship. An exception was H. Bellyse Baildon, the Arden editor (1904), whose arguments for its authenticity are sometimes of a curious kind—that scepticism about Shakespeare's authorship "is part of that general sceptical movement or wave which has landed us first in the so-called 'Higher Criticism' in matters of Religion, and finally in Agnosticism itself". Baildon must have felt confirmed in his views when that veteran agnostic and disintegrator J. M. Robertson published in 1905 *Did Shakespeare Write 'Titus Andronicus'?* (revised in 1924 as *An Introduction to the Study of the Shakespeare Canon*), his answer being a resounding "No". Most of the work done in this period was concerned with questions of authenticity and sources, and complicated theories involving the lost *Titus and Vespasian* and surviving Dutch and German seventeenth-century versions were evolved by such scholars as H. De W. Fuller and G. P. Baker (both in *PMLA*, XVI, 1901), belatedly echoed by John Munro, *Times Literary Supplement*, 10 June 1949, while more remote Byzantine sources were later explored by W. Dibelius (*Shakespeare Jahrbuch*, XLVIII, 1912), and F. Granger, *Times Literary Supplement*, 1 April 1920. More recently, the 'Roman Background' in Seneca and Ovid has been examined by R. A. Law (*Studies in Philology*, XL, 1943), who suggests that the author also made use of some of Plutarch's Lives. The rediscovered eighteenth-century chapbook now in the Folger Library has come to be regarded as probably representing, in substance, the play's sole immediate narrative source. It is fully analysed by R. M. Sargent (*Studies in Philology*, XLIV, 1949). A tendency to belief in composite authorship of the play, and to giving Shakespeare a fairly large share in it as a reviser, is represented by T. M. Parrott (*Modern Language Review*, XIV, 1919), who saw Peele's as the other hand. He was followed and elaborated by A. K. Gray (*Studies in Philology*, XXV, 1928), and by J. S. G. Bolton (*Studies in Philology*, XXX, 1933). A still more elaborate form of the same view was argued by J. Dover Wilson in his edition of 1948. The present writer, in the new Arden edition of 1953, while sceptical about revision or divided authorship in the rest of the play, tentatively accepted the first Act and the opening soliloquy of the second as Peele's work—a view which he had attempted to support by statistical evidence about a syntactical peculiarity in an earlier article (*Journal of English and Germanic Philology*, XLIX, 1950). Scepticism about Peele's hand on grounds alike of language and structure has been expressed by A. M. Sampley in *Studies in Philology*, XXX (1933), and in *PMLA*, LI (1936); and a solely Shakespearian authorship has been ably defended by H. T. Price (*Journal of English and Germanic Philology*, XLII, 1943), who has also made a valuable contribution to the study of the play's language in *Papers of the Michigan Academy of Science, Arts and Letters*, XXI (1936 for 1935).

Titus is the only play of which the present century has produced a complete copy of a quarto earlier than any hitherto known. The unique copy of the 1594 quarto discovered in Sweden in 1904 was collated by W. Keller (*Shakespeare Jahrbuch*, XLI, 1905), but close study of it had to wait for the publication of a facsimile, edited by J. Q. Adams, in 1936, though earlier studies of value were made by J. S. G. Bolton (*PMLA*, XLIV, 1929), and R. B. McKerrow (*Library*, XV, 1934–5). H. T. Price contributed a study, largely concerned with spelling, to *English Institute Essays 1947* (1948).

The play's date is intimately involved with other problems, such as authorship and early theatrical history, and scholars are still divided between dates as far apart as 1589 and 1594. P. E. Bennett (*Notes and Queries*, n.s. II, 1955) gives good reason for dismissing the often-quoted passage from *A Knack to Know a Knave* as evidence for the existence of *Titus* in 1592.

More general literary criticism of *Titus* has tended to be buried among the scholarly speculations which have been surveyed. Apart from a general study by W. Keller (*Shakespeare Jahrbuch*, LXXIX, 1938), little of moment was published before Howard Baker's *Induction to Tragedy* (1939), which related the play to *A Mirror for Magistrates* and to *The Spanish Tragedy*, and minimized Senecan affiliations. Useful emphasis on its formal, even academic, qualities was provided by M. C. Bradbrook, *Shakespeare and Elizabethan Poetry* (1951), expanding briefer comments in her *Themes and Conventions of Elizabethan Tragedy* (1935), and by E. M. W. Tillyard, *Shakespeare's History Plays* (1944), who notes the political interests which link *Titus* with the Histories. Dover Wilson's view, developing suggestions in Mark Van Doren's *Shakespeare* (1939), that the more extravagant portions were written by Shakespeare with a burlesque intention, has not found much support. Perhaps more significant than any written criticism the play has provoked in recent years is the Stratford production of 1955, which left those who saw it sharply divided on its artistic value, but amply demonstrated its theatrical potentialities even for a present-day audience.

CANON, TEXT AND CHRONOLOGY

There has been no revolutionary change in the generally accepted account of the three Plutarch plays under any of these three heads. Only the most hardened disintegrators have raised serious doubts about authorship, chiefly in connexion with *Julius Caesar*, where J. M. Robertson, *The Shakespeare Canon*, I (1922), and W. Wells, *The Authorship of 'Julius Caesar'* (1923), claimed to detect the hands of Marlowe, Jonson and Beaumont.

For all three plays the Folio is the only authority, and the prevailing view, expressed, for example, by Sir Walter Greg in *The Shakespeare First Folio: Its Bibliographical and Textual History* (1955), has been that *Julius Caesar* was printed from a transcript, probably of the prompt-book, and *Antony and Cleopatra* and *Coriolanus* from author's "foul papers carefully prepared for production". The tendency to believe too readily in foul papers as copy has been challenged by Fredson Bowers, *On Editing Shakespeare and the Elizabethan Dramatists* (1955), who suggests that the intervention of a transcript is probable for these two plays.

Textual derangement has been suggested both in *Julius Caesar* and in *Antony and Cleopatra*. In *Julius Caesar*, the double announcement of Portia's death continues to divide critics, some crediting it to Shakespeare's intention (most recently G. Baldini in *Nuova Antologia*, CDLIII, 1951, and W. D. Smith in *Shakeapeare Quarterly*, IV, 1953), others believing in a double recension, with both versions preserved in the Folio text. Originally suggested by Resch in 1882, this view has been accepted in the present century by most editors—Macmillan, Furness, Kittredge, Dover Wilson, Sisson and Dorsch—and also by Chambers and Granville-Barker. It was elaborated by P. Kannengiesser (*Shakespeare Jahrbuch*, XLIV, 1908). Traces of revision have also been seen in the absence from the Folio text of the line censured by Ben Jonson, "Caesar did never wrong but with just cause"; the fullest recent discussion is that of Dover Wilson (*Shakespeare Survey*, 2, 1949).

One scene in *Antony and Cleopatra* that has come under suspicion of conflating Shakespeare's first and second thoughts is the Monument Scene (IV, xv). The fullest study of this is by B. Jenkin (*Review of English Studies*, XXI, 1945), which Dover Wilson's edition follows, and, in a modified form, M. R. Ridley's new Arden.

The textual problem in *Coriolanus* that has attracted most attention is the "frequent mislineations" noted by E. K. Chambers. It has been not very convincingly claimed by G. B. Harrison, *Adams Memorial Studies* (1948), that many of these, as they appear in the Folio, are not errors but correspond to Shakespeare's intentions.

There has been little disagreement on the approximate dating of these plays. *Julius Caesar* is firmly dated autumn 1599. The other two plays are less certainly dated, but most would agree with Chambers in placing *Antony and Cleopatra* about 1606–7 and *Coriolanus* 1607–8. Claims, first made by R. H. Case in his Arden edition (1906) and elaborated by Joan Rees, *Shakespeare Survey*, 3 (1953), that Samuel Daniel's 1607 revision of his *Cleopatra* shows the influence of *Antony and Cleopatra* are rejected by J. Schütze (*Englische Studien*, LXXI, 1936–7), and by E. Schanzer in a forthcoming number of *Review of English Studies*, who holds that, on the contrary, Shakespeare had read Daniel's earlier version and also "skimmed through the added material in the revised form".

SOURCES AND ANALOGUES

The nature of Shakespeare's indebtedness to Plutarch had already been extensively studied before 1900, and more recent study has not greatly modified the picture. Two more collections of the four relevant lives have been published, a very serviceable one, edited by R. H. Carr (1906), of the 1595 text, and Tucker Brooke's more elaborate edition in two volumes (1909) of the 1579 text. There is a comprehensive study dealing with Plutarch, M. H. Shackford's *Plutarch in Renaissance England with Special Reference to Shakespeare* (1929). J. Middleton Murry's essay on North's Plutarch in *Countries of the Mind, Second Series* (1931) contains perceptive comments, as does Sir Henry Newbolt's in *The Tide of Time in English Poetry* (1925). Relevant extracts from a possible subsidiary source, the 1578 translation of Appian's *Civil Wars*, have been edited by E. Schanzer under the title, *Shakespeare's Appian* (1956) with a discussion of the influence of Appian especially on the Antony of *Julius Caesar*. The earliest discussion in the century of Shakespeare's use of Plutarch was R. Büttner's (*Shakespeare Jahrbuch*, XLI, 1905), which was the first to note his debt to the 'Comparison of Alcibiades with Coriolanus'.

M. W. MacCallum's *Shakespeare's Roman Plays* (1910) contains lengthy discussions of his relationship to Plutarch, and of earlier Caesar plays. In the same year, H. M. Ayres (*PMLA*, XXV) dealt with 'Shakespeare's *Julius Caesar* in the Light of Some Other Versions'. This study, without claiming for Shakespeare any knowledge of earlier dramatic versions, sets his Caesar in the context of the bombastic heroes of Muret, Grévin and Garnier. Ayres was also the first to discuss in any detail the anonymous *Tragedy of Caesar and Pompey, or Caesar's Revenge*, privately acted by the students of Trinity College, Oxford, registered in 1606, and sometimes, on rather slight evidence, dated 1592–6. This play was more fully described by T. M. Parrott in *Modern Language Review*, V (1910), and published by the Malone Society in 1911. This edition provoked a Münster dissertation by W. Mühlfeld (1912), and an article by H. M. Ayres (*PMLA*, XXX, 1915), and there is an account of the play in F. S. Boas's *University Drama in the Tudor Age* (1914). Since then interest in this tedious play has understandably lapsed. The only obvious point of contact it has with Shakespeare's, the transformation of the 'evil spirit' of North's Plutarch into Caesar's ghost, is not enough to prove indebtedness in either direction, and recent claims by E. Schanzer (*Notes and Queries*, CXCIX, 1954) that *Caesar's Revenge* is second only to Plutarch as a source for Shakespeare would carry little conviction even if it were more certain than it is that the play preceded Shakespeare's and was accessible to him.

Few confident claims have been made for Shakespeare's indebtedness to other Caesar plays. In his 1910 article, Ayres mentioned a few parallels with Pescetti's *Cesare* (1594), regarding them as mere coincidence. G. Sarrazin (*Englische Studien*, XLVI, 1912–13), was more impressed by them, and thought that Shakespeare had come across a translation or adaptation of the play, which is also the subject of A. Boecker's *A Probable Italian Source of Shakespeare's 'Julius Caesar'* (1913). H. B. Charlton sums up the position well when he writes in *The Senecan Tradition in Renaissance Tragedy* (1921), "Pescetti is nearer to Shakespeare than the others [among the Senecan dramatists] simply because he develops more motives within the story than do the others". The only surviving certainly pre-Shakespearian Caesar play in English, Kyd's translation of Garnier's *Cornélie* (1594), has not been much discussed. There is only one substantial study, by Joan Rees (*Modern Language Review*, L, 1955), who thinks that Shakespeare may have seen a challenge in "the unintelligible coexistence of braggart and hero in *Cornelia*", and also that Shakespeare's Brutus may owe some of his "turning away from the particular to the grandiloquent general" to Kyd's.

Among minor sources from which Shakespeare has been thought to take hints in *Julius Caesar* may be mentioned Elyot's *Governour*, different passages of which have been cited by Douglas Bush (*Modern Language Notes*, LII, 1937), and by the present writer (*Notes and Queries*, n.s. III, 1956). Sources for the portents before Caesar's death were discussed by M. H. Shackford (*Modern Language Notes*, XLI, 1926). An unplausibly long list of classical sources for Antony's funeral oration was compiled by E. Staedler, a disintegrationist, in *Neuphilologische Monatsschrift*, X (1939).

On the other two plays, there are still fewer miscellaneous studies to record. Dover Wilson, in his edition of *Antony and Cleopatra* (1950), found it difficult to believe that Shakespeare had not read the Countess of Pembroke's *Antonius*, and his arguments are strengthened by E. Schanzer (*Notes and Queries*, n.s. III, 1956). Ethel Seaton's '*Antony and Cleopatra* and the Book of Revelation' (*Review of English Studies*, XXII, 1946) illuminates Shakespeare's creative use of thematically apt material; and P. D. Westbrook (*PMLA*, LXII, 1947) claims Horace's *Odes*, I, XXXVII as a source for the emphasis on Cleopatra's dying pride and the predominance of her determination not to grace Caesar's triumph.

It seems unlikely that discoveries of major importance about Shakespeare's sources in these plays remain to be made. But after a period of quiescence, during which, however, R. W. Chambers, *Shakespeare's Hand in 'Sir Thomas More'* (1923), published some valuable incidental remarks on the adaptation of Plutarch in *Coriolanus*, a more critical study of the *use* made by Shakespeare of his sources has begun. An early example is H. Heuer's 'Shakespeare und Plutarch: Studien zu Wertwelt und Lebensgefühl im *Coriolanus*' (*Anglia*, LXII, 1938), whose subtitle indicates the intention of linking source-study with deeper critical problems. Another article which makes the discussion of Shakespeare's use of his sources ancillary to the study of his art is Maria Wickert's 'Antikes Gedankengut in Shakespeares *Julius Caesar*' (*Shakespeare Jahrbuch*, LXXXII–III, 1946–7), particularly valuable on the "spirit of Caesar" and Shakespeare's recreation of the classical notion of a "daimon" or "genius", and also on the rhetorical background of the speeches of Brutus and Antony. The latter topic had also engaged R. W. Zandvoort in 'Brutus's Forum Speech in *Julius Caesar*' (*Review of English Studies*, XVI, 1940; reprinted in his *Collected Papers*, 1954). The recent comprehensive study by V. K. Whitaker, *Shakespeare's Use of Learning* (1953), also lays stress on the word 'use', and may serve as a bridge to more general studies of Shakespeare's reading, especially in the classics, such as T. W. Baldwin's monumental *William*

Shakspere's Small Latine and Lesse Greeke (1944), J. A. K. Thomson's *Shakespeare and the Classics* (1952), and, on a smaller scale, F. S. Boas's 'Aspects of Classical Legend and History in Shakespeare' (*Proceedings of the British Academy*, XXIX, 1944) and E. Wolff's 'Shakespeare und die Antike' (*Die Antike*, XX, 1944; expanded in *Antike und Abendland*, I, 1945). A comprehensive study of Shakespeare's sources by Kenneth Muir is in preparation.

THE BEGINNING OF THE CENTURY

A. C. Bradley, as has been noted, did not deal with any of the Roman plays in his *Shakespearean Tragedy*. But he did not ignore them, and his essays on *Antony and Cleopatra* (dated 1905 and printed in *Oxford Lectures on Poetry*, 1909) and *Coriolanus* (*Proceedings of the British Academy*, V, 1911–12; reprinted in *A Miscellany*, 1929) gain something from being briefer and less imbedded in philosophizing than his studies of the four 'great tragedies'. The essay on *Antony and Cleopatra* in particular gives reasons for regarding it as inferior to the earlier tragedies that still deserve careful consideration.

There are not many other critical essays of value from the early years of the century, though R. H. Case's introduction to the Arden *Antony and Cleopatra* (1906)—like his later one to *Coriolanus* (1922)—is characteristic of a sound and perceptive scholar. E. K. Chambers' introductions to all three plays, later collected in *Shakespeare: a Survey* (1925), also belong to this period. In a careful study of the views of earlier German scholars, W. Münch, *Shakespeare Jahrbuch*, XLII (1906), dealt with the contrast between Aufidius and Coriolanus, finding the former less crudely handled than some critics had maintained. The most solid work, covering all aspects of the plays, was M. W. MacCallum's *Shakespeare's Roman Plays and their Background* (1910), which can still be read with respect and, more often than not, with assent, though scarcely with exhilaration. The equipment of a Roman historian who was also a sane and sensitive critic was brought to bear by W. Warde Fowler on 'The Tragic Element in Shakespeare's *Julius Caesar*' (*Transactions of the Royal Society of Literature*, XXIX, 1911; reprinted in *Roman Essays and Interpretations*, 1920)—an essay of which Bradley wrote, "I am sure nothing so good has been printed on this play" (quoted in R. H. Coon, *William Warde Fowler: an Oxford Humanist*, 1934, p. 178).

FROM BRADLEY TO GRANVILLE-BARKER

The following years were not rich in criticism of these plays. The best-known trend in the Shakespeare criticism of this period was that variously known as 'realist', 'historical' and 'sceptical', and perhaps most conveniently described simply as that of Stoll and Schücking. L. L. Schücking's *Die Charakterprobleme bei Shakespeare* (1919; English translation 1922) dealt at some length with *Julius Caesar* and *Antony and Cleopatra*. The account of the characterization of Caesar is sound in so far as it insists (principally against Brandes) that the greatness of Caesar is presupposed throughout, but unduly rigid in dismissing all that has seemed self-dramatizing and bombastic in Caesar's language as simply a case of the primitive dramatic technique of direct self-revelation. Schücking's woodenness of mind comes out still more strongly in his account of Cleopatra, who is, for him, a different woman in the first three acts from what she is in the last two. Cleopatra is also the subject of E. E. Stoll's only extended treatment of any of the

Roman plays (*Modern Language Review*, XXIII, 1928; reprinted in *Poets and Playwrights*, 1930), in an essay which well illustrates that the customary collocation with Schücking needs to be made with reservations. For Stoll, the separate characterizations Schücking gives of his two Cleopatras are, each of them, still too psychological, and his own solution is an imaginative unity conveyed through speech. This essay is not an extreme example of Stoll's methods, and indeed, in its broad outline it presents a generally accepted view, though rather lacking in finesse.

The best briefer essays of this period are on *Coriolanus*. J. Middleton Murry's 'A Neglected Heroine of Shakespeare' (*Countries of the Mind*, 1922), together with some questionable reassignment of speeches, gives a sensitive appreciation of Virgilia, and incidentally of the "quality of Roman relentlessness and inevitability" which he has more space to discuss, along with other aspects of the play, in a more general essay in *Discoveries* (1923). There is a useful study of 'The Structure of *Coriolanus*' by A. H. Tolman in *Modern Language Notes*, XXXVII (1922), which is relevant also to Shakespeare's use of Plutarch. This essay is reprinted in *Falstaff and Other Shakespearean Topics* (1925), a book which also contains some miscellaneous comments on various aspects of *Julius Caesar*.

THE LAST THIRTY YEARS

In 1927, the first series of Granville-Barker's *Prefaces to Shakespeare* was published, containing that to *Julius Caesar*. (Those on *Antony and Cleopatra* and on *Coriolanus* followed in 1930 and in 1947). G. Wilson Knight was soon to publish *The Wheel of Fire* (1930; revised edition 1949) and *The Imperial Theme* (1931; revised edition 1951). Much subsequent criticism can be associated with one or the other of these two critics, though some recent work has, rightly and naturally, adopted eclectic methods. Granville-Barker had given a first sample of his treatment of Shakespeare in 'From *Henry V* to *Hamlet*' (*Proceedings of the British Academy*, XI, 1924–5), in which *Julius Caesar* was described as "the turning-point of Shakespeare's career", and *Antony and Cleopatra* as "in some ways the most perfect, and altogether, I think, the most finely spacious piece of play-making he ever did".

The *Julius Caesar* Preface, though it does justice to the play's structural qualities, is one of Granville-Barker's less remarkable pieces. *Antony and Cleopatra* afforded more scope for his emphasis, against anachronistic criticism, on the theatrical virtues of the play as originally staged. It is noteworthy that he here postpones analysis of the characters until he has dealt with questions of construction, staging and verse, whereas in the earlier Preface the characters had been given pride of place, with Brutus at their head. Finally the *Coriolanus* Preface, the last that he lived to complete, suffers somewhat from expansion to book-length, though it is much shorter than the *Hamlet* or the *Othello*. The action of the play is followed and commented on in unnecessary detail, and there is little in the volume, conscientious as it is, that remains vividly in the mind.

G. Wilson Knight has also dealt with all three plays. His first book, *The Wheel of Fire*, contains an essay on 'Brutus and Macbeth' which brings out resemblances that earlier critics had not sufficiently stressed; and more than half of *The Imperial Theme* is devoted to the Roman plays. There is ample (perhaps too ample) documentation of the language and imagery of *Julius Caesar* as "a play of love and fire", and the essay entitled 'The Eroticism of *Julius Caesar*' gives a salutary challenge to assumptions about the relations of the characters, and the poetic impact they make on us. The very lengthy treatment of *Antony and Cleopatra* is less satisfying and the piling up of detail makes it difficult to get a clear impression. The much briefer essay on *Coriolanus*, on the other hand, shows Knight at his best, bringing out the predominating style of the play, and its congruence with the character of the hero.

About the same time Caroline Spurgeon published her *Shakespeare's Imagery and what it tells us* (1935), whose treatment of the principal tragedies follows closely her earlier 'Leading Motives in the Imagery of Shakespeare's Tragedies' (*Shakespeare Association Pamphlet* 15, 1930). This discusses the pervading 'world' imagery in *Antony and Cleopatra*, and deals rather unsympathetically with *Coriolanus*, which she finds "somewhat languid and artificial". A substantial study of a single play, indebted to Wilson Knight, is R. Binder's *Der Dramatische Rhythmus in Shakespeares 'Antonius und Cleopatra'* (1939).

A number of other books in this period have dealt at length with these plays. The most thorough study of them in relation to the political conceptions of Shakespeare's time is J. E. Phillips' *The State in Shakespeare's Greek and Roman Plays* (1940), which, like other works of this kind, probably exaggerates the importance of Shakespeare's attachment to the commonplaces of political orthodoxy. A salutary contrast is John Palmer's refreshingly unprofessional, and rather old-fashioned, *Political Characters of Shakespeare* (1945), including essays on Brutus and Coriolanus, which demonstrate what can still be done, with little technical equipment, by a critic who knows the world of politics and the text of Shakespeare. These plays figure also in Brents Stirling's *The Populace in Shakespeare* (1949), and *Julius Caesar* in H. B. Charlton's *Shakespearian Tragedy* (1948), which treats it as a history rather than a tragedy in the full sense. The most substantial work dealing with *Antony and Cleopatra* and *Coriolanus* is Willard Farnham's *Shakespeare's Tragic Frontier* (1950), which argues that the later tragedies are distinguished from the earlier by having "deeply flawed" heroes whose nobility "seems inseparable from their flaws". Some of Farnham's views are ably challenged by R. Roth (*Modern Philology*, XLIX, 1950–1).

Briefer studies are J. W. Draper's 'Political Themes in Shakespeare's Later Plays' (*Journal of English and Germanic Philology*, XXV, 1936), which sees an increasing concern for classical local colour in *Antony and Cleopatra* and *Coriolanus*, and P. A. Jorgensen's 'Shakespeare's Coriolanus: an Elizabethan Soldier' (*PMLA*, LXIV, 1949), indicating Coriolanus's deficiency in generalship, as well as his unsuitability for civil life, in the light of contemporary experience, and 'Enobarbus' Broken Heart and the Estate of English Fugitives' (*Philological Quarterly*, XXX, 1951). A recent essay in the same tradition is L. Borinski's '"Soldat" und "Politiker" bei Shakespeare und seinen Zeitgenossen' (*Shakespeare Jahrbuch*, XCI, 1955). The most distinguished recent essay dealing with more than one of the plays is perhaps L. C. Knights' 'Shakespeare and Political Wisdom: a Note on the Personalism of *Julius Caesar* and *Coriolanus*' (*Sewanee Review*, LXI, 1953; reprinted in *Some Shakespearean Themes*, 1957), which shows how the plays "refresh our sense of the actual where today it is most urgently needed". Also of value for two of the plays is J. I. M. Stewart's *Character and Motive in Shakespeare* (1949). Few have written as penetratingly on the two Caesars in *Julius Caesar*—the public figure, and the man "opposing to the first falterings of the mind an increasingly rigid and absolute assertion of the Caesar idea", and the chapter on Cleopatra argues with wit and cogency against Schücking's primitivistic notions of Shakespeare's art. Roy Walker in 'The Northern Star: An Essay on the Roman Plays' (*Shakespeare Quarterly*, II, 1951), discusses questions of imagery. Huntington Brown's 'Enter the

Shakespearean Tragic Hero' (*Essays in Criticism*, III, 1953), distinguishes between the unsympathetic heroes, including Coriolanus (and Titus), and the sympathetic ones, including Brutus and Antony. He sees in the sympathetic heroes "a common inward character more or less different from the individual outward one"—something which makes us aware of an "inner everyman". M. MacLure, 'Shakespeare and the Lonely Dragon' (*University of Toronto Quarterly*, XXIV, 1955), discusses Coriolanus and Antony as examples of the hero dedicated to honour, involved in a political situation.

The rest of what has been done on the plays in the last thirty years can most conveniently be dealt with play by play.

The excellent essay by Sir Mark Hunter, 'Politics and Character in Shakespeare's *Julius Caesar*' (*Transactions of the Royal Society of Literature*, n.s. X, 1931), was one of the first among modern attempts to correct the tendency to over-idealize Brutus and give him too central a place in the play. A recent expression of the same point of view—though it contains the questionable assumption that Brutus is "the dramatic hero"—is the Introduction to T. S. Dorsch's new Arden edition (1955). The important point that the play is an example of revenge tragedy was touched upon by Percy Simpson in *Proceedings of the British Academy*, XXI (1935), reprinted in *Studies in Elizabethan Drama* (1955), and was illustrated by L. B. Campbell in *Modern Philology*, XXVIII (1930–1). Shakespeare's attitude towards Caesar has preoccupied a number of scholars, their views ranging from that of L. Morsbach, *Shakespeares Cäsarbild* (1935), which sees nothing but unmitigated admiration of Caesar on Shakespeare's part, to the Introduction to J. Dover Wilson's edition (1949), according to which Shakespeare is concerned to depict "Caesarism" as "a secular threat to the human spirit". A useful corrective to some rash assertions in this Introduction about medieval and renaissance ideas of Caesar is provided by D. S. Brewer in *Review of English Studies*, n.s. III (1952). M. Deutschbein, 'Die Tragik in Shakespeares *Julius Caesar*' (*Anglia*, LXII, 1938), sees the tragedy as consisting in the way the "honourable" Brutus is forced to dishonourable means, and in the vulnerability of the Caesar who has thought himself superior to "danger". D. Klein defends Cassius in *Shakespeare Association Bulletin*, XIV (1939), and S. Musgrove has a general study of the play in a lecture published by the Australian English Association in 1941. R. M. Frye (*Quarterly Journal of Speech*, XXXVII, 1952) uses Antony's speech in establishing a distinction between the "specific" reaction to rhetoric and the "non-specific" to poetry. Two studies emphasize the peculiar contribution made by Brutus's sacrificial attitude to the horror of the assassination: Leo Kirschbaum's 'Shakespeare's Stage Blood and Its Critical Significance' (*PMLA*, LXIV, 1949), which also comments on the shock of the hero's blood-smeared entry in *Coriolanus*, and Brents Stirling's 'Or Else This Were a Savage Spectacle' (*PMLA*, LXVI, 1951). The play is approached through the imagery by R. A. Foakes in *Shakespeare Quarterly*, V (1954). Finally E. Schanzer has two essays, 'The Problem of *Julius Caesar*' (*Shakespeare Quarterly*, VI, 1955), suggesting that "the main purpose of Shakespeare's dissociation of the corporeal and spiritual Caesar throughout the play is to show up the futility and foolishness of the assassination", and 'The Tragedy of Shakespeare's Brutus' (*ELH*, XII, 1955), treating the play as "the first of the poet's tragedies in what we have come to think of as the peculiarly Shakespearean mode", with Brutus's "inner conflict" as the centre of interest.

The comparison of *Antony and Cleopatra* with *All for Love* was used by F. R. Leavis (*Scrutiny*, V, 1936–7) as a means of bringing out Shakespeare's "superiority in concreteness, variety and sensitiveness". John Wilcox, in *Papers of the Michigan Academy of Science, Arts and Letters*, XXI (1936 for 1935), dealt with the play "as a sympathetic retelling of a great love between two intense, sincere lovers", opposing interpretations which give greater prominence to the political and historical side. Eva Buck's 'Cleopatra, eine Charakterdeutung' (*Shakespeare Jahrbuch*, LXXIV, 1938) described with some subtlety how Cleopatra destroys Antony's "absolute masculinity" and seeks to overcome the tragedy of her love by "making the hostile masculine principle her own", while Antony "flees from the political sphere to the personal". Cleopatra is also the centre of Leo Kirschbaum's essay in *Shakespeare Association Bulletin*, XIX (1944), which stresses the unity of presentation, especially as reflected in imagery. There are general essays by Lord David Cecil (W. P. Ker Memorial Lecture, 1944; reprinted in *Poets and Storytellers*, 1949), who considers that the play's interest is "largely political" and that "the private life is, as it were, a consequence of the public life", and by G. S. Griffiths (*Essays and Studies*, XXXI, 1946 for 1945)— enthusiastic but rather over-written. The play has appeared in both the major modern editions, J. Dover Wilson's in the New Shakespeare (1950) and M. R. Ridley's in the new Arden (1954). Dover Wilson lays the main stress on "vitality" as the "true theme" of this "Hymn to Man"; Ridley, in his briefer comments, suggests a similar judgment, though finding Dover Wilson liable to the "generous error" of being carried too far by his admiration of the central figures. Both editors devote some space to discussing whether Cleopatra's denunciation of Seleucus is a "put-up-job". E. M. Waith, 'Manhood and Valor in Two Shakespearean Tragedies' (*ELH*, XVII, 1950), writes of the conflicting ideals of the soldier-hero as seen by Caesar and Cleopatra, and suggests that they are reconciled in the "magnanimity" of Antony's final achievement. The question of religious colouring in the language of the play, especially in relation to the hint of apotheosis in the final scenes, has aroused disagreement. At one extreme, S. L. Bethell, in *Shakespeare and the Popular Dramatic Tradition* (1944), saw the play as a sort of allegory of opposing values, conveying the message that "the good life may be built upon the Egyptian, but not upon the Roman. It is a way of saying that the strong sinner may enter heaven before the prudential legislator. In *Antony and Cleopatra* the strong sinners meet their purgatory here". Many will be more inclined to agree with J. F. Danby who held, in an essay in *Scrutiny*, XVI (1949), reprinted in *Poets on Fortune's Hill* (1952), that Shakespeare holds the balance more evenly between "the World and the Flesh, Rome and Egypt, the two great contraries that maintain and destroy each other", and that the specifically religious is kept out of the play. Four recent studies in *Shakespeare Quarterly* are evidence of continuing disagreement. D. G. Cunningham, VI (1955), attempts to read something approaching Christian repentance into the Cleopatra of the last Act, but is adequately answered by E. S. Donno, VII (1956). D. Stempel, VII (1956), pouring contempt on romantic criticism, forces the play into the strait-jacket of Renaissance order-theory, and sees it as a "tragic satire" like the *Coriolanus* of O. J. Campbell's theory; while in the same number J. S. Stull uses a new interpretation of II, v, 103–6 as evidence for "Cleopatra's Magnanimity".

Studies of *Coriolanus* have dealt largely with the problems presented by the hero, and his relation to the political context in which he is placed. In *Church Quarterly Review*, CXVII (1933–4), Geraldine Hodgson sought to answer the charge of "comparative emptiness" brought by Dover Wilson in *The Essential Shakespeare* (1932), seeing instead "the intolerable tragedy of intrinsic nobility wantonly self-ruined" by a typically Renaissance pride. A number of themes that have been prominent in more recent discussions figure in E. Baumgarten's 'Gemeinschaft und Gewissen in Shakespeares *Coriolan*' (*Die Neueren Sprachen*, XLIII, 1935), which notes the ironic treatment of the hero, his isolation within his community, and the peculiar nature of his hatred for the common people—"he discharges his own feeling of guilt on those 'base' objects" —and gives a subtle discussion of how the various groups and individuals to whom he is opposed are used to explore the nature of his "conscience". A little later came D. A. Traversi's discriminating essay in *Scrutiny*, VI (1937–8), particularly valuable on the impression the play gives of "an iron social framework which permits...no community of interests" between the two sides, and on the hero's corresponding failure in sensitivity. A later study which arrives at comparable results through an examination of "verbal music" in relation to character is Una Ellis-Fermor's 'Some Functions of Verbal Music in Drama' (*Shakespeare Jahrbuch*, XC, 1954). A. H. King, in a series of 'Notes on *Coriolanus*', *English Studies*, XIX–XX (1937–8), dealt mainly with details of interpretation, but also wrote well on the temper of the play as "a tragedy of choleric humour"—a description which points forward to O. J. Campbell's more one-sided treatment of it as a "tragical satire" in the Jonsonian manner in *Shakespeare's Satire* (1943). The Jonsonian affinities were also discussed by E. Honig, 'Sejanus and Coriolanus: a Study in Alienation' (*Modern Language Quarterly*, XII, 1951). An approach from one particular aspect was attempted by the present writer in "Animal Imagery in *Coriolanus*' (*Modern Language Review*, XLII, 1947), stressing its clear-cut and rather schematic nature. Some points touched on in this essay were more fully worked out, and placed in a wider context, by F. N. Lees, '*Coriolanus*, Aristotle and Bacon' (*Review of English Studies*, n.s. I, 1950), who argues that the Aristotelian dictum "an unsocial man is either a beast or a god", is reflected in a pattern of references throughout the play. More topical political connections were discussed by E. C. Pettet, '*Coriolanus* and the Midlands Insurrection of 1607' (*Shakespeare Survey*, 3, 1950). Specifically classical qualities, earlier discussed by M. St Clare Byrne in *National Review*, XCVI (1931), which may have made the play unattractive to the romantic English, were stressed by S. Rosati in *Nuova Antologia* CDLVIII (1953), who also noted the solitariness of the hero, and the conflict between his integrity and the Machiavellianism of Volumnia. Most recently of all, there has been a vigorous revival of controversy about Coriolanus himself. I. Ribner (*English Studies*, XXXIV, 1953), treats the play as a tragedy of pride and self-ignorance on the part of one who remains basically good. D. J. Enright, '*Coriolanus*: Tragedy or Debate?' (*Essays in Criticism*, IV, 1954), finds the figure of the hero "thin", and the whole play a success on an essentially lower level than that of the great tragedies; whereas I. R. Browning in his reply, '*Coriolanus*: Boy of Tears' (*Essays in Criticism*, V, 1955), gives a more penetrating analysis, with some of the same stresses as Baumgarten's 1935 essay, noting Coriolanus's lack of self-knowledge and the way in which "in striving to 'make a man' of him, his mother has (paradoxically) prevented him from achieving independent manhood".

It is perhaps significant that recent critics have shown a certain tendency to turn from the splendours of *Antony and Cleopatra* and from the headiness it inspires in some of its admirers, to the more sober qualities of the other two plays. A distrust of the extravagant and the one-sided is detectable in the best recent criticism, and the price that has sometimes been paid is some degree of dullness and unadventurousness. But the next major critic will have sound foundations to build on.

SHAKESPEARE'S 'SMALL LATIN'—
HOW MUCH?[1]

BY

J. DOVER WILSON

The question was already being asked in his life-time and no conclusive answer has yet been found. Certainly none will be offered in what follows; perhaps none ever will. Yet in a volume dealing in the main with Shakespeare's Roman Plays, it is well that the question should be posed and that some of the relevant evidence should at least be glanced at. I shall even dare to suggest a fresh line of approach, which, if followed up, *might* lead somewhere.

I begin, as everyone must, with Ben Jonson's claim that Shakespeare's plays were worthy to rank with those of the greatest Greek and Latin dramatists, though he had "small Latin and less Greek". It comes, of course, from the fine laudatio which Ben wrote for the First Folio edition of his dead friend's plays. For they were friends, we cannot doubt of that; and though his praise seems today in no way exaggerated, he probably felt a generous glow as he wrote it, felt indeed that he owed it to his "beloved, the author, Mr. William Shakespeare" to pitch it rather higher than the truth. Certainly, in the lines about Shakespeare's art, he attributed qualities to him which he denied in private talk and in notes he left behind him.[2] And there was one quality he could not allow him even in public—classical learning. It seems evident too that he never forgave him for writing *Julius Caesar*. We have four instances of his criticizing this play and they extend over a period of thirty years or more. No doubt its abiding popularity as compared with the failure of his own classical tragedies with London audiences explains this exasperation in part. But Shakespeare's real crime, one suspects, was that he, no scholar, whose only source for his Roman plays was an English translation of a French translation of Plutarch's *Lives of the Noble Grecians and Romans*, should have had the impudence to make the attempt.[3] Jonson had, and still has, many admirers, and he deserves them. But it must have been difficult to make friends with him and still more difficult to keep that friendship "in repair", to use a phrase of his namesake Samuel. That Shakespeare won his friendship and retained it to the end, as the lines in the First Folio show, is the greatest tribute to the urbanity of the man he called "my gentle Shakespeare" that has come down to us.

But to return to our text—"small Latin". How small? When we ask what chance he had of learning to read the ancients with ease, we have unhappily nothing but inference to go upon. There is proof that Peele, Lyly, Greene and Marlowe were all university men; the probability is that Shakespeare was not, though the records of Oxford and Cambridge are by no means complete for his epoch. On the other hand, there is no absolute certainty that he even attended the Stratford Grammar School, though we may legitimately assume it since being the son of Alderman John Shakespeare he was entitled to do so without payment. And the Stratford Grammar School was probably at this time a good example of its type. The master's salary being exceptionally large would attract good scholars. We have too a Latin letter written in 1598 by Richard Quiney, a boy of eleven, to his father, one of Shakespeare's friends, at that time in

12

London. Even if we suppose this to be largely the composition of the master, who seized an opportunity of showing off a promising lad to a prominent citizen of the town, the boy must have had some hand in it and Richard Quiney senior must have been expected to understand it.[4] Now, if Shakespeare was at the same school a quarter of a century earlier he probably left it when about two years older than little Richard. Rowe, his earliest biographer, wrote in 1709 that Shakespeare's father

who was a considerable dealer in wool, had so large a family...that though he was the eldest son, he could give him no better education than his own employment. He had bred him, 'tis true, for some time at a Free School, where 'tis probable he acquired that little Latin he was master of. But the narrowness of his circumstances, and the want of his assistance at home forced his father to withdraw him from thence, and unhappily prevented his further proficiency in that language.[5]

Rowe is a late witness and in other details his *Life* is often open to serious question, while this passage has been hotly contested (like every other early statement about Shakespeare). But Edmund Chambers sees no reason for doubting it and notes that it agrees with what we know from the corporation records of the financial circumstances of John Shakespeare when William was about thirteen or fourteen years of age.[6] Rowe tells us that most of his facts were the fruit of inquiries made at Stratford by the actor Thomas Betterton. And it was another actor who supplies us with evidence that seems to conflict with Betterton's. About 1681 the antiquary John Aubrey recorded the following note as coming from William Beeston, himself an actor and the son of Christopher Beeston who had been a member of Shakespeare's company:

Though as Ben Johnson sayes of him, that he had but little Latine and lesse Greek, He understood Latine pretty well: for he had been in his younger yeares a Schoolmaster in the Countrey.[7]

A great deal has been heard about Beeston's testimony of recent years from those who argue in favour of Shakespeare's knowledge of the Classics. But candidly considered it cannot be said to carry us very far. Even if it means that the master at Stratford, knowing a bright boy when he saw one, induced William Shakespeare to return and help him as an usher with the junior boys, in return for a fee which would make it worth John Shakespeare's while to release him from the shop, not much knowledge would be required for such instruction. The curriculum of a modern grammar school is of course far less classical than that of its predecessor three or four centuries ago. But the capacity of the boy-mind is much the same; and I have myself been a grammar-school master in my younger years, drilled boys of fourteen and fifteen in Latin accidence, and corrected their exercises. On the other hand, if Shakespeare added to the family income by serving as usher at the Grammar School for three or four years before he found his way to London, that would have given him an opportunity of adding to his own knowledge, not only by teaching, but also by learning and borrowing books from the masters in charge, even though he seems to have repaid one of them, the Welshman Thomas Jenkins, who was master 1575-9, by immortalizing him as the hot-tempered Hugh Evans in *The Merry Wives*, whom incidentally he represents examining a boy called William "in his accidence".

But Dryden, while admitting Jonson's disparagement, made a far more effective reply to it than speculative inferences from Beeston's debatable statement. "Those who accuse him", he wrote in his *Essay of Dramatic Poesy*, "to have wanted learning give him the greater commendation; he was naturally learned; he needed not the spectacles of books to read Nature"—and by Nature he meant in particular, as all did at that period, human nature—"he looked inwards, and found her there".[8] Such was the opinion of most informed persons in the generation after Shakespeare; Milton's description of him as "Fancy's child", warbling "his *native* woodnotes wild" being a more romantic way of saying the same thing. Nor are latter-day attempts to explain away views of this character as clichés, or the expression of a myth, very persuasive. Even if not correct in all its details the following incident from Rowe's *Life*, for example, cannot be wholly fictitious:

In a Conversation between Sir *John Suckling*, Sir William *D'Avenant*, *Endymion Porter*, Mr. *Hales of Eaton*, and *Ben Johnson*; Sir *John Suckling*, who was a profess'd admirer of *Shakespear*, had undertaken his Defence against *Ben Johnson* with some warmth; Mr. *Hales*, who had sat still for some time, hearing *Ben* frequently reproaching him for want of Learning, and Ignorance of the Antients, told him at last, That if [i.e. though] Mr. *Shakespear* had not read the Antients, he had likewise not stollen any thing from 'em; (a Fault the other made no Conscience of) and that if he would produce any one Topick finely treated by any of them, he would undertake to shew something upon the same Subject at least as well written by *Shakespear*.[9]

Hales was one of the best scholars of the age and this remark of his in varying forms is quoted by three other writers, one of them Dryden, before Rowe gave it currency. Moreover, those whom Rowe names as present were all men who either might have known Shakespeare personally or were alive before his death. Conversely, there would have been many other persons still alive in 1709 who had been acquainted with some of them and able to contradict the story if incorrect. But the very manner in which Rowe tells it gives it the stamp of truth. And I suspect that his only error was to make Ben Jonson one of the company. The other versions do not, and the fact that Ben's views were the subject of the discussion would naturally suggest the idea of his being there to voice them.

Opinion on the matter, once it passed beyond the reach of human memory, has fluctuated to and fro, like opinion on so much else about Shakespeare. Shortly after the publication of Rowe's *Life* an attempt was made to reverse the judgment of Ben Jonson and prove that Shakespeare was a good classical scholar, whereat a Cambridge don, Richard Farmer, who had for his day a surprising knowledge of Elizabethan literature, issued his famous *Essay on the Learning of Shakespeare* (1767) in which he traced to forgotten English translations of the period most of the allusions the dramatist was supposed to have taken straight out of the Classics. Farmer convinced the scholars of his day, and held the field down to recent times. With the great advances made during the last half century in our knowledge of Elizabethan life and thought, "the Jonson versus Shakespeare question" has, however, flared up with renewed ardour. And readers of this paper may like to have a list of the more important books and articles bearing upon the matter: R. K. Root, *Classical Mythology in Shakespeare*, 1903; H. R. D. Anders, *Shakespeare's Books*, 1904; Henry Jackson, *Lecture on Shakespeare*, 1912 (see pp. 272–89 of *Henry Jackson, O.M.*, 1926, by R. St J. Parry); J. S. Smart, *Shakespeare, truth and tradition*, 1928; E. I. Fripp, 'Shakespeare's Use of Ovid's Metamorphoses' in *Shakespeare Studies*, 1930; Douglas Bush, *Mythology and the Renaissance tradition in English Poetry*, 1932; P. Alexander, *Shakespeare's Life and Art*, 1939; T. W. Baldwin, *William Shakspere's Small Latin and Lesse Greek*, 1944; F. P. Wilson,

'Shakespeare's Reading' in *Shakespeare Survey* 3, 1950; J. A. K. Thomson, *Shakespeare and the Classics*, 1952; Percy Simpson, 'Shakespeare's Use of Latin Authors' in *Studies in Elizabethan Drama*, 1955.[10]

Of these Root, Anders, and Bush take little or no part in the argument, being rather concerned with the more useful task of establishing facts. For the rest Smart, Fripp, Alexander, Baldwin and Simpson are inclined to credit Shakespeare with a good deal more classical learning than either Jackson or Thomson will allow, in which connexion it is perhaps relevant to observe that while the former are well known Elizabethan scholars the other two are eminent classicists and probably the best who have ever given their minds to the subject. F. P. Wilson occupies a some-what middle position in a judicious summing up. But the most ambitious and certainly the most voluminous of them all is Baldwin of Illinois. In an obvious attempt to settle the problem for good, he gives us a portentous monograph, in two volumes, and running over 1500 pages, which consists for the most part of a minute examination of what was actually taught in the grammar schools of that day. But as Thomson, who is a shrewd critic as well as a learned classic, observes:

Professor Baldwin tells us in very great detail what Shakespeare *could* have learned at school. But the hard fact is that we do not know what amount of schooling Shakespeare had....Moreover I cannot believe that Professor Baldwin has sufficiently considered that a practised man of letters is continually picking up information—even information contained in books—from other people.[11]

And he remarks elsewhere that at the time of the Renaissance the classics were in the air men breathed. Elizabethan literature, unlike modern, is "full of classical names, allusions, quotations", so that anyone who could read at all became acquainted with them, while "an almost continuous succession of masques, shows, revels, processions, royal progresses and the like, in each of which there was sure to be one or more characters drawn from ancient history or mythology, brought some knowledge of Greece and Rome even to the most illiterate".[12] Henry Jackson, making much the same point, remarks how dangerous it is to assess the attainments of a sixteenth- or seventeenth-century writer by reference to twentieth-century standards, and appositely cites as a witness Samuel Pepys, who was already thirty years of age and a prominent civil servant when he found himself obliged to employ a tutor to teach him the multiplication table and was yet greatly shocked that Sir George Carteret did not know what the letters S.P.Q.R. stood for; "which ignorance" he says, "is not to be borne in a privy Councillor, methinks; a schoolboy should be whipt for not knowing it". And what did he read to Mistress Pepys before bed-time? Translations of Ovid's *Metamorphoses* and of *Aesop's Fables*! Such was the light literature of the age before novels existed.[13]

It is, too, a standing temptation among scholars to imagine poets to be like-minded with them-selves. Thomson, for example, quotes the following from one of Tennyson's letters:

There is, I fear, a prosaic set growing up among us, editors of booklets, bookworms, index-hunters, or men of great memories and no imagination, who *impute themselves* to the poet, and so believe that *he*, too, has no imagination, but is for ever poking his nose between the pages of some old volume in order to see what he can appropriate. They will not allow one to say "Ring the bell" without finding that we have taken it from Sir P. Sidney, or even to use such a simple expression as the ocean "roars" without finding out the precise verse in Homer or Horace from which we have plagiarized it.[14]

Tennyson could and did read the ancients with ease. But suppose we knew as little about the upbringing of John Keats as we do about that of William Shakespeare, would not the editors and index-hunters have long since claimed a wide acquaintance of Greek authors for the poet who gave us *Endymion*, *Hyperion* and the *Ode on a Grecian Urn*?

Yet we can be certain that Shakespeare was at least able to read Latin at need, since we can point to definite books or passages which he must have used and which as far as our knowledge goes were only available to him in the Latin language. For the writing of *Macbeth*, for example, he seems to have equipped himself by a study of Seneca and in particular of the *Hercules Furens* in the original.[15] Or, to take another instance, one of the main sources of *The Rape of Lucrece* was the account of the expulsion of the Tarquins in Book II of Ovid's *Fasti*, and it may be accepted as almost certain that Shakespeare read this in the Latin since no contemporary translation of the *Fasti* has been discovered.[16] Yet a close comparison of the poem with Ovid leads to surprising results. Let me once again quote Thomson, who gives us the best exposition of this point.

Here and there in *Lucrece*, there are touches which can hardly have been suggested by Painter or taken from any other English source known to us. For example:

> Her breasts...
> A pair of maiden worlds unconquered,
> Save of their Lord no bearing yoke, they knew   (407–9)

is surely a development of line 804 of the *Fasti*:

> nunc primum externa pectora tacta manu.

> A captive victor that hath lost in gain.   (730)

That is clearly suggested by Ovid's

> quid, victor, gaudes? haec te victoria perdet.

Here is another clear instance. Shakespeare says (1604–5)

> Three times with sighs she gives her sorrow fire,
> Ere once she can discharge one word of woe.

Ovid sings (*Fasti*, II, 823):

> ter conata loqui, ter destitit.

This is fairly conclusive evidence that Shakespeare had read the Latin *Fasti* or that part of it which told the story of Lucrece.... What strikes the candid reader, comparing *Lucrece* with the passage in the *Fasti*, is the absence rather than the presence of evidence for a direct use of the Latin. In a poem dealing in such elaboration of detail with so singular an incident as the Rape the astonishing thing would be if the Latin original were not echoed, over and over again. And it is the astonishing thing that happens. Apart from one or two echoes or imitations Shakespeare might as well not have read the *Fasti* at all. We may suppose that he did read it in a cursory way, lay it down and write *Lucrece*, as he had written *Venus*, entirely from his own resources.[17]

I have quoted that at length because I think it goes near to the heart of the matter. At any rate all Shakespeare's other dealings with the classics, so far as they can be observed, seem to conform to the same pattern.

There is, for example, his treatment of classical mythology, allusions to which are of course frequent in the plays. It would be absurd to expect in him or indeed in any other poet of the age the precise correspondence we should look for in a poet today or even in Milton, by whose time an author's conscience in such matters had become far more exact than it was a generation earlier. Spenser's scholarship can hardly be questioned. Yet he does not hesitate, when it suits his book in *The Tears of the Muses*, to make Apollo, and not Jupiter, the father of those "sacred sisters nine". Renwick's comment on this, that "Renaissance scholarship was more genial than exact" and that the ancient myths were a poetic inheritance to use as the poet pleased,[18] is a reminder that the myths were still alive in Shakespeare's day, as they had been throughout the Middle Ages; the outstanding example being the tale of Troilus and Cressida, which was almost entirely a medieval invention, and had grown into a great "matter" at the hands of four poets, Benoît de Sainte-Maure, Boccaccio, Chaucer and Henryson, before it came to Shakespeare's. Thus when his Antony cries to the spirit of Cleopatra, just about to cross the river of Death as he supposes,[19]

> Stay for me!
> Where souls do couch on flowers, we'll hand in hand,
> And with our sprightly port make the ghosts gaze:
> Dido and her Aeneas shall want troops,
> And all the haunt be ours—

it is perhaps idle or at any rate unfair to note that in the sixth book of the *Aeneid* Dido dwells in Hades with her husband Sychaeus and repulses with scorn the advances of the repentant Aeneas. Shakespeare has supplied a different end to the story. And one has only to read "her Sichaeus" for "her Aeneas", as the classicist Warburton did in the eighteenth century, to see how right Shakespeare was.

Yet for us, who are committed by the terms of our reference to be the prosaic book-worms Tennyson condemned, the question remains: was the invention deliberate or involuntary? We may even dare to wonder whether ignorance rather than forgetfulness may not be the explanation of the confusion in *2 Henry IV* (II, ii, 85) between the firebrand which Althaea plucked from the flames before the birth of Meleager and the firebrand Hecuba dreamed of before the birth of Paris, or the reference in *Love's Labour's Lost* (v, ii, 582) to Hercules' slaying Cerberus with his club, perhaps by confusion with the slaying of the three-headed Geryon,[20] or the spelling "Ariachne" in *Troilus and Cressida* (v, ii, 152) for Arachne, the spinner who became a spider, by confusion with Ariadne who was concerned with another kind of thread altogether.

Further, when we say he read Ovid or Seneca in the original, what do we mean by "read"? Read, with ease and enjoyment, or read laboriously with a lexicon, and with the aid of a translation if one was available, or merely consulted now and again so as to check or illuminate a translation lying before him? His verbal memory must have been prodigious, so that it is more than likely he carried away from school passages of Latin verse that his master set him to learn. We all do, but generally only a few scraps; and, unless we become classical scholars, the memory for such passages will probably fade as time goes on. What Shakespeare learnt in this way would, on the other hand, probably remain with him for the rest of his life, to be drawn upon, when needed for the writing of his plays and poems. A "good sprag memory", with which Sir Hugh Evans credits little William, is not necessarily however accompanied by linguistic ability. Thus Shakespeare's acquaintance with certain pieces of Latin poetry in the original, such as the story of Lucrece in Ovid or the *Hercules Furens* of Seneca, does not prove that he could read other Latin poems or plays at sight.

Moreover, his evident familiarity with Arthur Golding's Ovid, a familiarity so intimate that Golding's actual words, at times even his additions, recur to his mind and appear in his verse, is not easily accounted for if he read the original Ovid with facility, still less if, as Edgar Fripp held, a copy of *Metamorphoses* in Latin was "devoured" by him at an early age, so that "the difficulty was not to bring the boy to this school-book but to keep him from it".[21] Golding is not a book found today in every gentleman's library. Let me therefore quote a passage from it. Here are the lines in which he translates Ovid's fine description of the horses of the Sun running away with headstrong Phaeton.

> They girded forth, and cutting through the Cloudes that let their race,
> With splayed wings they overflew the Easterne winde a pace.
> The burthen was so lyght as that the Genets felt it not.
> The wonted weight was from the Waine, the which they well did wot.
> For like as ships amids the Seas that scant of ballace have
> Doe reele and totter with the wynde, and yeeld to every wave;
> Even so the Waine for want of weight it erst was wont to beare
> Did hoyse aloft and scayle and reele, as though it empty were.
> Which when the Cartware did perceyve, they left the beaten way,
> And taking bridle in the teeth began to run astray.
> The rider was so sore agast, he knew no use of Reyne,
> Nor yet his way: and though he had yet had it been in vayne,
> Bicause he wanted powre to rule the horses and the Wayne.[22]

Golding's "wain" is his translation of Ovid's "currus",[23] and one would hardly find two more suitable words to characterize the creaking lumbering fourteeners of the English on the one hand the smooth-running polished hexameters of the Latin on the other. Ezra Pound the American poet, we are told, admires Golding's verse: I am very sure Shakespeare, a different kind of poet, did not. And with this sample before them most lovers of English poetry will, I think, ask with Thomson: "How could a man, who read Ovid's Latin with ease and pleasure, *bear* to read Golding instead?"[24]

Yet there is ample proof that Shakespeare did read it, and a high probability that he knew portions of it by heart. The last two lines just quoted, which are Golding's paraphrase of

> nec scit qua sit iter, nec, si sciat, imperet illis,

clearly inspired Richard II's

> Down, down, I come like glistering Phaeton
> Wanting the manage of unruly jades.[25]

"Glistering" too, though Golding does not actually apply the epithet to Phaeton himself, is a favourite word of his and Shakespeare I do not doubt had in mind "the bright and fierie beames

That glistred rounde about"[26] the head of Phoebus, who later transferred them to the head of Phaeton. Then there are the two references to Jove's stay in the humble cottage of Philemon (*Much Ado*, II, i, 99–102; *As You Like It*, III, iii, 11). In both the point of the jest turns on the word "thatched"; in *As You Like It* "a thatched house"; in *Much Ado* a thatched "roof". And both may well be echoes of Ovid's line describing Philemon's "domus" as "stipulis et canna tecta palustri".[27] Nevertheless, there are at least grounds for suspecting the source to be the English and not the Latin version, since Golding translates the words,

> The *roofe* thereof was *thatched* all with straw and fennish reede,[28]

whereas Ovid never even directly refers to a roof at all. Similarly, when Ovid relates in his first book how men were content in the Golden Age to feed on wild berries

> et quae deciderant patula Iovis arbore glandes,

which Golding translates

> And by the acornes dropt on ground from Ioves brode tree in fielde,

one suspects again it was Golding rather than the original that Shakespeare recalled in the pretty exchange he gives to Celia and Rosalind about the discovery of Orlando in the Forest of Arden where men "fleet the time carelessly as they did in the Golden World". "I found him under a tree", says Celia, "like a dropped acorn"; to which Rosalind replies "It may well be called Jove's tree, when it drops forth such fruit".[29] Clearly Shakespeare *might* have got it from Ovid direct. Yet when one notes that his "Jove's tree" and "drop" are also found in Golding, is one guilty of Fluellen's salmon-fallacy if one infers a connexion? In any event it seems clear that when writing *As You Like It* Shakespeare looked up or called to mind the passage about the Golden Age in the first book of the *Metamorphoses*. And it is interesting to notice that *Henry V*, which belongs to the same period of his career, appears to show traces of the same influence. For it can hardly be doubted that when the Constable of France exclaims to his fellow nobles

> O, for the honour of our land
> Let us not hang like roping icicles
> Upon our houses' thatch[30]

and Grandpré a few scenes later speaks of the English horses with

> The gum down-roping from their pale-dead eyes,[30]

the word "roping", an unusual one and not found elsewhere in Shakespeare, was derived from

> Then Isycles hung roping down[31]

which occurs in Golding fifteen lines later than that line about the acorns dropped from Jove's tree just quoted. Furthermore, Ovid's words are

> et ventis glacies adstricta perpendit[31]

whence it is evident that 'roping', which means of course "hanging down like a rope", was Golding's addition.

But Shakespeare's best known borrowing from Ovid is Prospero's speech renouncing magic,[32] a speech full of echoes of Medea's incantation in Book VII of the *Metamorphoses*. And we have only to set the first line

> Ye elves of hills, brooks, standing lakes, and groves

beside Ovid's

> aureaque et venti montesque amnesque lacusque,
> dique omnes nemorum,

and Golding's translation of this

> Ye Ayres and windes: ye Elves of Hilles, of Brookes, of Woods alone,
> Of standing Lakes.

to render Golding's influence indisputable. The coincident "brooks" might be accidental; but "ye elves of hills" and the addition of the epithet "standing" to *lacus* cannot be.[33] There are, too, several other echoes later in the speech, as Malone first pointed out. On the other hand Churton Collins noted that Golding has nothing corresponding to Ovid's "convulsaque robora", which clearly inspired Shakespeare's "rifted Jove's stout oak". He must therefore have been acquainted also with the Latin. Surely the commonsense interpretation of this apparent contradiction is that when he came to write Prospero's speech he naturally recalled Medea's incantation from Golding, because it was there in his mind, and, having done so, turned up the passage in the original Ovid for any further hints which might be useful. In other words, he probably had a good deal of the Golding version by heart, but had to consult the Latin one in a book.[34]

It looks to me, in short, as if the copy of *Metamorphoses* which he "devoured", as Fripp claims, at an early age was not the Latin version but the English. Golding's verse might be wooden and his diction often absurd, but he offered an inexhaustible mine to a young poet; for the book was a kind of encyclopaedia of classical story.[35] Cowden Clarke, writing of Keats' schooldays, tells us that "he became an omnivorous reader...but the books that he read with most assiduity were Tooke's *Pantheon*, Lemprière's *Classical Dictionary*, which he seemed to learn, and Spence's *Polymetis*". Golding must have done for Shakespeare very much what these did for Keats. And the formal education of the two poets was, it appears, similarly scanty. For Keats was taken from school before reaching the age of sixteen: never learnt Greek; and though acquiring some knowledge of Latin "could hardly have reached that stage of scholarship in which the influence of classical literature begins to make itself felt".[36] It was, however, when he was about seventeen or eighteen that the poet in him first awoke. An introduction to Spenser did this for him, and once introduced, he went through *The Faerie Queene*, Cowden Clarke writes, like "a young horse through a spring meadow ramping". Shakespeare was fifteen when *The Shepherd's Calendar* appeared. Was it Spenser also who made him conscious of his inheritance? The question is, perhaps, an idle one. But before we begin looking for his Latin sources we ought surely to exhaust the possibilities of the native poetry available in the mid-sixteenth century. For we can be certain that before he was twenty-five he had read and absorbed any English poem he found worth absorbing. Personally I think he jibbed at boring, ill-languaged stuff like *The Mirror for Magistrates*, except for Sackville's magnificent Induction, in which rather than in the sixth book of the *Aeneid* I see his inspiration for Clarence's dream.[37] And as a good deal of early Elizabethan verse *was* boring, his golden treasury would be a slim volume, apart from Chaucer and such poems as he needed for his plots like Arthur Brooke's *Romeus and Juliet*, which he must have known almost by heart.[38]

Pondering these matters one day, it occurred to me that I might try a little experiment: I would take a passage in which Shakespeare was clearly appealing to the classically minded in his audience, and see how much of it could be traced directly to classical sources. And, being under the impression that he brushed up his Latin a little when he came to the great tragedies, or after he came to know Ben Jonson, I turned to the comedies and found in the first fourteen lines of the fifth act of *The Merchant of Venice* the sort of passage I had in mind. They form the opening bars of Shakespeare's moonlight sonata, in which four love-lorn personages of classical story are summoned up to usher us in by contrast to the happiness of Belmont. Everyone knows the passage. Yet it must be quoted for reference in what follows, and after all it cannot be read or heard too often.

Enter Lorenzo and Jessica

Lor. The moon shines bright: in such a night as this,
When the sweet wind did gently kiss the trees
And they did make no noise—in such a night,
Troilus methinks mounted the Troyan Walls,
And sighed his soul towards the Grecian tents,
Where Cressid lay that night.

Jes.   In such a night
Did Thisbe fearfully o'ertrip the dew
And saw the lion's shadow ere himself
And ran dismayed away.

Lor.   In such a night
Stood Dido with a willow in her hand
Upon the wild sea-banks, and waft her love
To come again to Carthage.

Jes.   In such a night
Medea gathered the enchanted herbs
That did renew old Aeson.

It is absurd to think of Shakespeare digging that glorious stuff out of books: it was all in his head, below the threshold of consciousness as the psychologists say, ready to spring to life and song. Yet spontaneous as it no doubt was, it of course goes back to reading at some time or other. How much of it derives from the Latin originals? The Troilus passage does not at any rate, since, as already noted, his story is a medieval one. But, as an illustration of how Shakespeare's mind was working, it is worth pointing out that these six lines are a distillation of six stanzas of Chaucer's *Troilus and Criseyde*—"night", "bright moon", "sighs", "walls" of Troy, Grecian "tents", the "sweet wind", the "soul" of Troilus, all are there.[39]

As for Thisbe, thereby hangs a tale of blended memories, memories of Chaucer—this time of his *Legend of Good Women*—on the one hand, and of Golding's Book IV, 67–201, on the other. But to get the full story one must take the lines in *The Merchant* with the comic interlude of Pyramus and Thisbe in *A Midsummer Night's Dream*, since both sources are there echoed also.[40] The Mechanicals went to Golding for, among other things, the "cranny", for the "courtesy" of the wall, and for Thisbe's "tarrying". But Chaucer supplied Wall with his "lime" and "stone", while Chaucer's line

> And as she ran her wimpel leet she falle[41]

reappears in Shakespeare as

> And as she fled her mantle she did fall.[42]

Furthermore when he makes Bottom-Pyramus exclaim

> O wicked wall through whom I see no bliss[43]

he is directly echoing Chaucer's

> And every day this wal they wolde threte,
> And wisshe to god, that it were doun y-bete.
> Thus wolde they seyn—"alas! thou wikked Wal"[44]

—a personification which probably inspired Bottom with the idea that "some man or other must present Wall". Whether Jessica's brief tribute to Thisbe echoes Chaucer or Golding is uncertain. But her reference to "dew" is assuredly derived either from the former's "dew of herbes wete"[45] or the latter's "dewie grasse",[46] which are their renderings of Ovid's "pruinosae herbae"[47] (frosty grass).

The most interesting of all is Dido, since she seems to provide evidence that Shakespeare was drawing upon memory, and memory alone. Here again his Chaucerian source is *The Legend of Good Women*, but in this case he has, no doubt unconsciously, gone to the wrong love-lorn lady, since it was Ariadne, deserted by Theseus and not Dido deserted by Aeneas, who stood upon the shore and beckoned her lover to return; a confusion first noted by Malone.[48] Chaucer's Ariadne, however, is taken from the tenth letter of Ovid's *Heroides*, and Root maintains "there is no reason to suppose that Shakespeare had Chaucer in mind rather than Ovid".[49] But there *is* a reason and it lies in the words "Upon the wild sea-banks", which Shakespeare gives us in place of Chaucer's "strond" or Ovid's "litus", and borrowed from the "yle amid the wilde see"[50] at which Chaucer tells us, but Ovid does not (at any rate in the *Heroides*[51]), Theseus first put in after sailing from Crete. This little change, whether conscious or not, was a stroke of genius; and Shakespeare added a like stroke to it, this time of his own unaided invention. In Ovid Ariadne, relating how she tried to signal to her treacherous lover as he sailed away, says

> candidaque inposui longae velamina virgae,[52]

which is in modern English "I set white garments upon a tall rod" and appears rather crudely in Chaucer as

> Her kerchef on a pole up stikked she.[53]

The kerchef has disappeared in Shakespeare and the pole become a willow branch, symbol of lost or unrequited love. Thus by double or treble alchemy we get the golden

> In such a night
> Stood Dido with a willow in her hand
> Upon the wild sea-banks, and waft her love
> To come again to Carthage,—

lines noted by Matthew Arnold as "drenched and intoxicated with the fairy dew...of natural magic", and as the perfect example of transposition from the classical into the romantic key.[54]

Shakespeare's wayward dealings with Dido would make an interesting digression upon my theme, but one too long for this place. It would be ridiculous, however, to suppose that he was ignorant of her story. Had he not, probably a little before he wrote the lines just quoted, made Hermia swear to Lysander

> And by the fire which burned the Carthage queen,
> When the false Troyan under sail was seen?[55]

And after 1593 he certainly knew, and knew well, Marlowe's *Tragedy of Dido*, while there was always Chaucer's *Legend of Dido, Queen of Carthage*, even if the *Heroides* was a closed book to him. And knowing these things might it not have occurred to him later that he had mixed her up with Ariadne? If so, that was no reason for going back and altering the passage. Nobody in the audience would be likely to detect a solecism. Besides, why should not he make Dido wave a willow upon the wild sea-banks (before committing herself to the flames) if he wished? As for going back and altering, his fellow players boasted, Ben Jonson tells us, that he "never blotted out line",[56] by which, I take it, they meant, not that he never thrust his quill too deeply into the ink—the blots on his signatures prove he could do that—but that he never needed to correct, or never cared to correct, what he had once written. Certainly he would not have cared to correct these Dido lines, for he must have known how lovely they were.

But let us not forget Medea, last of our moonlit lovers. The four speeches begin "In such a night", as do the three following in which Lorenzo and Jessica strive to "out-night" each other; and it may well be that what led Shakespeare to select these incidents of classical story was the part the moon plays in them all. For, though Medea is a lover like the other three, and a deserted lover like Troilus and Dido, it is not of love but of her gathering herbs by moonlight that Jessica speaks. Now of this, or of old Aeson's rejuvenation, Chaucer made no mention in his *Legend of Medea*: Shakespeare takes it from the seventh book of the *Metamorphoses*,[57] and I feel sure once again from Golding. In a couple of lines verbal links are hardly to be expected; yet Jessica's "enchanted herbs"[58] and "renew"[59] are both found in Golding's version. I would rather stress however Shakespeare's familiarity with the story evidenced in other plays. That Golding's translation of it indubitably lies behind Prospero's speech in *The Tempest* has already been shown. The expression "triple Hecat" which Golding uses twice[60] occurs also at V, i, 391 of *A Midsummer Night's Dream*. When again Laertes alludes to the supreme life-giving qualities of a cataplasm

> Collected from all simples that have virtue
> Under the moon[61]

Shakespeare was alluding, and perhaps expecting his judicious spectators to realise he was alluding, to Medea's diligent search throughout Greece during nine moonlit nights for

> herbs that can by vertue of their juice
> To flowring pride of lustie youth old withred age reduce,

as Golding elegantly puts it.[62] I suspect too that the witches in *Macbeth* owe not a little to Ovid's Medea. Certainly, the cauldron scene has much in common with his account of the brewing of her bronze pot and the ingredients she casts into it. In short Shakespeare's mind often turned to this particular passage of the *Metamorphoses* and the evidence, taking it all round, once again seems to prove that what it turned to was Golding's English and not the original Latin.

The upshot then of our little experiment is that every scrap of the Lorenzo and Jessica duet, for all its classical panoply, was derived from native sources. Is it not possible that the same thing would prove true for most of the other classical allusions in Shakespeare were all the facts known? In any case the paramount influence of Golding is incontestable. Nor was it confined to Shakespeare's mythological references, as the occurrence of "roping icicles" in *Henry V* warns us. To assess it fully a comparison of Shakespeare's vocabulary as a whole with that of Golding would be needed—a vast undertaking!

To the question then at the head of this article, I can find no better answer than one given by Dr Johnson two hundred and twenty years ago and with that I will conclude, as it serves to sum up most of what I have been trying to say.

There has always prevailed a tradition that Shakespeare wanted learning, that he had no regular education, nor much skill in the dead languages. *Johnson* his friend affirms, that *he had small Latin, and no Greek*; who besides that he had no imaginable temptation to falsehood, wrote at a time when the character and acquisitions of *Shakespeare* were known to multitudes. His evidence ought therefore to decide the controversy, unless some testimony of equal force could be opposed.

Some have imagined, that they have discovered deep learning in many imitations of old writers; but the examples which I have known urged, were drawn from books translated in his time; or were such easy coincidences of thought, as will happen to all who consider the same subjects; or such remarks on life or axioms of morality as float in conversation, and are transmitted, through the world in proverbial sentences....

It is most likely that he learned *Latin* sufficiently to make him acquainted with construction [i.e. capable of translating Latin word by word], but that he never advanced to an easy perusal of the *Roman* authors.[63]

The common sense of the first two paragraphs seems to me to dispose of not a few claims in favour of Shakespeare's learning advanced by learned men who desire to have him of their company. And if discoveries since Johnson's day suggest that he hardly allows for quite enough Latin in the first half of his final sentence, to those who would say the same of the second half I reply in Scottish "Not proven".

NOTES

1. This paper was first delivered in an earlier form as a presidential address to the Scottish Classical Association in 1951, was delivered again in September 1955 as a lecture to the Shakespeare Conference Stratford-upon-Avon, and has now been revised for publication.

2. See *Conversations with Drummond* (*Ben Jonson*, ed. Herford and Simpson, I, 133) and *The Discoveries* (*id.* VIII, 583–4) "In effect", wrote Herford (II, 447) these qualifications of the praise "are developments of the verse-tribute, not contradictions of it". In other words, even the praise implied criticism.

3. See my article on 'Ben Jonson and *Julius Caesar*', *Shakespeare Survey*, 2 (1949).

4. For the letter see J. S. Smart, *Shakespeare: truth and tradition*, p. 40, or E. I. Fripp, *Shakespeare, man and artist*, II, 498.

5. Cited by E. K. Chambers, *William Shakespeare*, II, 264. I modernize the spelling.

6. Chambers, *op. cit.* I, 17.

7. Cited by Chambers (*op. cit.* II, 254), who comments (*id.* I, 22): "The statement is not in itself incredible. The course at Stratford, even if not curtailed, would hardly have qualified him to take charge of a grammar school; but his post may well have been no more than that of an usher or an *abecedarius.*"

8. *Essays of John Dryden*, ed. W. P. Ker, I, 80.

9. Cited in Chambers, *op. cit.* II, 211.

10. *Shakespeare's Use of Learning* by V. K. Whitaker (The Huntington Library, 1953), which did not reach my hands until just before this article was sent to press, follows Baldwin in the main.

11. Thomson, *Shakespeare and the Classics* (1952), p. 153.

12. *Ibid.* pp. 36–8.

13. See Parry, *Henry Jackson, O.M.* (1926), pp. 275–80.

14. Thomson, *op. cit.* p. 153.

15. See *Macbeth* (New Cambridge Shakespeare), Introduction, p. xliii, n. 1 and the notes there referred to.

16. For *Venus and Adonis* he could have found all he wanted in Golding; and Bush has shown that for the story of Lucrece in Livy he relied mainly if not entirely upon a version of it in Painter's *Palace of Pleasure* (1566).

17. Thomson (*op. cit.* pp. 43–4), who gives the following translations of the lines from Ovid:

Breasts now for the first time touched by a stranger's hand...	(II, 804)
Why victor, dost thou triumph? This victory will destroy thee...	(II, 811)
Three times she strove to speak, three times she failed...	(II, 823)

By some oversight he assigns the wrong line-numbering to the first two lines, as he does also in his reference on p. 43 to the whole passage.

18. See W. L. Renwick's note, p. 206 of his edition of Spenser's *Complaints*.

19. *Antony and Cleopatra*, IV, xiv, 50–4.

20. The two three-headed monsters are mentioned by Ovid in the same line: *Metamorphoses*, IX, 185 (Golding, 226–7).

21. E. I. Fripp, *op. cit.* I, 102.

22. *Metamorphoses*, II, 158–70 (Ovid), 209–21 (Golding). Cited from the edition of Golding by W. H. D. Rouse (1904).

23. It is only fair to Golding to note that "wain" apart from its ordinary meaning of "an oxdrawn waggon" was the accepted neo-classical word for "quadrigae", a four-horse chariot such as Phoebus drove.

24. Thomson, *op. cit.* p. 154.   25. *Richard II*, III, iii, 178.

26. Golding, II, 53–4, 164–5. Cf. "glister" in 156.   27. *Metamorphoses*, VIII, 630.

28. Golding, VIII, 806. My italics.

29. *Metamorphoses*, I, 106; Golding, I, 121: *As You Like It*, III, ii, 247 ff.

30. *Henry V*, III, v, 22–4; IV, ii, 48.   31. *Metamorphoses*, I, 120; Golding, I, 136.

32. *Tempest*, v, i, 33 ff.   33. *Metamorphoses*, VII, 197; Golding, VII, 265–6.

34. Root detects the same blend of Phaer with the original Aeneid in the *Tempest* masque. Cf. *Classical Mythology in Shakespeare*, p. 77.

35. See Fripp 'Shakespeare's Use of Ovid's *Metamorphoses*' in his *Shakespeare Studies*.

36. De Selincourt, *The Poems of John Keats*, pp. xxi–xxii, from which I take the quotations from Cowden Clarke and the other particulars about Keats in this paragraph.

37. See the Introduction to *Richard III* (New Cambridge Shakespeare), pp. xxiii–viii.

38. See the Introduction to *Romeo and Juliet* (New Cambridge Shakespeare), p. xi.

39. *Troilus and Criseyde*, Book V, stanzas 92–7.

40. This section of the article was originally written in 1951 (see n. 1), since when Kenneth Muir has unravelled a much fuller story as regards the English sources of the interlude. See his 'Pyramus and Thisbe: a study in Shakespeare's Method' (*Shakespeare Quarterly*, Spring 1954), which notes the parallels with Golding's "cranny" and "courtesy" and with Chaucer's "Thus wolde they seyn, 'allas! thou wikked wal'".

41. *Legend*, 813.   42. *Midsummer Night's Dream*, V, i, 143.

43. *Ibid.* 181.   44. *Legend*, 754–6.

45. *Ibid.* 774.   46. Golding, IV, 102.

47. *Metamorphoses*, IV, 82.

48. *Malone's Shakespeare* (1821), V, p. 135.

49. R. K. Root, *Classical Mythology in Shakespeare* (1903), p. 57. Ovid's Dido (*Heroides*, 7), it is true, often refers to the stormy seas upon which Aeneas put forth.

50. *Legend*, 2163.

51. Perhaps Chaucer took this detail from *Metamorphoses*, VIII, 174–5 where Ovid says Theseus sailed to Dia (i.e. Naxos) with the daughter of Minos "comitemque suam crudelis in illo/litore destituit".

52. *Heroides*, X, 41.

53. *Legend*, 2202.

54. *Celtic Literature* (1867), p. 168.

55. *Midsummer Night's Dream*, I, i, 173.

56. *Discoveries*, see *Ben Jonson*, ed. Herford and Simpson, VIII, 583.

57. *Metamorphoses*, VII, 159–293; Golding, VII, 220–381.

58. Golding, VII, 142; cf. 284, 295, etc.

59. Golding, VII, 381.

60. Golding, VII, 136. (Ovid "triformis dea"), 318 (Ovid "Hecate").

61. *Hamlet*, IV, vii, 144–6.

62. Golding, VII, 284–5.

63. Preface to his edition of Shakespeare (1765), cited in Sir Walter Raleigh, *Johnson on Shakespeare* (1908), pp. 34–5.

SHAKESPEARE AND
THE ELIZABETHAN ROMANS[1]

BY

T. J. B. SPENCER

Shakespeare has, at various times, received some very handsome compliments for his ancient Romans; for his picture of the Roman world, its institutions, and the causation of events; for his representation of the Roman people at three critical stages of their development: the turbulent republic with its conflict of the classes; the transition from an oligarchic to a monarchic government which was vainly delayed by the assassination of Julius Caesar; and the final stages by which the rule of the civilized world came to lie in the hands of Octavius Caesar. These are quite often praised as veracious or penetrating or plausible. Moreover, the compliments begin early, and they begin at a time when no high opinion was held of Shakespeare's learning. The name of Nahum Tate, for example, is not a revered one in the history of Shakespeare studies; yet in 1680 he wrote:

I confess I cou'd never yet get a true account of his Learning, and am apt to think it more than Common Report allows him. I am sure he never touches on a Roman Story, but the Persons, the Passages, the Manners, the Circumstances, the Ceremonies, all are Roman.[2]

And Dryden, too, in conversation said "that there was something in this very tragedy of *Coriolanus*, as it was writ by Shakespeare, that is truly great and truly Roman".[3] And Pope (for all his comparison of Shakespeare to "an ancient majestick piece of *Gothick* Architecture") declared in his Preface that he found him

very knowing in the customs, rites, and manners of Antiquity. In *Coriolanus* and *Julius Caesar*, not only the Spirit, but Manners, of the *Romans* are exactly drawn; and still a nicer distinction is shewn, between the manners of the *Romans* in the time of the former and of the latter.[4]

The odd thing is that this veracity or authenticity was approved at a time when Shakespeare's educational background was suspect; when the word "learning" practically meant a knowledge of the Greek and Roman writers; when the usual description of Shakespeare was "wild"; when he was regarded as a member of what Thomas Rymer called "the gang of the strolling fraternity".

There were, of course, one or two exceptions; Rymer wrote, towards the end of the seventeenth century, in his most cutting way about *Julius Caesar*:

Caesar and *Brutus* were above his conversation. To put them in Fools Coats, and make them Jack-puddens in the *Shakespear* dress, is a *Sacriledge*.... The Truth is, this authors head was full of villainous, unnatural images, and history has only furnish'd him with great names, thereby to recommend them to the World.[5]

There was, too, the problem of Shakespeare's undignified Roman mobs. It was obvious that Cleopatra's vision of a Rome where

> mechanic slaves
> With greasy aprons, rules, and hammers, shall
> Uplift us to the view

was derived from Shakespeare's own London. And Casca's description: "The rabblement hooted and clapped their chopped hands and threw up their sweaty night-caps..."—this was the English populace and not the Roman *plebs*. Dennis thought that the introduction of the mob by Shakespeare "offends not only against the Dignity of Tragedy, but against the Truth of History likewise, and the Customs of Ancient *Rome*, and the majesty of the *Roman* People".[6] But the opinions of Rymer and Dennis were eccentric; the worst they could say against Shakespeare's Romans was that they were not sufficiently dignified; and this counted for very little beside the usual opinion of better minds that Shakespeare got his Romans right.

More surprising, therefore, was Shakespeare's frequent neglect of details; and it was just at *this* time that the scholars and critics (if not the theatrical and reading publics) were becoming sensitive to Shakespeare's anachronisms, his aberrations from good sense and common knowledge about the ancients, and were carefully scrutinizing his text for mistakes. It was apparent that, when it came to details, Shakespeare's Romans often belonged to the time of Queen Elizabeth and King James. And the industrious commentators of the eighteenth century collected a formidable array of nonsense from his plays on classical antiquity: how clocks strike in ancient Rome; how Cleopatra has lace in her stays and plays at billiards; how Titus Lartius compares Coriolanus's *hm* to the sound of a battery; and so on. Above all, it could be observed that Shakespeare was occasionally careless or forgetful about ancient costume. Coriolanus stood in the Forum waving his hat. The very idea of a Roman candidate for the consulship standing waving his hat was enough to make a whole form of schoolboys break into irrepressible mirth. Pope softened the horror by emending *hat* to *cap*; and Coriolanus was permitted to wave his cap, not his hat, in the texts of Theobald, Hanmer, Warburton, and Dr Johnson, and perhaps even later. What seemed remarkable and what made the eighteenth-century editors so fussy about these anachronisms was Shakespeare's inconsistency in his historical reconstructions: his care and scrupulosity over preserving Roman manners, alongside occasional carelessness or indifference. The very reason they noticed the blunders was that they jarred against the pervading sense of authenticity everywhere else in the Roman plays.

I take it that Dryden and Pope were right; that Shakespeare knew what he was doing in writing Roman plays; that part of his intention was a serious effort at representing the Roman scene as genuinely as he could. He was not telling a fairy tale with Duke Theseus on St Valentine's Day, nor dramatizing a novelette about Kings of Sicilia and Bohemia, but producing a *mimesis* of the veritable history of the most important people (humanly speaking) who ever lived, the concern of every educated man in Europe and not merely something of local, national, patriotic interest; and he was conscious of all this while he was building up his dramatic situations and expositions of characters for the players to fulfil. It can, therefore, hardly fail to be relevant to our interpretations of the plays to explore the views of Roman history in Shakespeare's time. It is at least important to make sure that we do not unthinkingly take it for granted that they were the same as our own in the twentieth century to which we belong or the nineteenth century from which we derive. It is worth while tracing to what extent Shakespeare was in step with ideas about ancient Rome among his contemporaries and to what extent (and why) he diverged from them.

"Histories make men wise." Ancient, and in particular Roman, history was explored as the material of political lessons, because it was one of the few bodies of consistent and continuous historical material available. Modern national history (in spite of patriotism) could not be regarded as so central, nor were the writers so good; and the narratives in the scriptures were already overworked by the parson. Roman history was written and interpreted tendentiously in Europe in the sixteenth century, as has happened at other times. In writing his Roman plays Shakespeare was touching upon the gravest and most exciting as well as the most pedantic of Renaissance studies, of European scholarship. Although Shakespeare himself turned to Roman history after he had been occupied with English history for some years, nevertheless it was Roman history which usually had the primacy for the study of political morality. Yet in spite of the widespread interest in ancient culture among educated persons, the actual writing of the history of the Greeks and Romans was not very successful in England in the sixteenth century. There was no history of the Romans in Shakespeare's lifetime comparable (for example) to the *History of Great Britain* by John Speed or the *Generall Historie of the Turkes* by Richard Knolles. Sir Walter Raleigh did not get very far in his *History of the World* and dealt only with the earlier and duller centuries of Rome. Probably the reason for the scarcity of books of Roman history and their undistinguished nature was that the sense of the supremacy of the ancients and of the impudence of endeavouring to provide a substitute for Livy and Tacitus, was too strong.[7] So explained William Fulbecke, who published a book called *An Historicall Collection of the Continuall Factions, Tumults, and Massacres of the Romans* in 1601 and dedicated it to Sackville, Lord Buck-hurst (the primary author of *A Mirror for Magistrates*). "I do not despaire" (wrote Fulbecke) "to follow these Romanes, though I do not aspire to their exquisite and industrious perfection: for that were to climbe above the climates: but to imitate any man, is every mans talent." His book is a poor thing. And so is Richard Reynoldes' *Chronicle of all the Noble Emperours of the Romaines* (1571). And the translations of the Roman historians, apart from North's Plutarch, before the seventeenth century are not particularly distinguished. But for this very reason the books on Roman history are useful evidence for the normal attitude to the Romans and their story in Shakespeare's lifetime. For it is not so much what we can find in Plutarch, but what Shakespeare noticed in Plutarch that we need to know; not merely Plutarch's narrative, but the preconceptions with which his biographies could be read by a lively modern mind about the turn of the seventeenth century; for

> men may construe things after their fashion
> Clean from the purpose of the things themselves.

It is by no means certain that we, by the unaided light of reason and mid-twentieth-century assumptions, will always be able to notice the things to which Shakespeare was sensitive.

First then, the title of William Fulbecke's book is worth attention: *An Historicall Collection of the Continuall Factions, Tumults, and Massacres of the Romans and Italians during the space of one hundred and twentie yeares next before the peaceable Empire of Augustus Caesar.* There is not much of the majesty of the Roman People (which Dennis desiderated) in these continual factions, tumults and massacres. In his preface Fulbecke writes:

The use of this historie is threefold; first the revealing of the mischiefes of discord and civill discention.... Secondly the opening of the cause hereof, which is nothing else but ambition, for out of this seed groweth a whole harvest of evils. Thirdly the declaring of the remedie, which is by humble estimation of our selves, by living well, not by lurking well: by conversing in the light of the common weale with equals, not by complotting in darke conventicles against superiors.[8]

Equally tendentious is what we read on the title-page of the translation of Appian as *An Aunciente Historie and exquisite Chronicle of the Romanes Warres, both Civile and Foren* in 1578;

In the which is declared:
Their greedy desire to conquere others.
Their mortall malice to destroy themselves.
Their seeking of matters to make warre abroad.
Their picking of quarels to fall out at home.
All the degrees of Sedition, and all the effects of Ambition.
A firme determination of Fate, thorowe all the changes of Fortune.
And finally, an evident demonstration, That peoples rule must give place, and Princes power prevayle.

This kind of material (the ordinary stuff of Roman history in the sixteenth century) does not lend itself to chatter about the majesty of the Roman people. In fact, the kind of classical dignity which we associate perhaps with Addison's *Cato* or Kemble's impersonation of Coriolanus is not to be taken for granted in Shakespeare's time. The beginning of Virgil's *Aeneid*, with its simple yet sonorous *arma virumque cano*, might by us be taken as expressive of true Roman dignity. Richard Stanyhurst, however, in his translation of Virgil in 1582 rendered it:

Now manhood and garboyles I chaunt....

"Garboyles", it will be remembered, was Antony's favourite word to describe the military and political exploits of Fulvia.

So much for Roman history as "garboyles". Secondly, besides the "garboyles" and encouraging them, there was a limitation in viewpoint due to the fact that the moral purpose of history in general, and of Roman history in particular, was directed towards *monarchs*. When Richard Reynoldes published his *Chronicle of all the noble Emperours of the Romaines, from Julius Caesar orderly.... Setting forth the great power, and devine providence of almighty God, in preserving the godly Princes and common wealthes* in 1571, he gave the usual panegyric: "An historie is the glasse of Princes, the image most lively bothe of vertue and vice, the learned theatre or spectacle of all the worlde, the councell house of Princes, the trier of all truthes, a witnes of all tymes and ages..." and so forth. The really important and interesting and relevant political lessons were those connected with *princes*. It was this that turned the attention away from republican Rome to monarchical Rome: the Rome of the Twelve Caesars and their successors. Republican Rome was not nearly so useful for models of political morality, because in sixteenth-century Europe republics happened to be rather rare. (Venice, the important one, was peculiar, not to say unique, anyway.) Republics were scarce. But there were aspiring Roman Emperors all over the place.

Sometimes the political lesson was a very simple one. In dedicating his *Auncient Historie and exquisite Chronicle of the Romanes Warres* in 1578, the translator states:

How God plagueth them that conspire againste theyr Prince, this Historie declareth at the full. For all of them, that coniured against *Caius Caesar*, not one did escape violent death. The which this Author hathe a pleasure to declare, bycause he would affray all men from disloyaltie toward their Soveraigne.

We need not, perhaps, put too much emphasis upon this argument, because the book was being dedicated to the Captain of the Queen's Majesty's Guard. But more sophisticated writers showed the same interest. Sir Walter Raleigh in his *History of the World* on occasions pointed the suitable political moral. But the problems that interested him and set him off on one of his discussions were those relevant to the political situation in the sixteenth and early seventeenth centuries. The story of Coriolanus, for example, does not interest him at all; he compresses Livy's fine narrative into nothingness, though he spares a few words for Coriolanus's mother and wife who prevailed upon him "with a pitiful tune of deprecation".[9] But the problem of the growth of tyranny fascinates him. He never got as far as Julius Caesar. He had to wind up his *History* at the beginning of the second century B.C. But he gets Caesar into his discussion. The problem of the difference between a benevolent monarchy and an odious tyranny, and the gradations by which the one may merge into the other—that was the real interest; and Imperial Rome was the true material for that.

So that, in spite of literary admiration for Cicero, the Romans in the imagination of the sixteenth century were Suetonian and Tacitan rather than Plutarchan. An occasional eccentric enthusiasm for one or both of the two Brutuses does not weigh against the fact that it was the busts of the Twelve Caesars that decorated almost every palace in Europe. And it required a considerable intellectual feat to substitute the Plutarchan vision of Rome (mostly republican) for the customary line of the Imperial Caesars. Montaigne and Shakespeare were capable of that feat. Not many others were. The Roman stuff that got into *A Mirror for Magistrates* naturally came from Suetonius and historians of the later Caesars. One of the educators of Europe in the sixteenth century was the Spaniard Antonio de Guevara. His *Dial of Princes* (which was a substitute for the still unprinted *Meditations* of the Emperor Marcus Aurelius) was translated by North with as much enthusiasm as Plutarch was. Guevara, whose platitudinous remarks on politics and morals—he was a worthy master for Polonius—gave him a European reputation, naturally turned to Imperial Rome to illustrate his maxims and observations on life. The Emperor Marcus Aurelius was his model of virtue (though he included love-letters from the Emperor to a variety of young women in Rome—which seems rather an incongruous thing to do for the over-virtuous author of the *Meditations*); and when Guevara wanted examples of vices as well as virtue, to give more varied moral and political lessons, he again naturally turned to the Roman monarchs. His *Decada*, in fact, gives lives from Trajan onwards. Among them appears a blood-curdling life of a certain Emperor Bassianus, a name which we shall not remember from our reading of Gibbon, but one with which we are thoroughly familiar from *Titus Andronicus*. This account of Bassianus is a shocking thing, translated with considerable energy into English in 1577 by Edward Hellowes in *A Chronicle, conteyning the lives of tenne Emperours of Rome* and dedicated to the Queen. The life of Bassianus (whom we know by his nickname of Caracalla—but Renaissance writers had too much respect for Roman Emperors to use only their vulgar nicknames) is one of almost unparalleled cruelty: how he slew his brother in the arms of his mother; how he slew half the Vestal Virgins because (so he said) they were not virgins, and then slew the other half because (so he said) they were. I will not say that it is a positive relief to pass from the life of Bassianus by Guevara to Shakespeare's *Titus Andronicus* (and there to find, by the way, that Bassianus is the better of the two brothers). Still, we feel that we are in the same world. *Titus Andronicus* is Senecan, yes; and it belongs to what Mr Shandy would call "no year of our Lord"; and its *sources* probably belong to medieval legend. Yet, as made into the play we know, it is also a not untypical piece of Roman history, or would seem to be so to anyone who came fresh from reading Guevara. Not the most high and palmy state of Rome, certainly. But an authentic Rome, and a Rome from which the usual political lessons could be drawn. *Titus* was entered in the Stationers' Register in 1594 as "a Noble Roman Historye", and it was published the same year as a "Most Lamentable Romaine Tragedie", and by sixteenth-century standards the claim was justified. One could say almost without paradox that, in many respects, *Titus Andronicus* is a more typical Roman play, a more characteristic piece of Roman history, than the three great plays of Shakespeare which are generally grouped under that name. The Elizabethans had far less of a low opinion of the Low Empire than we have learned to have. In fact, many of the qualities of Romanity are in *Titus*. The garboils; the stoical or Senecal endurance; the many historical properties: senators and tribunes and patricians. It was obviously *intended* to be a faithful picture of Roman civilization. Indeed, the political institutions in *Titus* are a subject that has been rather neglected.[10] They are certainly peculiar, and cannot be placed at any known period in Roman history, as can those in *Coriolanus* or *Julius Caesar*; and they afford a strange contrast with the care and authenticity of those later plays. In *Titus Andronicus* Rome seems to be, at times, a free commonwealth, with the usual mixture of patrician and plebeian institutions. Titus is himself elected emperor of Rome on account of his merits, because the senate and people do not recognize an hereditary principle of succession. But Titus disclaims the honour in favour of the late Emperor's elder (and worser) son. Titus is a devoted adherent (not to say a maniacal one) of the hereditary monarchical principle in a commonwealth that only partly takes it into account, and he eventually acknowledges his mistake. He encourages, by his subservience, the despotic rule on which Saturninus embarks, passing to a world of Byzantine intrigue, in which the barbarians (Southern and Northern, Moors and Goths), both by personalities and armies, exert their baneful or beneficent influence. And finally, by popular acclaim, Lucius is elected emperor "to order well the state" (says the second Quarto). Now, all these elements of the political situation can be found in Roman history, but not combined in this way. The play does not assume a political situation known to Roman history; it is, rather, a summary of Roman politics. It is not so much that any particular set of political institutions is assumed in *Titus*, but rather that it includes *all* the political institutions that Rome ever had. The author seems anxious, not to get it all right, but to get it all in. It has been suggested that *Titus Andronicus* was the work of a fairly well-informed scholar. It seems to be a quintessence of impressions derived from an eager reading of Roman history rather than a real effort at verisimilitude. Still, I think that *Titus* would easily be recognized as typical Roman history by a sixteenth-century audience; the claim that it was a "noble Roman history" was a just one.

Bearing this in mind, one can see why Plutarch was no rival to Suetonius (and his imitators and followers) as a source of impressions of the Romans. Suetonius's rag-bag of gossip, scandal, piquant and spicy *personalia*, provided the material for a large proportion of the plays written on Roman themes, including a number of University plays. Indeed the estimate of the popularity of Plutarch in the sixteenth century seems to have been rather exaggerated—at least, the popularity of Plutarch's *Lives*. It was Plutarch's *Moralia* which were most admired, and most influential, those essays on such subjects as 'Tranquillity of Mind', and 'Whether Virtue can be Taught', and so forth, which constantly provided exercises for translation, including one by the Queen herself. These things came home to men's business and bosoms far more than the parallel lives of the Greeks and Romans, and were admired for much the same reason as Dr Johnson's *Ramblers* and Martin Tupper's *Proverbial Philosophy*: they perfectly hit the moral preoccupations of the time; and were the model for Montaigne, and thence for Bacon. It was really the eighteenth century that was the great age of Plutarch's *Lives*, when there were two complete new translations, many partial ones, and frequent convenient reprints. In Shakespeare's time the *Lives* were confined to large and cumbrous folios. We, when we want to study the relation between Shakespeare's Roman plays and Plutarch's lives, can turn to those handy selections prepared for the purpose by Skeat or Tucker Brooke or Carr. Or, if we are prompted by curiosity or conscience to set about reading the whole thing, we can turn to the manageable volumes of the Tudor Translations or to the handy little pocket volumes of the Temple Classics. But Shakespeare, when he read Plutarch, could not turn to a volume of selections illustrating Shakespeare's Roman plays. He had to take a very heavy folio in his hands. We have to read 1010 folio pages in the 1579 edition before we come to the death of Cleopatra. (It need not be suggested that Shakespeare read 1010 folio pages before *he* came to the death of Cleopatra.) It is certainly not a literary experience comparable with picking up a novelette like *Pandosto* or *Rosalynde*, or reading a little book about the Continual Factions, Tumults and Massacres of the Romans. It was rather a serious thing for a busy man of the theatre to do. It was probably the most serious experience that Shakespeare had of the bookish kind.

In Shakespeare's three principal Roman plays we see a steadily advancing independence of thought in the reconsideration of the Roman world. In *Julius Caesar*, it seems to me, he is almost precisely in step with sound Renaissance opinion on the subject. There has been a good deal of discussion of this play because of a supposed ambiguity in the author's attitude to the two principal characters. It has been suggested, on the one hand, that Brutus is intended to be a short-sighted political blunderer who foolishly or even wickedly struck down the foremost man in all the world; Dante and survivals of medieval opinion in the sixteenth century can be quoted here. We have, on the contrary, been told, on very high authority in Shakespeare studies, that Shakespeare followed the Renaissance admiration for Brutus and detestation for Caesar. It has also been suggested that Shakespeare left the exact degrees of guilt and merit in Caesar and Brutus deliberately ambiguous in the play, to give a sense of depth, to keep the audience guessing and so make the whole dramatic situation more telling. But all this, it seems to me, obscures the fact that the reassessment and reconsideration of such famous historical figures was a common literary activity in the Renaissance, not merely in poetry and drama (where licence is acceptable), but in plain prose, the writing of history. It seems hardly legitimate to talk about "tradition", to refer to "traditional" opinions about Caesar and Brutus, when in fact the characters of each of them had been the subject of constant discussion. In the nineteenth century you could weigh up the varying views of Caesar held by Mommsen or Froude or Anthony Trollope or Napoleon III of France, and read their entertaining books on the subject. It was not so very different in the sixteenth century. I am not suggesting that Shakespeare read the great works on the life and character of Julius Caesar by Hubert Goltz (1563) or by Stefano Schiappalaria (1578) where everything about him was collected and collated and assessed and criticized. But other people did. And Shakespeare, writing a play of the subject, could hardly live in such intellectual isolation as to be unaware of the discussion. It would, I think, be quite wrong to suggest by quotation from any one writer such as Montaigne that Caesar was generally agreed to be a detestable character. On the contrary, the problem was acknowledged to be a complicated and fascinating one; and the discussion began early, and in ancient times. Men have often disputed (wrote Seneca in his *De Beneficiis*, a work translated both by Arthur Golding and by Thomas Lodge), whether Brutus did right or wrong. "For mine owne part, although I esteemed *Brutus* in all other thinges a wise and vertuous man, yet meseemeth that in this he committed a great errour"; and Seneca goes on to explain the error: Brutus

imagined that such a Citie as this might repossesse her ancient honour, and former lustre, when vertue and the primitive Lawes were either abolished, or wholly extinguished; Or that Iustice, Right, and Law, should be inviolably observed in such a place, where he had seene so many thousand men at shocke and battell, not to the intent to discerne whether they were to obay and serve, but to resolve under whom they ought to serve and obay. Oh how great oblivion possessed this man! how much forgot he both the nature of affaires, and the state of his Citie! to suppose that by the death of one man there should not some other start up after him, that would usurpe over the common-weale.

Likewise William Fulbecke (writing in 1586, though his book was not published until 1601), while seeing the calamities Caesar was bringing upon the Roman state, could not praise Brutus for permitting himself to participate in political assassinations:

M. Brutus, the chiefe actor in Caesars tragedie, was in counsel deepe, in wit profound, in plot politicke, and one that hated the principality whereof he devested Caesar. But did Brutus looke for peace by bloudshed? did he thinke to avoyd tyrannie by tumult? was there no way to wound Caesar, but by stabbing his own conscience? & no way to make Caesar odious, but by incurring the same obloquie?[12]

Fulbecke summarized his position in the controversy: "Questionlesse the Romanes should not have nourished this lyon in their Citie, or being nourished, they should not have disgraced him."

In writing *Julius Caesar* and *Antony and Cleopatra* Shakespeare was keeping within a safe body of story. Those persons had been dignified by tragedies in many countries of Europe and many times before Shakespeare arose and drove all competitors from the field. But with *Coriolanus* it was different. There was apparently no previous play on the subject. It was more of a deliberate literary and artistic choice than either of the other two Roman plays. He must have discovered Coriolanus in Plutarch. As for Caesar and Cleopatra, he presumably went to Plutarch knowing that they were good subjects for plays. But no one had directed him to Coriolanus. The story was hardly well known and not particularly attractive. The story of the ingratitude he suffered, the revenge he purposed and renounced, was told by Livy, and, along with one or two other stories of Roman womenfolk (Lucretia, Virginia), it was turned into a *novella* in Painter's *Pallace of Pleasure*; there is a mention in *Titus Andronicus*. More than *Julius Caesar* or than *Antony and Cleopatra, Coriolanus* (perhaps by the rivalry or stimulation of Ben Jonson) shows a great deal of care to get things right, to preserve Roman manners and customs and allusions. We have, of course, the usual Roman officials, and political and religious customs familiarly referred to; and we have the Roman mythology and pantheon. But we are also given a good deal of Roman history worked into the background. Even the eighteenth-century editors who took a tooth-comb through the play for mistaken references to English customs could find very little; and it requires considerable pedantry to check these. Moreover, in *Coriolanus* there is some effort to make literary allusions appropriate. The ladies know their Homer and the Tale of Troy. The personal names used are all authentically derived from somewhere in Plutarch; Shakespeare has turned the pages to find something suitable. He is taking great care. He is on his mettle. Dozens of poetasters could write plays on Julius Caesar or on Cleopatra. Dozens did. But to write *Coriolanus* was one of the great feats of the historical imagination in Renaissance Europe.

Setting aside poetical and theatrical considerations, and merely referring to the artist's ability to "create a world" (as the saying is), we may ask if there was anything in prose or verse, in Elizabethan or Jacobean literature, which bears the same marks of careful and thoughtful consideration of the ancient world, a deliberate effort of a critical intelligence to give a consistent picture of it, as there is in Shakespeare's plays. Of course, Ben Jonson's *Catiline* and *Sejanus* at once suggest themselves. The comparison between Shakespeare's and Ben Jonson's Roman plays is a chronic one, an inevitable one, and it is nearly always, I suppose, made to Jonson's disadvantage. At least it had its origin in their own time; for Leonard Digges tells us, in his verses before the 1640 *Poems*, that audiences were ravished by such scenes as the quarrel between Brutus and Cassius, when they would not brook a line of tedious (though well-laboured) *Catiline*. Of course, Ben Jonson's two plays are superior to any other Roman plays of the period outside Shakespeare (those of Lodge, Chapman, Massinger, Marston, or Webster, or the several interesting anonymous ones). But when Ben Jonson's are compared with Shakespeare's, as they cruelly must, their defect is a lack not so much of art as of sophistication. There is a certain naïvety about Ben Jonson's understanding of Roman history. Of course, in a way, there is more obvious learning about *Catiline* and *Sejanus* than about Shakespeare's Roman plays. There must have been a great deal of note-book work, a great deal of mosaic work. It is possible to sit in the British Museum with the texts of the classical writers which Jonson used around you and watch him making his play as you follow up his references (not all, I think, at first hand). But the defect of Jonson's *Sejanus* is lack of homogeneity of style and material. Jonson mixes the gossip of Suetonius with the gloomily penetrating and disillusioned comments on men and their motives by Tacitus. It is the old story; "who reads incessantly and to his reading brings not a spirit and judgment equal or superior" is liable to lose the advantages of his reading. After all, it doesn't require very much effort to *seem* learned. What is so difficult to acquire is the judgment in dealing with the material in which one is learned. This is not something that can in any way be tested by collecting misspellings of classical proper names in an author whose works have been unfairly printed from his foul papers and prompt-book copies. Shakespeare brought a judgment equal or superior to whatever ancient authors he read however he read them. Ben Jonson did not; his dogged and determined scholarship was not ripe enough; he had the books but not always the spirit with which to read them. There are occasions when we can legitimately place parts of their plays side by side. Consider the portents which accompanied the death of Julius Caesar, something which obviously interested Shakespeare very much. His description of them in

Hamlet is unforgettable. His introduction of them in *Julius Caesar* is beautifully done. Some of the excitable Romans are prepared to believe any yarn about lions and supernatural fires and so forth. The amiable and unperturbed Cicero asks Casca:

> Why are you breathless? and why stare you so?

And he answers Casca's fustian about "a tempest dropping fire" with mild scepticism:

> Why, saw you any thing more wonderful?

His response to the contagious panic which Casca has acquired from

> a hundred ghastly women,
> Transformed with their fear; who swore they saw
> Men all in fire walk up and down the streets,

is to be quite unimpressed by anything that a lot of hysterical old women *swore they saw*; and he then leaves, with the remark that the weather is too bad for a walk that evening:

> Good night then, Casca: this disturbed sky
> Is not to walk in.

Compare this with the account of the portents that accompany the conspirators' oath and the blood-drinking in *Catiline*. (Jonson got little of it from the excellent Sallust but from an inferior source.) It is given no connexion with the varying emotions of the observers, there is no sceptical note: it merely seems to be there because "mine author hath it so". Indeed there is something medieval about it, and about Jonson's treatment of his characters in *Catiline*. He takes sides emphatically. He does what some critics would like Shakespeare to do in *Julius Caesar*; that is to tell us plainly which is the good man and which is the bad man. There is a sort of pre-Renaissance naïvety about Jonson's setting up Catiline as an example of unmitigated villany and Cicero as an example of unmitigated virtue. It is comparable with what you find in Chaucer or in Lydgate about the slaying of the glorious and victorious Julius Caesar by that wicked Judas-like figure called Brutus Cassius with bodkins hid in his sleeve. There is a sense of unreality about it, a recurring feeling that Ben Jonson doesn't really know what he is talking about—the feeling of hollowness you get when Jonson starts praising Shakespeare by shouting

> Call forth thund'ring *Æschilus*,
> *Euripides*, and *Sophocles* to us,
> *Pacuvius*, *Accius*, him of *Cordova* dead,
> To life againe, to heare thy Buskin tread,
> And shake a Stage....

Is this the writing of a well-informed person? We can stand for Seneca, of course. But it is hard to include the Greek tragedians, too little known and too little available to make the comparison intelligent; and as for Accius and Pacuvius, there could be few criticisms more pointless than to ask anybody to call forth their meagre fragments, those ghostly writers, mere names in biographical dictionaries. Perhaps it is only Ben Jonson's fun. I would like to think so. But I doubt it. I fear he wants to be impressive. Like a medieval poet, he has licence to mention the names of great authors without their books.

There may very well be, in Shakespeare's writings, a good many vestiges of the medieval world-picture. His mind may have been encumbered, or steadied, by several objects, orts, and relics of an earlier kind of intellectual culture. But it is scarcely perceptible in his Roman plays, which can be brought to the judgment bar of the Renaissance revivification of the ancient world, and will stand the comparison with the major achievements of Renaissance Humanism (as Ben Jonson's will not). We find there a writer who seems in the intellectual current of his times. Shakespeare had what might be described as the scholarship of the educated creative writer—the ability to go and find out the best that is known and thought in his day; to get it quickly (as a busy writer must, for Shakespeare wrote more than a million words in twenty years); to get it without much trouble and without constant access to good collections of books (as a busy man of the theatre must, one often on tour and keeping up two homes); and to deal with his sources of information with intelligence and discrimination. The favourite notions of learning get around in ways past tracing. Anyone who is writing a play or a book on any subject has by that very fact a peculiar alertness and sensitivity to information and attitudes about his subject. Shakespeare did not write in isolation. He had friends. It would be an improbable hypothesis that he worked cut off from the intellectual life of his times. Indeed, all investigations of the content of his plays prove the obvious: that he was peculiarly sensitive to the intellectual tendencies of his age, in all spheres of thought. His scholarship was of a better quality than Jonson's, because (one might guess) he was a better listener, not so self-assertive in the company of his betters, and was therefore more able, with that incomparable celerity of mind of his, to profit from any well-informed acquaintance.

Finally, in understanding the picture of the ancient world in these plays, the part played by Shakespeare himself in creating our notions of the ancient Romans should not be forgotten. It has become difficult to see the plays straight, to see the thing in itself as it really is, because we are all in the power of Shakespeare's imagination, a power which has been exercised for several generations and from which it is scarcely possible to extricate ourselves. It is well known, I believe, that Shakespeare practically created the fairies; he was responsible for having impressed them on the imagination, the dainty, delightful, beneficent beings which have become part of the popular mythology. To suggest that Shakespeare also practically created the ancient Romans might be regarded as irresponsible. Still, the effect that Shakespeare has had on the way the Romans exist in our imaginations is something that might well be explored. We have had in England no great historian of Rome to impose his vision of the Roman world upon readers. Gibbon begins too late; and the English historians of Rome who wrote in the sixteenth, seventeenth and eighteenth centuries are mediocre and practically unread. We have had, on the one hand, no Mommsen; on the other, we have had no Racine, no Poussin, no David, no Napoleon. But since the early nineteenth century generations of schoolboys have been trained on *Julius Caesar* and *Coriolanus*. When English gradually penetrated into the schools as a reputable subject, it was in the sheep's clothing of Shakespeare's Roman plays that it entered the well-guarded fold; and so gave the *coup de grâce* to classical education in England. It can hardly be doubted that Shakespeare's *Julius Caesar* has had more effect than Caesar's own *Commentaries* in creating our impressions of his personality. Indeed, Shakespeare has had no serious rival on the subject of

Ancient Rome. Neither *All for Love* nor *Cato* has stood the test of time and changing tastes. Neither the importation of *Ben Hur* from America nor the importation of *Quo Vadis* from Poland has affected Shakespeare's domination over the imagination. Besides, they belong to the wrong period. Novel writers have generally turned to the age of the Twelve Caesars, rather than to the Republic, for precisely the same reasons as did Shakespeare's contemporary play-wrights; it is so much more lurid; there are so many more "garboyles". The spirit of Suetonius lives on. Shakespeare, perhaps, chose with a better instinct or with surer taste.

NOTES

1. A lecture delivered to the Shakespeare Conference at Stratford-upon-Avon, 6 September 1955.

2. Letter before *The Loyal General, A Tragedy* (1680); *The Shakspere Allusion Book...1591 to 1700* (Oxford, 1932), II, 266.

3. Reported by Dennis; see D. Nichol Smith, *Eighteenth Century Essays on Shakespeare* (Glasgow, 1903), p. 309.

4. D. Nichol Smith, *op. cit.* pp. 53, 62.

5. *A Short View of Tragedy* (1693), p. 148.

6. D. Nichol Smith, *op. cit.* p. 26.

7. Cf. A. Momigliano, *Contributo alla storia degli studi classici* (Rome, 1955), pp. 75-6: "To the best of my knowledge, the idea that one could write a history of Rome which should replace Livy and Tacitus was not yet born in the early seventeenth century. The first Camden Praelector of history in the University of Oxford had the statutory duty of commenting on Florus and other ancient historians (1622)....Both in Oxford and Cambridge Ancient History was taught in the form of a commentary on ancient historians."

8. Sig. A2.

9. *The History of the World*, IV, vii, §i; *Works* (Oxford, 1832), V, 531-2.

10. William Watkiss Lloyd in 1856 made some pertinent remarks (*Critical Essays on the Plays of Shakespeare* (1894), p. 352).

11. Lodge's translation in *The Workes of Lucius Annaeus Seneca, Both Morall and Naturall* (1614), pp. 30-1; *Of Benefits*, II, xx.

12. *Op. cit.* sig. Z1ᵛ.

THE METAMORPHOSIS OF VIOLENCE
IN *TITUS ANDRONICUS*[1]

BY

EUGENE M. WAITH

It is surprising to find Shakespearian critics in agreement, yet almost to a man they have concurred in their verdict on the merits of *Titus Andronicus*. The word which most nearly sums up their feelings is "disgust". Ravenscroft called the play "a heap of rubbish"; Coleridge said that it was "obviously intended to excite vulgar audiences by its scenes of blood and horror—to our ears shocking and disgusting"; Dover Wilson recently called it a "broken-down cart, laden with bleeding corpses from an Elizabethan scaffold".[2] Only a few critics have had so much as a word of praise for this early Shakespearian tragedy.[3]

The features of *Titus Andronicus* which have had such enduring power to repel the critics are easy to identify. The succession of extraordinarily violent episodes has given rise to the opinion that the play is crude—fit only for "vulgar audiences". The florid style of many of the speeches has seemed appallingly overwrought. Now it is a curious fact that this second feature should logically lead to a quite different opinion about the play. Miss M. C. Bradbrook has well characterized the tone as "cool and cultured".[4] If the style is crude in a way, it is not the crudity of the bear-baiting pit or the Elizabethan scaffold. The trouble seems to be an excess of refinement, or an overloading with classical allusion—surely caviare for the bear-baiting crowd.

Taken separately, these two features of *Titus Andronicus* have seemed bad enough; taken together, they have served to damn the play utterly, for even if we grant the author of a thriller his right to bring the heroine on the stage, "her hands cut off, and her tongue cut out and ravisht" (II, iv, stage direction), must we endure a description of the "crimson river of warm blood, like to a bubbling fountain" on her "roséd lips" (II, iv, 22–4)? The combination of crude violence with this sort of fanciful description is so incongruous that Dover Wilson has suggested that Shakespeare was burlesquing the style of his contemporaries.[5] Though this view has not so far prevailed, the incongruity has troubled every critic. It has seemed impossible to see a meaningful relationship between action and style.

A further objection to the play is the flatness of the characters. Critics have complained that only Titus and Aaron have any life in them, while the formal, rhetorical style tends to make of all the rest purely emblematic figures. Once again, style is to blame: caught in some fantastic pose in the midst of their most violent actions, the characters are petrified by a blast of eloquence —plunged, as it were, in the deep-freeze of rhetoric.

There is, however, a relationship between the violence of *Titus Andronicus* and the style in which it is written. My object in this paper is to examine that relationship with the intention, not of rehabilitating the play, but of placing it in a stylistic development of some consequence for the English drama. The direct source of *Titus Andronicus* appears to have been a prose account which survives in an eighteenth-century chapbook. This account purports to be translated from the Italian, which may have been a tale of the order of those in the *Gesta Romanorum*. The exact nature of this source must remain a matter for speculation. We can be sure, however, that behind it lie the stories of the rape of Lucretia, of Appius and Virginia, probably of Thyestes, and most certainly of the rape of Philomela. Shakespeare of course knew these stories as well as the Titus-story which they influenced. How much he may have been affected by Seneca is debatable. Though *Titus Andronicus* used to be called a Senecan play, critics such as Howard Baker and E. M. W. Tillyard[6] have shown the many respects in which it is not Senecan, and it seems fair to conclude that however important the Senecan model may have been, Ovid exerted a more direct influence. References in the play leave no doubt that his telling of the Philomela story in his *Metamorphoses* was fresh in Shakespeare's mind. This well-known fact provides a point of departure. We may ask how Ovid renders the violence of Tereus' attack and of the dire revenge of Philomela and her sister Procne, and what meaning he sees in these dreadful events.

If we turn to the latter part of Book VI and begin reading this story, we shall be struck immediately by the emphasis on pathos: King Pandion's tearful farewell to his daughter Philomela, and his injunction to Tereus to "guard her with a father's love";[7] the rape itself in a "hut deep hidden in the ancient woods", where Philomela, far from all help, calls vainly for her father and sister; the efforts of Itys, the little son of Procne by Tereus, to throw his arms around his mother's neck as she murders him. Along with the feelings of the victims we find other emotions: the raging lust of Tereus at the sight of Philomela, Procne's fierce devotion to revenge, Philomela's unspeakable joy as she hurls the head of Itys in his father's face. At such feelings we can only be horrified. But if the mixture of pity and horror is reminiscent of the Aristotelian account of tragedy, the ending of the story hardly fulfils our expectations of tragedy. Every schoolchild who has been brought up on the explanatory notes to *The Waste Land* knows what follows: Tereus draws his sword after the cannibalistic feast, and pursues the revenging sisters, who turn into a nightingale and a swallow as he turns into a hoopoe. Of the sisters, Ovid's final words are "One flies to the woods, the other rises to the roof. And even now their breasts have not lost the marks of their murderous deed, their feathers are stained with blood" (VI, 668–70). Of Tereus, "Upon his head a stiff crest appears, and a huge beak stands forth instead of his long sword. He is the hoopoe with the look of one armed for war" (VI, 672–4). This is not "How are the mighty fallen!" nor "How horrible!" nor yet "How pathetic!" It is more as if Ovid were saying, "Strange, isn't it?"

We cannot expect to penetrate Ovid's meaning by looking at only one out of his vast collection of myths. When we read one or more entire books of the *Metamorphoses* certain predominant attitudes toward the material begin to emerge. The theme of metamorphosis, which gives the work its title, is a vital part of the meaning. It appears in several variant forms. Most obviously there are the physical transformations, such as those I have just mentioned, or of Ceyx and Alcyone, also changed into birds, of Daphne or Myrrha into trees, of Niobe into stone, of Hecuba into a dog. These characters also undergo a kind of psychic transformation. In certain cases the change is of a moral order: Tereus, possessed by lust, becomes a cruel monster; so do Procne, Philomela, and Hecuba when they devote themselves to revenge; Niobe is changed from a proud boaster to a suppliant, paralysed by grief. It is tempting, of course, to equate these two sorts of metamorphosis by saying that the physical change symbolizes the moral change and the punishment fits the crime. This is a temptation that the commentators of the Middle Ages and the Renaissance did not resist. To take one example from the hundreds of possible ones, when

George Pettie comes to the end of his retelling of the story of Tereus, he says of the three principal characters, "and as Ovid reporteth [they] were turned into birds, meaning they were not worthy human shape or the use of reason, which were such cruel monsters altogether devoid of ruth and reason".[8] If one succumbs to this sort of interpretation, it is easy enough to see a moral emblem in the transformation of Hecuba into a dog after she has gouged out Polymestor's eyes, or in the change of proud Niobe into a weeping stone. But one is apt to have misgivings about some of the other cases, even though the hardened allegorizers apparently had none. If Tereus, Procne and Philomela were turned into birds, so were Ceyx and Alcyone, those models of marital devotion. Were they also unworthy of human shape? Ovid tells us only that the pity of the gods was responsible for the transformation. Then too we notice that while Daphne is turned into a tree to save her from Apollo's embraces, Myrrha is turned into a tree after her incestuous union with her father to keep her from contaminating either the world of the living or the world of the dead. The teaching of this last story is, to say the least, rather oblique, and in none of the instances we have just been considering is there any clear-cut moral transformation.

Psychic metamorphosis of another sort is clearly common to all the stories I have cited. In the execution of their vengeance Procne and Philomela are transported by emotions which rise steadily to the point of obliterating their normal characters; when Tereus discovers what vengeance has been taken on him, he too is transported by overmastering emotions. At this moment of crisis the feelings of the three characters are alike in intensity, though as different as exultant vengeance mixed with fear is from grief mixed with rage. In each case the emotion is unbearable; the character is literally beside himself. And this is the moment in which all three are metamorphosed. In Ovid's telling of the story of Niobe we watch the mounting intensity of the mother's grief to the point where it can no longer find expression in words and her tongue is frozen to the roof of her mouth. This is the moment of her transformation. The mingled love and grief of widowed Alcyone are similarly unbearable, like the virginal terror of Daphne, and the fear, the guilt, and above all the utter weariness of Myrrha, fleeing alone, month after month. These examples suggest that Ovid was more interested in the transforming power of intense states of emotion than in pointing a moral. Hecuba's story makes this especially clear. Her suffering is extraordinary as is the vengeance to which it drives her. Ovid's comment on her transformation into a dog is this: "Her sad fortune touched the Trojans and her Grecian foes and all the gods as well; yes, all, for even Juno, sister and wife of Jove, declared that Hecuba had not deserved such an end" (XIII, 573–5). In this case the actual transformation is anticipated in the description of the moment in which vengeance is planned. When the body of Polydorus is discovered, the Trojan women shriek, but Hecuba, like Niobe, is dumb with grief and stands immovable as a rock, looking at the corpse of her son. When her anger rises, however, Ovid tells us that she is "wholly absorbed" by the idea of vengeance and goes off to Polymestor like a lioness whose suckling cub has been stolen from her. Two sorts of transformation are suggested here of which only the latter, the raging animal, materializes. But in both are portrayed the transforming power of great emotion.

I have dwelt upon this point at length both because the tendency to allegorize is by no means absent from some modern criticism and because the emphasis on emotional states is important in itself. Seneca the Rhetorician observed in his *Controversiae* (II, 2, 12) that Ovid, who had a considerable reputation as an orator, was not so interested in argument as in the depiction of character and behaviour. In the *Metamorphoses* this interest appears chiefly in the representation of the various passions and their extraordinary effects on various natures, human or divine. Yet, despite such variety, one of the lasting impressions from reading this work is of the unity of all creation, informed by one vital force. The idea, as Miss Bradbrook has pointed out, is closely related to that of Lucretian Nature.[9] In the moments of greatest emotional stress Ovid's characters seem to lose not only individuality but even humanity as if sheer intensity of feeling made them indistinguishable from other forms of life. Often a physical transformation completes the suggestion. Thus, in the depiction of these legendary figures individuality is built up only to be obliterated by an impersonal force working from within. Character and personality miraculously give way to naked, abstract emotion.

It is obvious that incidents of great violence lend themselves well to the portrayal of character under emotional stress. Outrage is the prime mover in the story of Philomela, forcing the protagonists to that final crisis in which they lose themselves utterly. And in some of the other gruesome stories, such as the battle of the Lapiths and the centaurs, where physical transformation is rather a minor part of the action, the violent carnage is in itself a powerful means of portraying the senseless fury which has transformed both men and centaurs.

Ovid's style reinforces in several ways the effects I have been describing. Both horror and pathos are pointed up by brilliant touches, often given in a very few words. When Tereus boards the ship with Philomela in his power he exclaims to himself, "We have won!" (VI, 513). This single utterance conveys the elation of a man who thinks of his lustful scheme as an exciting game. The brief description of the "hut deep hidden in the ancient woods" is most evocative, and the gesture of Itys, seeking to embrace his mother, condenses the pathos of an entire incident.

At the same time, the elegant urbanity of these narrations implies a considerable detachment. With great suavity Ovid leads us from one story to another, scarcely seeming to alter the tone of his voice, as if the story of Philomela did not really affect him very differently from that of Pelops, which it follows. His use of narrators further increases the psychic distance. The story of Venus and Adonis, for instance, is one of a group of stories told by Orpheus, and it is interrupted by the story of Atalanta, which Venus tells Adonis. Perspective opens within perspective.

The seemingly illogical combination of emotional excitement and psychic distance contributes to the effect of impersonalization. The metamorphosis of the character is of absorbing interest; the individual who is transformed is only interesting as an example of metamorphosis. Ovid's descriptions of violence illustrate such an attitude. The battle of the Lapiths and the centaurs contains some sensationally gory exploits by the infuriated opponents. Ovid does not spare detail, but his descriptions are sometimes surprisingly matter of fact. A flaming brand plunged into an open wound is like the hot iron which the blacksmith plunges in water (XII, 276–7); a mangled body is compared to a common and pleasant household sight (XII, 434–8). In the story of Philomela, the tongue, when it has been cut out, is compared to the severed tail of a snake, still twitching (VI, 557–60). In every case the visual image is exact and thus the horror more vivid, yet at the same time our minds are turned away from the individual as a whole to a minute contemplation of what has happened to one part of his body. Looking thus through the microscope, as it were, we momentarily forget the sufferer in the overwhelming reality of the wound, and beyond the wound we glimpse its analogies in an everyday world. The comparisons are often extended, usually unexpected, sometimes even fanciful, always neatly phrased. What may seem at first an incongruous elegance is perfectly suited to the process of transforming a character into an emotional state. Violence, as Ovid describes it, is an emblem of the transformation. In a sense, it is itself transformed in the process into an object of interested but somewhat detached contemplation.

It would be risky to assume that this descriptive technique or the reduction of character to abstract passions had for Augustan Romans or for Renaissance Englishmen the inhibiting effect upon emotional response which I think they have for us today. It is less risky to suggest that even if these devices were considered very moving, the effect they produced was less that of sharing a great emotional experience with another human being than of wonder at the extraordinary manifestations of familiar emotions raised to a most unfamiliar pitch. Ovid sometimes points up this effect by a comment. Of Alcyone leaping into the sea, "It was a wonder that she could do it" (XI, 731); of Procne and Philomela fleeing from the enraged Tereus, "You would have thought they were on wings; they *were* on wings!" (VI, 667–8). We are left with these moments of wonder, caught in a series of vivid pictures, elegantly framed by the style of a master-narrator.

Before turning to *Titus Andronicus* to see how certain Ovidian effects are reproduced in the play, a few words must be given to a matter previously alluded to—the attitude of Renaissance readers towards the *Metamorphoses*. Douglas Bush points to the multiple attitude composed of the medieval moralizing tradition, the beginnings of a new paganism which admired Ovid's depictions of nature and of love, and perhaps most important of all, the great respect for Ovid as a model of style.[10] In generation after generation students were encouraged to imitate him.

The new pagan attitude towards Ovid left, so far as I know, no coherent interpretation of the *Metamorphoses*. One can only surmise that from this point of view the stories might have seemed to illustrate the miraculous vitality of nature. As for the grammarians and textual critics, the Italian Regio will serve as an example of their attitude towards violence. His frigid observation on the description of Philomela after her rape is that Ovid "beautifully expressed virgin fear" by comparing her to a lamb and a dove. Clearly, it is elegance of style which interests Regio.[11]

There remains the moralizing tradition. By and large, the Renaissance commentators did not pursue the medieval *Ovide Moralisé* to its *o altitudo!* of allegorical interpretation. Golding, the famous Elizabethan translator of Ovid, lays greatest stress on a general point of moral philosophy: not all "that bear the name of men" are truly men; many are like beasts or even worse than beasts.[12] The notion is essentially what emerges from Pettie's interpretation of the story of Tereus, Procne, and Philomela. In addition to this kind of lesson there appeared to the Renaissance commentators to be certain broad underlying themes in Ovid's work. His account of the Creation interested them especially. They found it in accordance with the Biblical story, and some of them, as T. W. Baldwin has shown,[13] also saw in it the transformation of chaos into order by the power of love as portrayed in Hesiod and Plato. Such Biblical and philosophical associations seemed to provide an important theme of order versus chaos in the *Metamorphoses*. Golding gives a political formulation of the theme in a passage which also brings in the theme of transformation: if the States, which are God's representatives on earth, "Decline from virtue unto vice and live disorderly, / To eagles, tigers, bulls, and bears" they change both themselves and their people.[14] To allegorical interpreters like Golding the most violent episodes were obviously acceptable as rewards of wickedness or emblems of disorder.

The theme of *Titus Andronicus* is too commonplace to attribute to any one source. It is, I take it, the opposition of moral and political disorder to the unifying force of friendship and wise government, a theme in which Shakespeare was interested all his life. Tillyard noted several years ago the relation of this tragedy to the history plays,[15] and it extends to the Roman plays, to *King Lear*, *Macbeth* and much else that Shakespeare wrote. Marcus states the theme at the end of the play:

> You sad-faced men, people and sons of Rome,
> By uproar severed, as a flight of fowl
> Scattered by winds and high tempestuous gusts,
> O, let me teach you how to knit again
> This scattered corn into one mutual sheaf,
> These broken limbs again into one body.
>
> (v, iii, 67–72)

The rape and mutilation of Lavinia is the central symbol of disorder, both moral and political, resembling in this respect the rape of Lucrece as Shakespeare portrays it. The connexion between the two sorts of disorder is made explicit in the play's two references to Tarquin, once as ravisher (IV, i, 64–5) and once as the evil, exiled king (III, i, 299). The association is still present in Shakespeare's mind many years later, when he has Macbeth speak of "wither'd murder" moving "with Tarquin's ravishing strides" (II, i, 55).

The integrating force, which through most of the play is too weak to impose itself upon chaos, appears in the guise of friendship, brotherly love, justice, and gratitude. Marcus addresses Titus at the beginning of the play as the "friend in justice" to the people of Rome (I, i, 180), and at the end calls Lucius "Rome's dear friend" (v, iii, 80). Brotherly love is demonstrated in the bizarre episodes of Quintus losing himself in the effort to help his brother Martius out of the pit, and of Marcus offering his hand for that of Titus. The absence of brotherly love appears in the first scene in the quarrel of Saturninus and Bassianus, and injustice and gratitude are the subjects of complaint throughout the play.

The theme of *Titus Andronicus* is at least consonant with what many interpreters supposed Ovid to be saying. Friendship is one of the ordering forces; Golding uses this word in translating Ovid's account of how the strife between the elements was ended. He says that God, separating "each from other did them bind / In endless friendship to agree" (I, 24–5). Titus laments the departure of justice by quoting "Terras Astraea reliquit" from Ovid's description of the iron age, just before the time of the giants and the flood. Disorder is represented by the acts of wanton violence and one of the most powerful metaphors in the play, "Rome is but a wilderness of tigers" (III, i, 54), seems to echo Golding's lines about disorder in the state.

We may ask then whether any of the characterization is in an Ovidian mode. "Tiger" is one of several animal and bird epithets applied to the passionate Tamora, whose story would fit easily into the scheme of the *Metamorphoses*. When we first see her, she is a captive "distressèd queen", pleading for mercy to her son. We must sympathize, though we are given very little time to do so, with her protest against Titus's inflexibility: "O cruel, irreligious piety!" (I, i, 130). Demetrius then compares her to Hecuba, who was given the opportunity to revenge the loss of her son on Polymestor. The allusion reminds one of the guile and the ferocity of Hecuba in carrying out her vengeance and of her final transformation into a dog. The end of Tamora's career is quite consistent with this introduction. Her disguise as Revenge, though part of her plot to deceive Titus, obviously labels for us the passion which dominates her character. She dies a victim of an outrage prompted by the outrage in which she had assisted, and the last words of the play leave no doubt of her complete assimilation into the animal kingdom:

> As for that ravenous tiger, Tamora,
> No funeral rite, nor man in mourning weed,
> No mournful bell shall ring her burial;
> But throw her forth to beasts and birds of prey.
> Her life was beastly and devoid of pity,
> And being dead, let birds on her take pity.

Golding or Pettie could not make the moral more clear.

The character of Tamora is so intimately related to the character of Titus, for which it is a foil, that the two must be discussed together. Once more we have a story which could easily be put with the *Metamorphoses*. We see Titus at the beginning a man of absolute integrity but cursed, somewhat like Coriolanus, with an unbending and blind fixity of character. If his piety, ignoring all pleas for mercy, warrants Tamora's adjective, "cruel", his slaying of Mutius and his refusal to have him entombed deserve the charges of injustice, impiety, and barbarity brought by his brother and sons. His choice of a principle rather than a man, when he throws the election to Saturninus, is palpable folly. Thus his closely related virtues and faults are well established in the first act. In the succeeding acts the cruelties of his enemies are heaped upon him in a steady succession. After he has cut off his hand, the unbearable horror of his situation causes him to exclaim,

> Is not my sorrow deep, having no bottom?
> Then be my passions bottomless,...
> If there were reason for these miseries,
> Then into limits could I bind my woes.   (III, i, 217–18, 220–1)

If this speech suggests some of the attitudes I have pointed to in Ovid, so do the comments of Marcus after the messenger has brought Titus the heads of his sons:

> These miseries are more than may be borne!...
> Ah! now no more will I control thy griefs:...
> Now is a time to storm, why art thou still?   (III, i, 244, 260, 264)

From this point the character of Titus is markedly altered by grief. Although Marcus says that Titus is "so just that he will not revenge" (IV, i, 129), it gradually becomes clear that revenge is his obsession. At first he takes refuge in fantasy, but when he finally has Chiron and Demetrius in his power his words reveal clearly his true state of mind and do so in a series of Ovidian allusions. After a grisly account of his plans for the banquet, he says:

> This is the feast that I have bid her to,
> And this the banquet she shall surfeit on;
> For worse than Philomel you used my daughter,
> And worse than Progne I will be revenged....
> Come, come, be every one officious
> To make this banquet, which I wish may prove
> More stern and bloody than the Centaurs' feast.   (V, ii, 193–6, 202–4)

Here surely is a psychic metamorphosis which provides one of the truly powerful moments in the depiction of the hero. His cruelty is monstrous yet, thanks to the indications of the first act, not incredible.

Because of this consistent development Titus is a more successful character than Tamora, who is not always depicted as the woman obsessed by revenge. In the second act we find her more lustful than revengeful, while Aaron, described in terms of the same birds and beasts to which Tamora is compared, becomes in a sense the projection of her revenge. But unfortunately for the unity of design, Aaron, though a brilliant dramatic creation, belongs to the un-Ovidian tradition of Barabas and Eleazar. His villainy invites a less complicated response than does the obsessive behaviour of Tamora and Titus.

Although the references to Procne and to the battle of the Lapiths and the centaurs show the horrifying effect of the fixation on revenge, Titus, unlike Tamora, is not finally shown as bestial or degenerate. His slaying of Lavinia, also somewhat prepared for by the first act, has overtones of nobility, though Saturninus' comment "unnatural and unkind", is uncomfortably close to the truth. The final comments on his character are all praise and pity, sharply contrasted with the abuse heaped on Aaron and Tamora. Marcus gives the core of the defence:

> Now judge what cause had Titus to revenge
> These wrongs, unspeakable, past patience,
> Or more than any living man could bear. (v, iii, 125–7)

So at the end it is Titus rather than Tamora who produces an effect like that of Ovid's Hecuba, for whom even the gods felt pity when revenge had dreadfully transformed her. Or we might describe the difference by saying that the depiction of Tamora is in the mode of the moralized Ovid, while the depiction of Titus more closely resembles Roman Ovid.

The underlying theme of *Titus Andronicus*, to which I have referred, is not so important an organizing principle as Shakespeare's themes are in his later tragedies. I think that, like Ovid, he was more interested here in portraying the extraordinary pitch of emotion to which a person may be raised by the most violent outrage. The passions of Titus transcend the limits of character to become in their own right, so to speak, phenomena of nature: his grief, like the Nile, "disdaineth bounds" (III, I, 71). The grotesqueries of his mad scenes contribute to this effect, and the end is pure frenzy. If the violence of the play serves the theme as an emblem of disorder, it also serves as both agent and emblem of a metamorphosis of character which takes place before our eyes. Character in the usual sense of the word disintegrates completely. What we see is a personified emotion.

We come finally to Lavinia, the third character who may profitably be seen against this Ovidian background. She has been one of the chief stumbling-blocks to the appreciation of the play: to many critics she has seemed smug in her contemptuous speeches to Tamora (II, iii, 66 ff.), and intolerably pathetic or ludicrous thereafter. Dover Wilson gave the most unkindest cut of all when he likened her to "a little puppy-dog", trotting after Titus with his severed hand in her teeth.[16] Yet as an inhabitant of the Ovidian world she is neither absurd nor difficult to understand. Her proud self-confidence with Tamora clearly points up the shocking suddenness of her change to a weeping suppliant—an initial metamorphosis somewhat comparable to Niobe's.

Lavinia's second metamorphosis is accomplished in a description which has proved to be the most unpalatable passage in the play. It is also the most Ovidian. This is the passage in which Marcus compares Lavinia to a tree whose branches have been cut, her blood to a river, a bubbling fountain, her lips to roses, her cheeks to the sun, her lost hands, once more, to the leaves of a tree (II, iv, 16–57). In a somewhat different category is the comment on her loss of blood "As from a conduit with three issuing spouts", a comparison reminiscent of Ovid's description of the death of Pyramus: "...the spouting blood leaped high; just as when a pipe has broken at a weak spot in the lead..." (IV, 121–3). Like Ovid's comparisons, these of Shakespeare's are unexpected, fanciful, and yet exact. Miss Bradbrook has pointed to Shakespeare's use of opposites in description in *Venus and Adonis* and here in *Titus Andronicus*. The imagery of the description of Lavinia is meant, she believes, to "work by contrast.... The writer is saying by means of the images, 'Look here upon this picture, and on this'."[17] It is the "contrast of remembering happiness in misery" to which she refers, and agreeing that the observation is just, I should like to add some other ways in which contrast works here. These pleasant and familiar images of trees, fountains, and conduits bring the horror that has been committed within the range of comprehension. They oblige us to see clearly a suffering body, yet as they do so they temporarily remove its individuality, even its humanity, by abstracting and generalizing. Though not in themselves horrible, they point up the horror; though familiar, they point up the strangeness. The suffering becomes an object of contemplation.

This technique of description is not inappropriate to this sort of situation. The trouble is that it is a narrative rather than a dramatic device. Though many writers have used it in plays, its function is to present to the mind's eye something which is not on the stage for the physical eye to see. When Duncan is described, "His silver skin lac'd with his golden blood" (*Macbeth*, II, iv, 118), there is also an incongruity between mortal wounds and decorative language, but Duncan himself is not there to compete with the description. The imagination of the spectator is free to contemplate a spectacle simultaneously horrible and kingly. The narrative intrusion is brief and clearly separated from dramatic action. For the Ovidian description of Lavinia to work as it might work in the *Metamorphoses* an even greater freedom is required. A physical impersonation of the mutilated Lavinia should not block our vision.

Though this objection sounds like Lamb's criticism of *King Lear*, I believe it is more valid because of the different way in which metamorphosis is related to the meaning of *Titus Andronicus*. In *King Lear* the transformation brought about by extraordinary suffering is not a loss of humanity but a step toward greater understanding. Dramatic action reinforces at every point what the poetry suggests. In Ovid's *Metamorphoses* the unendurable emotional state robs the character of his humanity and the story ends, so to speak, with a point of exclamation. It is easy to see that the melodramatic tale of Titus, Tamora, and Lavinia, partly inspired by Ovid, is susceptible of the full Ovidian treatment. It ends logically with what Joyce might have called an "epiphany" of the state of mind at which each of the principal characters has arrived. This would be shown by a physical metamorphosis or by a passage of description or by both together. In *Titus Andronicus* we have the many speeches insisting upon what is extraordinary in the situation of the hero—what makes it beyond human endurance—but the final transformation which would complete the suggestion cannot take place. We have the description which almost transforms Lavinia, but in the presence of live actors the poetry cannot perform the necessary magic. The action frustrates, rather than re-enforces, the operation of the poetry.

A simple formulation of the source of critical dissatisfaction with the play might seem to follow logically here: the style is inappropriate. Shakespeare, like some Elizabethan builders, has reached out for a bit of classical design and has come up with some decoration which does not fit his basic structure. But this pronouncement rests on an oversimplification, for the Ovidian borrowing in *Titus Andronicus* has more significance than the mere application of decorative detail.

In taking over certain Ovidian forms Shakespeare takes over part of an Ovidian conception which cannot be fully realized by the techniques of drama. This is the conception of the protagonist as a man so worked upon that by sheer intensity of passion he ultimately transcends the normal limits of humanity. I believe that there is a reason why such a treatment of character might appeal to an Elizabethan writer of tragedy, and hence why he might attempt what seems to us a patently impossible task.

In describing the proper effect of tragedy many Renaissance critics emphasized what they called "admiration". In the sixteenth century the word was sometimes used with approximately its modern meaning, but usually retained its basic meaning of "wonder" or "astonishment". The point of exclamation was commonly referred to as a "note of admiration". In a familiar passage of his *Defense of Poesie* Sidney speaks of tragedy "stirring the affects of admiration and commiseration",[18] where "admiration" oddly replaces Aristotle's terror. Minturno makes admiration the final aim of all poetry but particularly of tragedy. "That especially belongs to the tragic poet which fills the hearer with astonishment by horrifying him or moving him to compassion.... Whoever suffers a marvellous thing, if it is horrifying or causes compassion, will not be outside the scope of tragedy, whether he be good or whether he be evil".[19] There is no doubt that such ideas about tragedy were in the air at the end of the sixteenth century and hence that playwrights, whether or not they had read the theorists, might look for material and language suitable to arouse admiration. Seneca was obviously a rich mine, but often it was the Latin writers of verse narrative who furnished models; astonishing passages were freely borrowed or imitated from Virgil, Lucan, Statius. Marlowe and Chapman each developed what might be called a rhetoric of admiration; one thinks of Tamburlaine's "high astounding terms" and of the "glaring colours" which "amazed" the young Dryden.[20] By the time of Buckingham's *Rehearsal*, "to elevate and surprise" are the chief objectives of the satirized playwright. This genre of tragedy is most uncongenial to our times. We are inclined to deny that it is tragedy at all and to dismiss it as mere posturing and rant. Even in its own day it never lacked the mockery of critics.

Titus Andronicus is Shakespeare's contribution to a special tragic mode. Its final spectacle is both horrible and pathetic, but above all extraordinary. Ovid more than Seneca or the epic poets was the model for both characterization and style, with the result that Shakespeare's rhetoric of admiration, as seen in such lines as Marcus' description of Lavinia, is more elegantly florid than that of his contemporaries. The hero, in this respect like Tamburlaine or Bussy D'Ambois, is almost beyond praise or blame, an object of admiration.

NOTES

1. A lecture delivered at the International Shakespeare Conference at Stratford-upon-Avon, 9 September 1955.

2. Edward Ravenscroft, *Titus Andronicus, or The Rape of Lavinia* (1687), sig. A2; *Coleridge's Shakespearean Criticism*, ed. T. M. Raysor (Cambridge, Mass., 1930), II, 31; *Titus Andronicus*, ed. J. Dover Wilson (Cambridge, 1948), p. xii.

3. I do not deal in this article with the problem of authorship, which has been thoroughly treated most recently by J. C. Maxwell in the new Arden Edition (London, 1953), pp. xxiv–xxxiv; I agree with him that the play is substantially Shakespeare's. I am deeply indebted to all the critical apparatus of this edition.

4. M. C. Bradbrook, *Themes and Conventions of Elizabethan Tragedy* (Cambridge, 1935), p. 99.

5. *Titus Andronicus*, ed. Wilson, pp. li–lvi. Departing from the usual practice of *Survey*, I have taken all quotations from the play from this edition since the readings which Wilson takes from Q1 are preferred by most modern editors to those of F printed in the standard Globe edition.

6. Howard Baker *Induction to Tragedy* (University, Louisiana, 1939), pp. 119–39; E. M. W. Tillyard, *Shakespeare's History Plays* (New York, 1946), pp. 135–41.

7. Ovid, *Metamorphoses, with an English translation* by Frank J. Miller, Loeb Classical Library (London, 1936), VI, 499, 521. Unless otherwise indicated, all the English translations from Ovid are Miller's or are closely modelled on his.

8. *A Petite Pallace of Pettie His Pleasure*, ed. I. Gollancz (1908), I, 70.

9. M. C. Bradbrook, *Shakespeare and Elizabethan Poetry* (1951), pp. 51–3.

10. Douglas Bush, *Mythology and the Renaissance Tradition in English Poetry* (Minneapolis, 1932), pp. 68–81.

11. Ovid, *Metamorphoses*, ed. R. Regio (Venice, Bonetus Locatellus, 1493), sig. G7.

12. Epistle, ll. 55–62; *Shakespeare's Ovid...*, ed. W. H. D. Rouse (1904), p. 2 (I have modernized the spelling).

13. T. W. Baldwin, *On the Literary Genetics of Shakespeare's Poems and Sonnets* (Urbana, Ill., 1950), pp. 49–72.

14. Preface to the Reader, ll. 89–92; *Shakespeare's Ovid*, p. 16.

15. *Op. cit.* p. 139.

16. *Titus Andronicus*, ed. Wilson, p. xi.

17. Bradbrook *Shakespeare and Elizabethan Poetry*, pp. 64, 108.

18. *Literary Criticism Plato to Dryden*, ed. Allan H. Gilbert (New York, 1940), p. 432; see also pp. 459–61.

19. Gilbert, pp. 292–3. On "admiration" see also Marvin T. Herrick, 'Some Neglected Sources of *Admiratio*', *Modern Language Notes*, 62 (1947), 222–6; and J. V. Cunningham, *Woe or Wonder* (Denver, 1951).

20. Dedication of *The Spanish Friar*.

FROM PLUTARCH TO SHAKESPEARE:
A STUDY OF CORIOLANUS[1]

BY

HERMANN HEUER

Coriolanus is not a popular play. It is, as Middleton Murry pointed out, unpalatable to the modern taste. Its hero is "unsympathetic", even "alien", being a martyr not to the cause of liberty but to the aristocratic idea. Those who sympathize with the play may accordingly render themselves a little suspect as to their basic predilections. But even apart from the political implications of a certain antipathy against the play, it has sometimes, because of its alleged comparative poverty in poetic appeal, rather superciliously been deemed appropriate intellectual food for dry-as-dust schoolmasters or antiquarian philologists. It has been regarded as the privilege of pedants to admire *Coriolanus*. Thus the lover of the play finds himself between Scylla and Charybdis.

I myself own to a certain admiration for *Coriolanus*, and there is consolation in the thought that, despite the general unpopularity of the play, it has had at least some illustrious defenders:[2] Coleridge and Swinburne, Granville-Barker, Middleton Murry, and André Gide.[3] Thus I hope that I may steer a safe course under the protection of such a remarkable convoy.

This paper does not pretend to reopen the question of Shakespeare's sources—though Kenneth Muir has recently shown that this is still possible—but to add to the discussion concerning the peculiar process of transmutation to which the source-material has been subjected by the dramatist. A comparative study of the modifications would seem to offer satisfactory modes of approach to the play's meaning and might perhaps lessen the danger of discovering profundities of sense in places where (according to a phrase of Schücking's) "the brush of the painter may just as well have blundered". If translations as such more or less unconsciously introduce something of an author's habits of valuation and experience, and if such personal reshaping is often enough a cause of particular enjoyment when the translating authors, as Dryden says, "strike a little out of the common road", how much more fascinating is the spectacle of a creative artist refashioning his material and adapting it to his artistic vision and concept.

With regard to *Coriolanus* we are in the fortunate position of being able to trace such processes of alteration from the Greek original via Amyot and his translator North up to Shakespeare. In particular, the great scene in the fifth act provides us with an excellent example; Volumnia's famous speech is, I believe, the longest continuous passage in which Shakespeare relies closely on a particular source, while the entire scene offers a clear opportunity of our watching the dramatist's creative imagination at work. I hope to be able to show how certain concepts have been characteristically moulded on their way from Plutarch to Shakespeare and how, in particular, the dramatist adopted, rejected, modified, or supplemented them. In a passage where— according to MacCallum—there is a minimum of Plutarch and a maximum of North, Shakespeare's treatment of his original (North) must needs be instructive. MacCallum has, by the way, in the appendix to his well-known book[4] prepared a synopsis of four parallel versions of this great scene, pointing out some principal deviations in the French and English versions—without, however, explaining their significance.

Before turning to an examination of Shakespeare's scene, a word may be said on the general tone of the Greek original. Plutarch views Roman life and manners from his Greek angle. Even were we not sufficiently acquainted with his ethical and political views from his numerous theoretical writings, his deliberate presentation of Greek and Roman twin portraits would make it abundantly clear that the Greek virtues are his ideal. He does not really sympathize with the sternness of ancient Roman characters and he likes to contrast them with specimens of the harmonious culture and urbanity of Greece. To Plutarch, in spite of some moral reservations, the versatility and adaptable smoothness of Alcibiades is admirable, as contrasted with the crudity of Coriolanus. For him, Coriolanus exhibits a want of education:

> This man also is a good proofe to confirme some mens opinions. That a rare and excellent witte untaught, doth bring forth many good and euill thinges together: like a fat soile bringeth forth herbes & weedes that lieth unmanured.[5]

The characteristic quality of Coriolanus is anger, and anger occupies a particularly unfavourable position in a system of ethics which is built on the normative value of moderation. His want of refinement by education, and his lack of well-tempered political virtue, are both stressed. Coriolanus is repeatedly blamed; his achievements, in comparison with those of Alcibiades, are minimized, even his good qualities are relegated to the background. On the whole, Coriolanus serves as an example of a style and conduct which do not fit into the Greek ethical concept of personal culture. Plutarch is far from discovering a note of tragic greatness in the downfall of Coriolanus. There is nothing of the spirit of Greek tragedy about his figure.[6]

Amyot's French version of Plutarch aims at literal accuracy:

> ie confesse auoir plus étudié à rendre fidèlement ce que l'auteur a voulu dire que non pas à orner ou polir le langage.

At the same time he notes that Plutarch wrote rather "doctement et gravement" than "doucement et facilement", consequently he not only simplifies his long periods, but also interpolates explanations of his own. Many of his deviations from the Greek original seem designed to strengthen the psychological aspects of the work. There is a heightening of emotional touches: the dignity of Coriolanus, his emotional excitement, the way he welcomes his relatives, his offended silence are underlined by additional words or phrases. The language of affection is given freer play. Notice, for example, the expression "chauldes larmes". The Greek word "pathos" becomes "affection du sang", "affection naturelle". The stream of emotions is called "force d'un impetueux torrent". These and other alterations serve to introduce a dramatic quality and diverse stylistic devices add to it. Thus Amyot introduces irony by using the word "profit" in a passage of dramatic importance: "si tu en demoures vaincueur, il t'en restera ce *profit*, que tu en seras estimé *la peste et la ruine* de ton pais" (cf. the Greek ἀλάστως). He loves to animate his dialogues by argumentative insertions ("necessairement", "cuides-tu") which help to produce a certain atmosphere of logicality. He introduces the dialectical antithesis "rigueur"-"raison". In other passages in which he goes beyond the original, he seems to reveal a certain preoccupation with the desirability of a polished society ("aimable recueuil", etc.). In many of these novel ingredients one cannot fail to discover a remoulding of the original into specifically French patterns of thought. Notice, for example, the enthusiastic praise of "bonnes lettres" in another passage:

le plus grand fruit que les hommes rapportent de *la douceur et benignité* des Muses, *c'est à dire de la connoissance des bonnes lettres*, c'est qu'ils en domptent et adoucissent leur nature, *qui estoit auparavant sauvage et farouche*, trouvans avec le compas de la raison, le moyen, et reiettans le trop.

Amyot's translation may be described as a sympathetic version, but with a special emphasis of its own. It is interesting to observe how the marginal comments of later editions (such as that of 1621) stress the lessons implied in his rendering:

On ne saurait trop recommander aux grands et petits la connoissance des bonnes lettres.... Les ambitieux sont mal propres en la société humaine.

The version produced by North has, of course, still greater interest for us. North assimilates Plutarch in his English fashion, just as Amyot gives him a French colouring. The stylistic features of his translation have been aptly described by MacCallum,[7] who mentions his "full-blooded words", his "phrases racy of the soil", his "native homespun", his "indisputable Anglicity", his "native idiom" and the fact that he "naturalised" Plutarch among the English, thereby "meeting Shakespeare half-way".[8] A close scrutiny of North's version of Volumnia's speech undoubtedly confirms this general impression. The modifications introduced by North throw into stronger relief the concrete, the factual, the sensuous. Colourless expressions are replaced by crisp pictorial ones. Essentially important is the emphasis laid on elemental relations of life. Amyot's independent rendering "affection naturelle" ("affection du sang") remains unaltered ("natural affection"; "affection of his blood"). An entirely new feature, moreover, is the occurrence of the words "nature" and "natural", with the opposite notion of "unnatural", no less than five times within Shakespeare's scene: "And *Nature* so wrought with him, that the teares fell from his eyes";—"preferring love and *nature* before the malice and calamitie of warres";—"and I maye not deferre to see the daye, either that my sonne be led prisoner in triumphe by his *naturall* country men, or that he him selfe doe triumphe of them, and of his *naturall* countrie". Of peculiar importance is the following passage: "No man living is more bounde to shewe him selfe thankefull in all partes and respects then thy selfe: who so *unnaturally* sheweth all ingratitude." The French version has "asprement" here, which corresponds literally to the Greek πικρῶς: North paves the way to Shakespeare by using the word "unnaturally". It is evident from North's renderings that nature is conceived as the operative and guiding force, as the sacred order and ultimate appeal. Its negative reverse is the "unnatural" as opposed to the values implied in what is called "natural". The consequence of North's modifications is that the conflict, conceived psychologically or rather logically in the French version as one between "rigueur" and "raison", is now being transferred to a different plane. It is now a question of the acknowledgment or denial of the natural. The disruption of the natural bonds and of the naturally inherent order of human existence has become the decisive issue. Our observation that North thinks in terms of the natural and fundamental is confirmed by his characteristic phrasing elsewhere. It is he who introduces the expression "the nurse of their native country" (i.e. the country is the nurse, the foster-mother). This enhances the idea that the individual is connected with his country by inborn, instinctive ties and that these primitive impulses belong to the natural order. There is also fundamental forcefulness in his insertion of the word "womb" which neither Plutarch nor Amyot use: "but thy foot shall tread upon thy mother's womb that brought thee first into this world." Although such an introduction of the elemental and natural strongly increases the pathetic appeal, French additions like "chauldes larmes" and "picqué", bordering on the sentimental or the theatrical, are omitted: the element of the lachrymose does not fit into the atmosphere of a dispute where first principles come into play. Thus the sense of tragedy is heightened both by additions and omissions.

Another feature in North's translation is the stronger accent put on moral valuations. When he translates: "thy selfe *deservedly* shall carie the *shameful* reproache and burden of either partie", he inserts two extra touches of moral judgement. The demand for filial reverence receives a significant stress by the expression of a moral postulate: "acknowledging the duety and reverence they *ought* to bear unto them". North deviates characteristically from Amyot when he says: "And therefore it is *not only* honest, *but due unto me*, that without compulsion I should obtain my so just and reasonable request of thee." It is North again who underlines the inappropriateness of Coriolanus' treasonable behaviour by coupling his phrases with additional ones in such sentences as: "For as to destroye thy naturall country it is altogether *unmete* and unlawfull", or: "so were it not just, and *lesse honorable*, to betraye those that put their trust in thee." The same trend of moral criticism is indicated by various additional devices of irony or the replacing of French words like "juste" by such significant expressions as "honorable". The notion of personal honour gains central importance by the use of such terms for dishonourable behaviour as "unmete", "unlawfull", "shamefull", etc.

At the same time the idea of fatality is underlined by modifying words indicative of the limitation of the personal responsibility of the hero, such as by the significant addition of the word "only" in the following passage:

So as that which is thonly comforte to all other in their adversitie and miserie, to pray unto the goddes and to call to them for aide, is the *onely* thinge which plongeth us into most deepe perplexitie.

The deepest cause of confusion is thus an inexplicable paradox.

In North's story of Coriolanus there is a preoccupation, similar to that in Plutarch's and Amyot's, with educational considerations, but, whereas Amyot stresses "bonnes lettres" and "la douceur et benignité des Muses", North finds the educationally desirable thing to be "civil" and "courteous"; Coriolanus is "churlish", "uncivil", "rude" and "rough".

There is finally, in North's version, a stronger emphasis upon Coriolanus' exuberant vitality. The French word "gravité" is turned into "a certain insolent and stern manner". The word "force" is rendered by "stoutness", a word which Shakespeare takes over and which seems to imply over-bearing pride. There is a significant variation from the French original when Coriolanus is called "a man too full of passion and choller and too much given over to self-will and opinion". Here, however, no narrow-minded censoriousness seems to be intended. A "high mind" and "great courage" are expressly attributed to Coriolanus. They are mentioned as real, not as hypothetical qualities as in the French version.

Thus, from the total of a great many individual changes of the text—inconspicuous and trifling as they may sometimes appear at first sight—there results an entirely different cumulative effect. It is specially important to observe that with all his intensification of the moral tone and with all his emphasis on the practical and educational aspects, North has a pronounced sense of the natural and elemental, and to a certain extent also, of fatality and tragic greatness.

SHAKESPEARE'S HANDLING OF THE VOLUMNIA-SCENE

Shakespeare's drama attains its essential realization in the great Volumnia-scene. Differing from Plutarch, it is the culmination of a climax. Two attempts at reconciliation have already taken place. A delegation headed by Cominius, the soldier-friend, has been rudely rejected. Then Menenius Agrippa, against his better judgment, devotes himself to the thankless task. He throws his friendship with Coriolanus into the balance. In vain: his mission too is a failure—he returns broken-hearted. The first breach, however, has been effected in the hardened mood of the protagonist. Scarcely has he buckled himself to another semblance of insensibility, when he catches sight of the group of those dearest to him—his mother, his wife and his child. Thus the ensuing scene is most passionately accentuated by an appeal to Coriolanus as husband, father, and son. It represents the final assault on a mind that is already weakening like a bulwark crumbling under repeated attacks.

The development of the scene is noteworthy for its stressing of the element of unnaturalness. There are various interesting deviations from Plutarch: the gesture of maternal self-humiliation does not occur once but three times. There is a climax in the petitioning process. First mother, wife and son bestow their tribute of respect to Coriolanus as the enemy leader. Coriolanus is painfully aware of the enormity of this unnatural occurrence, yet he silences the voice of his natural feelings. Thereupon the genuflexion of his relatives takes place. It represents in itself, and even more so by its *mise-en-scène* (each kneeling before Coriolanus at the prompting of Volumnia), a further intensification of the motif of unnaturalness. Yet still Coriolanus, though deeply moved, justifies the unnatural appearance of his retributory scheme. Finally, there is the last and third desperate gesture of genuflexion associated with anxious prayer, exhortation and terrible maternal resignation.

Shakespeare emphasizes Volumnia's petition by the introduction of the additional parts of Virgilia and young Marcius—a further challenge to the fundamental instincts of husband and father—but the decisively new thing is the character conflict in Coriolanus. He grows increasingly conscious of the perverted delusion of his treason. Already in the great monologue (IV, iv, 12 ff. "O world, thy slippery turns!") he had come to perceive the ironic reversal of such natural forces as friendship, enmity, patriotism. "Fellest foes" were turning into new friends, friendship had been converted into "bitterest enmity". The worst, however, was this: "my birth-place hate I, and my love's upon this enemy town". This change had been inexplicable to him as if it were some weird magic: "some chance, some trick not worth an egg" had, it seemed to him, been at play. He was beginning to realize his loss of self-determination.

Now Coriolanus is made to feel his way of acting as a crime against his own kindred, as a horrifying hardening of his heart towards his wife and as the most monstrous negation of his filial respect for his mother. The consciousness is dawning on him that his deed amounts to the inhuman cancelling of the natural laws of existence, to an upheaval of natural order. "Great Nature" simply forbids the denial of "instinct", of "natural affection". Thus the tragic issue is transposed into a sphere of ultimate questionings. Shall the bonds of natural loyalty and piety be perversely torn? There are values which Coriolanus' nobler self cannot ultimately sacrifice. He cannot, without destroying his nobler substance, deny the value of his former life. The "violentest contrariety" (IV, vi, 73) as Menenius had termed his alleged treason will prove unbearable to him. Thus "Nature"9 becomes the key-word of the great scene. At first Coriolanus prepares himself to ignore the voice of nature:

> But, out, affection!
> All bond and privilege of nature, break!

Yet he is not able to play his part. The stupendous nature of his contradictions reveals itself to him:

> I melt, and am not
> Of stronger earth than others. My mother bows;
> As if Olympus to a molehill should
> In supplication nod: and my young boy
> Hath an aspect of intercession, which
> Great nature cries, "Deny not."

His language rises to awe-inspiring heights when it voices the monstrosity of a mother kneeling before her son and when it gives utterance to a reversal of all values amounting to the most unheard-of disturbance of the laws of existence:

> What is this?
> Your knees to me! to your corrected son!
> Then let the pebbles on the hungry beach
> Fillip the stars; then let the mutinous winds
> Strike the proud cedars 'gainst the fiery sun;
> Murd'ring impossibility, to make
> What cannot be, slight work.

The self-justification of Coriolanus cannot but admit the impression he conveys of perverted conduct:

> tell me not
> Wherein I seem unnatural.

There is an overwhelming expression of the tragic paradox into which he finds himself manoeuvred, when he suddenly awakens to a recognition of his true situation and faces the inevitability of his fate:

> Behold, the heavens do ope,
> The gods look down, and this unnatural scene
> They laugh at.

Here it becomes manifest how powerfully Shakespeare has developed the germinal idea of nature as he found it in the accentuations and valuations of North's English version of Plutarch: these lines suggest a scene of universal, of metaphysical, significance.

A number of other passages add to the general impression. There are striking homely images such as that of the hen and the chicken ("she—poor hen!—fond of no second brood, Has cluck'd thee to the wars, and safely home") or that of the stocks ("yet here he lets me prate like one i' the stocks"). North's image of the country as nurse receives even more emotional colouring ("the dear nurse of our country"); the expression "the country whereto we are bound", the taking over of Amyot's and North's word "affection" and of North's phrase "thou shalt tread on thy mother's womb", the more liberal language of the heart—everywhere this preoccupation with fundamental relations of life is visible. Coriolanus in Shakespeare's version is made to appear much more drastically as the "foreign recreant", as the apostate and sinner against the laws of nature, than in North's prose version; what we have here are North's germinal notions fostered and elaborated in dramatic manner.[10]

Some other distinctive features likewise show Shakespeare's dramatization as the continuation and completion of certain rudimentary ideas already discoverable in North's Plutarch. The motif of honour and that of personal ethics are raised to a more central position. In the Greek version Coriolanus' actions seem to be measured by the yardstick of rational logic. Shakespeare's valuations are different. The heroic ideal is not identical with that of the Greek *kalokagathia* but with that of nobleness. "The man was noble"—such will be the verdict of future historians (says Volumnia) when they will register the meritorious past in a traitor's life. "The man is noble" (v, vi, 126)—thus a Volscian nobleman defends the hero who is under the charge of treason. And after his death Coriolanus is awarded the tribute of nobleness even by Aufidius. Volumnia, in pleading with him harps upon the theme of nobleness by way of irony, sarcasm, desperate remonstrance. She, the advocate of her son's honour, launches against him the reproach, "thou art not honest". This is the ultimate accusation she can raise against her own son. Coupling it with that of degenerate unnaturalness ("this fellow had a Volscian to his mother") she demonstrates that "honesty", a prerequisite of "honour", is primarily rooted in a most elementary stratum of existence. The moral sphere is at bottom the natural sphere. Nature and morality are correlatives.

There is an interesting passage denoting that Coriolanus had hitherto endeavoured to attain some almost superhuman degree of moral excellence:

> Thou hast affected the fine strains of honour,
> To imitate the graces of the gods.

The verses immediately following allude to the disproportion between his willing and acting:

> To tear with thunder the wide cheeks o' the air,
> And yet to charge thy sulphur with a bolt
> That should but rive an oak.

One may perhaps look upon such passages as a kind of corrective of Plutarch's leading conception that Coriolanus typifies deficient self-education. Shakespeare shows him repeatedly as being by no means inaccessible to educational influences, particularly those of his mother and his friends. It is also the dramatist's intention that we should read Coriolanus' own ethos from the mind of his yet immature boy whom he has sought to instruct in the duties of nobility and whom he regards with paternal hope and pride. Shakespeare does not introduce—as Plutarch does—Coriolanus' children (nameless and in the plural), but he concentrates all the love of the hero on that one boy Marcius. Moreover, the hero's tragedy is not something that might have been avoided by education or instruction—rather are we confronted here with a problem of destiny.

With all his want of polish, his revulsion from the mob and his naive display of unbounded vitality, the solitary protagonist is meant to claim our sympathies as a tragic figure.[11]

It is noteworthy too that the conflict amounts to opposing pride to pity:

> He turns away:
> Down, ladies; let us shame him with our knees.
> To his surname Coriolanus 'longs more *pride*
> Than *pity* to our prayers.

Aufidius, his antagonist, refers with malicious satisfaction to the same conflict:

> I am glad thou hast set thy *mercy* and thy *honour*
> At difference in thee: out of that I'll work
> Myself a former fortune.

It will be remembered that in the French version this conflict was pivoted on "rigueur" and "raison". Shakespeare's characteristic contribution is the concept of "mercy".[12] Mercy, the spirit of generosity—not in itself incompatible with the requirements of honour—is to be the basis of Volumnia's proposal of peace. Coriolanus' limitation was that he had "shown too little mercy towards the people", and yet the victor of Corioli had intervened in favour of a "poor man" (not of "an honest wealthie man" according to Plutarch). This represents, as MacCallum has pointed out, an interesting digression from Plutarch and North, implying an extension of mercy beyond the narrow scope of class bias.

Still another thing may be gathered from an examination of this scene. It is Coriolanus' error to think that he might dispense with the established order of nature, defying its bonds and statutes by a proclamation of arbitrary autonomy:

> I'll never
> Be such a gosling to obey instinct, but stand,
> As if a man were author of himself
> And knew no other kin.

But whatever degree of proud emancipation an individual may boast of, he is not autonomous but remains intimately linked with his natural community, and has, in the long run, to acknowledge his primary connection with it. At bottom, Coriolanus' erroneous notion that he may stand alone and even denounce these natural bonds—the very springs of life—implies the reversal of his own most cherished conceptions of value. His tragedy consists in the imminent uprooting of his ethical consciousness, in the self-ironical paradox that, in a general confusion—his values being reversed—he is dangerously near becoming the destroyer of what he had formerly believed in and stood for. It is true that this utter catastrophe of his moral existence is warded off. It remains a mystery, however, that even temporarily, out of some inexplicable weakness, disposition or condition, in spite of the nobility of his mind, Coriolanus should have been prompted to trespass against the sacred laws of nature and his own treasured convictions—that merit and treason, honour and dishonour, greatness and delusion should have entered into such a bewildering alliance. Here is a sense of the unfathomable in Shakespeare, and the question why and how such demonic misguidance and such waste of noble energies could happen at all will be raised in vain.

Shakespeare's Coriolanus is presented almost as if he were a force of nature. He is compared to a thunderstorm, to the sea, to a planet:

> The shepherd knows not thunder from a tabor
> More than I know the sound of Marcius' tongue
> From every meaner man. (I, vi, 25)

> He waxed like a sea. (II, ii, 103)

> [He] struck Corioli like a planet. (II, ii, 117–18)

Menenius declares that "his nature is too noble for the world". Yet he is no god. The "spices" of his nature—pride and defect of judgment—are even termed a disease: one of the tribunes arrogantly states: "he is a disease that must be cut away", whereupon Menenius retorts "O! he's a limb that has but a disease". Fatality is inherent in the character of the protagonist; and a phrase from *Antony and Cleopatra* provides a pertinent comment: "Men's judgments are a parcel of their fortunes" (III, xiii, 32). Even so, we seem far away from Plutarch. Shakespeare's words are not "I see myself vanquished by thee alone" (North). The principle of explanation is not found on an entirely human and rational plane, but on a metaphysical one. In the chaotic disruption of character, in the disintegration of the natural order of being, Shakespeare exhibits Coriolanus as an exponent of the irrational in life and history. In Plutarch, Coriolanus serves as an example for the demonstration of the moral axiom that even an excellent character needs education. In his stock-taking the deviation from the Aristotelian[13] doctrine of the "mean estate" becomes prominent. Coriolanus lacks the proper mixture of gravity and affability, the requisites of "political virtue". He is neither rationally nor aesthetically well-balanced. Such unevenness of character, his passion, choler, self-will, opinion, wilfulness, are deprecated. For the Greeks wisdom, fortitude, and self-discipline were the three essential qualities of a man: Plutarch's Coriolanus is not in possession of these cardinal virtues. He may have valour, but he lacks wisdom and self-discipline.

How does Shakespeare proceed? He presents no psychological arithmetic, no moralizing systematization and certainly no petty rational outlook. Great characters for him do not represent equations that permit of smooth solutions. There ever remains an unanalysable remainder that defies rational explanation. For Shakespeare character is always wrapped in a cloak of mystery defying rational analysis. Even Menenius Agrippa, surely not a very mysterious personality himself, declares: "You know neither me, yourselves nor anything." Volumnia alluding to her son refers to those "mysteries which heaven will not have earth to know".

NOTES

1. A lecture delivered at the International Shakespeare Conference at Stratford-upon-Avon, 8 September 1955.

2. See the criticism mentioned in the Furness Variorum Edition of *Coriolanus* (1928), e.g. pp. 661, 665–6. Recently P. Alexander, *A Shakespeare Primer* (1951), p. 123, H. C. Goddard, *The Meaning of Shakespeare* (Chicago, 1951), U. Ellis-Fermor, *Shakespeare Jahrbuch* (1954), pp. 43 ff. have voiced equally commendatory views.

3. Lettre à Paul Valéry, 15 March 1898, in Gide-Valéry, *Correspondance 1890–1942* (Paris, 1955), p. 315.

4. *Shakespeare's Roman Plays and their Background* (1910).

5. Quoted from the 1595 facsimile edition in F. A. Leo, *Four Chapters from North's Plutarch* (London and Strasburg, 1878).

6. J. A. K. Thompson, *Shakespeare and the Classics* (1952) suggests "that, through the medium of North's Plutarch, Shakespeare divined the true spirit of Greek tragedy" (p. 250).

7. *Op. cit.* p. 158.

8. Cf. also F. O. Matthiessen, *Translation an Elizabethan Art* (Harvard University Press, 1931), ch. III, 'North's Plutarch'.

9. Cf. also J. F. Danby, *Shakespeare's Doctrine of Nature: A Study of King Lear* (1949). R. Speaight, *Nature in Shakespearian Tragedy* (1955); H. Heuer, 'Der Geist und seine Ordnung bei Shakespeare', *Shakespeare Jahrbuch*, lxxxiv–lxxxvi (1948–50), 52 ff.

10. Tucker Brooke overstates his case when he claims for the last all-decisive speech of Volumnia that it has "come straight and essentially unaltered out of North" (cf. Furness, *op. cit.* p. 621).

11. I fail to be completely convinced by the brilliant statements of O. J. Campbell (*Shakespeare's Satire*, 1943), Allardyce Nicoll (*Shakespeare*, 1952, p. 153) and L. C. Knights (*Poetry, Politics and the English Tradition*, 1954, p. 15), whose mainly satirical characterizations of Coriolanus seem to do insufficient justice to the tragic aspects of the play.

12. Cf. E. T. Sehrt, *Vergebung und Gnade bei Shakespeare* (Stuttgart, 1952).

13. For other possible connexions of the play with Aristotle see F. N. Lees, 'Coriolanus, Aristotle, and Bacon', *Review of English Studies*, n.s. I, April 1950.

THE COMPOSITION OF
TITUS ANDRONICUS

BY

R. F. HILL

This is not an essay in disintegration. Indeed, the study of *Titus Andronicus* and other First Folio plays makes me doubt the possibility of disintegrating an Elizabethan play-text to the satisfaction of anyone but the disintegrator and those already predisposed to his view. Yet, while criticizing the methods hitherto used in authorship problems, I shall propose one which has proved valuable in the case of *Titus Andronicus* and might therefore with profit be applied to other disputed plays. The method is, in the main, stylistic, and the discovery of certain eccentricities in the style of *Titus* leads to the conclusion that it is either Shakespeare's first play, an alternative to which I incline, or else the work of more than one author. To refine the second alternative, should this prevail, to establish which authors were concerned in the composition, must await a parallel full-scale investigation of the styles of Shakespeare's contemporary dramatists. And here I must state my faith that in any play of disputed authorship the most careful sifting of internal evidence cannot satisfactorily assign small patches, or even whole scenes or acts, to particular writers—except possibly in the case of a clear-cut division of work between act and act—since within any play there may be wide and inexplicable variations. Thus in *Titus*, Peele's authorship of Act I, often suspected on account of the flatness of the verse, its thin diction and Peelean tags, seems confirmed by the abundant alliteration, a device favoured by Peele. Unfortunately there is just as much alliteration in Act II, where there are a number of apparent parallels with *Venus and Adonis* and *The Rape of Lucrece*; and Act V, which has only a third of the alliteration found in either Acts I or II, is the weakest part of the play in respect of lapses into wordiness and tautology. The evidence for Shakespearian or non-Shakespearian authorship seems contradictory. No test can unthread the strands, or remove the layers of work like paint from a canvas, and subjective judgments are hazardous with the changeable taffeta of Elizabethan dramatic writing; this way it looks Peele, that way Shakespeare. Where collaboration was close, or where one author re-fashioned the work of another, the best we can hope for is to establish which authors were concerned; let us recognize and work within the inevitable limitations of our criteria for determining authorship.

The application of internal evidence to authorship problems in Elizabethan drama bristles with difficulties. How is one to discern the individual style? Shakespeare and his contemporaries drew from a common stock of classical knowledge; they largely shared a common diction, deriving from the Senecans, from Spenser and from translations of the Latin poets;[1] they shared, as a result of the traditional rhetorical training, common elements in their methods of amplification and ornamentation. Moreover, the Renaissance theory of imitation contributed further to this homogeneity, whilst the wholesale 'borrowing' of vendible phrases from fellow writers must strike the twentieth-century parallel passage sleuth as criminally irresponsible.

The identification of authorship through verbal parallels has been tried and found seriously wanting.[2] Verbal parallels may be explained as plagiarism, deliberate or unconscious. And even if one skirts the frightening possibility of mere coincidence, one is faced with the problem of independent derivation from a common source, a phenomenon by no means unlikely in a literature which drew so heavily upon the same stock of learning, often taking a meretricious eloquence from the numerous compendia of classical wisdom and story.[3] Vocabulary tests (i.e. identification of authorship by a count of so-called characteristic words and phrases) have also been discountenanced.[4] Metrical tests are meaningless when applied to short passages, or even to whole scenes, since such features as feminine endings and run-on lines are not spread evenly, but appear sporadically, sometimes related to a particular mood, character or style, and sometimes just 'happening'.[5] Imagery tests have not yet been much used, but have already been critically examined.[6] Nonetheless, such tests seem to me of value where they rely upon the incidence of image clusters which result from the unconscious association of ideas, for in probing the unconscious they reach to what is truly idiosyncratic.

It may seem foolhardy to venture where so many have lost their way. I venture because I believe that tests hitherto applied are not inherently valueless but that they were either insufficiently thorough-going or else pressed to conclusions beyond their legitimate scope. Tests must be comprehensive; if we are working with verbal echoes or with characteristic words and phrases we must evidently demonstrate that they cannot be paralleled in other dramatists; it does not help much to gather together a few clichés from a play of known authorship and then to look for these specifics in the disputed or anonymous play. The latter may well exhibit, in addition, stylistic peculiarities not present in the known play and these features, which may easily escape the reader's notice, since he comes *parti pris* finding only what he wishes to find, could equally well prove that the two plays are by different authors. The aim of this study, the first step in a long process, is to establish by a full and impartial analysis of a group of Shakespeare's early plays what elements in the style of *Titus* are un-characteristic of his early manner. A final evaluation of these eccentricities must await a similar analysis of the work of other dramatists; only with these findings could true idiosyncrasies be recognized and comparisons made with confidence.

So far as literature is susceptible of scientific method the authorship problem should be thus approached, since aesthetic judgments are too incalculable and disputable to win universal acceptance. Yet their value as corroborative evidence need not be pleaded, and for no purpose would anyone wish to have plays reduced to mere anatomical data. Any consideration of what is characteristic or un-characteristic of the early Shakespeare in the style of *Titus* must evidently be controlled by a parallel consideration of its other dramatic features. A short excursion into literary criticism will therefore form a prelude to the discussion of style.

Ever since Ravenscroft's remark[7] (incidentally the sole external evidence we have for doubting the authenticity of *Titus*) that Shakespeare gave only "some master-touches" to the play, critics have sought to absolve him of its banalities and crude physical horrors, finding only the character of Aaron, the 'fly' scene and a few verbal felicities worthy of the master-touch. This is an underestimate, for it does not take account of the great scene (III, i) in which the mind of Titus is shattered by successive blows of cruelty and grief. Its dramatic power is astonishing. Already apparently at the height of anguish because his plea for his sons' lives has been ignored and

Lucius banished, Titus is suddenly confronted with the mutilated Lavinia. There is no immediate outburst; only after the terrifying control of:

> Marcus. I bring consuming sorrow to thine age.
> Titus.　Will it consume me? let me see it, then.
> Marcus. This was thy daughter.
> Titus.　　　　　　　　　　　　Why, Marcus, so she is.

does the full tide of agony flow:

> What fool hath added water to the sea,
> Or brought a faggot to bright-burning Troy?

Then hope comes in the devilish person of Aaron and, in return for a promise that his sons shall be spared, Titus cuts off his hand. A few minutes later the hand is returned with the heads of his two sons. Titus is silent. Several speeches ensue in which the servant delivers his message and Marcus and Lucius express their horror. Lavinia kisses her father. At last his stunned incredulity finds words:

> When will this fearful slumber have an end?

In touching the chords of pity this situation is not far distant from Lear's stumbling lines over the body of Cordelia.

Yet this should not be allowed to obscure the fact that it is a *tour de force*, imposed upon characters scarcely worth human sympathy. The grief of Titus cannot pierce deeply because we are never shown that he was capable of fatherly love; he lives by codes of honour and justice whose stern dictates he only once mitigates with humanity. He reaps what he has sown. He is just to the letter in demanding the sacrifice of Alarbus, but our hearts go out to Tamora as her passionate plea for mercy falls upon deaf ears. Without a thought he murders Mutius, and his subsequent sorrow is for his wounded honour, not for the unnatural act he has committed. He shows no remorse. The tragic potentialities of the predicament of Titus in the first act—the conflicting demands of honour and nature—are neither realized nor developed. It is inevitable that the sufferings of such a man should lead only to revenge—as Tamora's did—and not to the self-knowledge which would ennoble him, and claim our sympathy. Lavinia, the heroine, when not being ignored, is wooden and never credible. The betrothed of Bassianus, and apparently deeply in love with him if her words in the forest scene are to be believed, she makes no protest when handed over to Saturninus, and has to be forcefully carried off by her athletic, and no doubt astonished, lover. She is famous for her chastity, yet there is something rank in her "nice-preserved honesty" as her gentle tongue bandies fish-wife terms with Tamora:

> Under your patience, gentle empress,
> 'Tis thought you have a goodly gift in horning.　　　　　　　　　(II, iii, 66–7)

Lucius, whose role as saviour of Rome we are expected to applaud at the end of the play, treats Tamora's anguish with fearful brutality:

> Away with him [Alarbus]! and make a fire straight;
> And with our swords, upon a pile of wood,
> Let's hew his limbs till they be clean consumed.　　　　　　　　(I, i, 127–9)

Marcus Andronicus alone among the 'good' characters wins our respect and understanding.

What ought to strike one as strangest of all in this play is the absence of any human or moral frame of reference. The virtues of love, generosity, self-sacrifice, tolerance and goodness light up, if fitfully at times, the darkest and most frivolous of Shakespeare's plays; indeed, they are what make Shakespeare Shakespeare. One might argue that in portraying Rome as a "wilderness of tigers", he saw everyone tainted to some degree with barbarity, and that he meant us to understand that the inhumanities would continue after the final curtain. This would at least be an unexpressed moral judgment. Yet such an explanation does not satisfy. It is obvious that in the accession of Lucius we are supposed to see the restoration of moral sanity after the interregnum of evil, just as we do in the case of Richmond, Malcolm, and Edgar. Unfortunately, he is just as unsuited to that role as Titus and Lavinia are to that of suffering goodness. Shakespeare's really 'good' characters excel in goodness; the deficiencies of 'good' and 'bad' in *Titus* remind one rather of Marlowe's pattern.

The play has been praised for the excellence of its structure and this has sometimes been regarded as an indication of Shakespearian authorship, despite the fact that *The Spanish Tragedy* suggests that the plotting of *Titus* was by no means beyond Kyd. Besides, when examined closely, the structure has serious weaknesses. There is, of course, the transference of initiative and interest from Tamora to Aaron, but much worse is the sag in the play after III, i until the denouement. This is painfully obvious in the theatre. At the end of III, i Titus says, "Let's kiss and part, for we have much to do"; yet the following scene, merely harping upon the grief which had been expressed much more powerfully in the previous scene, develops nothing and ends with the quiet decision to read "Sad stories chanced in the times of old". If this is intended as a preamble to the discovery of the story of Philomena, it seems unnecessarily long-winded. The 'arrow' scene (IV, iii), presumably inserted to illustrate the madness of Titus, is clumsily executed and quite unessential to the action—in fact it is a positive hindrance to Titus since his purpose should be to lull the suspicions of Saturninus, not to incense him further. The impression grows that in this and in the 'Revenge-Rape-Murder' scene (v, ii) the author is attempting to mask the thinness of the plot with some theatrical 'business', for at the close of IV, i the villainy has been discovered and it remains only for Titus to seize the sons of Tamora and arrange the banquet. A flimsy reason is provided by Tamora to justify the 'Revenge' scene:

> For now he firmly takes me for Revenge;
> And, being credulous in this mad thought,
> I'll make him send for Lucius his son;
> And, whilst I at a banquet hold him sure,
> I'll find some cunning practice out of hand,
> To scatter and disperse the giddy Goths.   (v, ii, 73–8)

But Lucius had already agreed to a meeting at his father's house (v, i, 155–65) so that the 'Revenge' scene becomes no more than a foolishly elaborate means of putting Chiron and Demetrius into the hands of Titus. With regard to the motives of the Goths in desiring to free their enemies from a tyrannous emperor perhaps the less said the better. While it is true that Shakespeare was not always attentive to the details of his plots, this brief and incomplete survey of the shortcomings of *Titus* should warn us against making the merits of its structure an argument for Shakespearian authorship.

An examination of the dramatic qualities of *Titus* leaves one puzzled by the oddnesses, the curious mixture of strength and weakness. Can one categorically say of anything in the play "Shakespeare could not even in his earliest writing have done this"? The magnificent scene in the third act, the pathos of the fly killing episode, Aaron's strange blend of villainy and engaging paternal affection, all seem beyond the reach of any of his contemporaries; while the inconsistencies, the physical horrors, and the lapses of taste are about what one might expect from a first dramatic essay in the Senecan-Ovidian manner. Yet even this scheme need not necessarily exclude the humanity one expects from Shakespeare. Marlowe made Edward II die in lonely misery but Shakespeare's compassion gave Richard II the faithful groom and a brave death. Why then is he so relentless in his treatment of Titus and Lavinia? Or how does one account for the general amorality of the play? It seems a gratuitous refinement to say that there is an implied moral judgment in the portrayal of an un-Christian society in which evil begets evil. In all his other plays Shakespeare makes the moral issues clear in the balance of character and by direct statement, both of which are, to say the least, blurred, in *Titus*. Moreover, this almost symbolic representation of an ethical idea one would expect not in a writer's nonage but in his maturity, *after* a sequence of plays in which moral issues were expressed through a simple opposition of the forces of good and evil. Besides, the conclusion of *Titus* does attempt to conform to this second, more customary pattern; it fails to convince because of uncertainty of moral direction and characterization in the remainder of the play. Uncertainty of treatment—is this the result of collaboration or merely the stumbling of a writer unable to compass the manifold problems of his first play? Characterization, structure, dialogue, motivation, poetry, all to be brought into strict harmony for the expression of a governing theme—should we wonder at the faltering of a young dramatist, especially when his tragic models were themselves imperfect? It remains to be seen what direction is given by a consideration of style.

Since the Elizabethan art of language is based squarely upon rhetoric, a fundamentally self-conscious approach, it seems reasonable to analyse style in the same terms. In the imitation of their Latin authorities the Elizabethan rhetoricians schematized innumerable twists and turns of language, so that such analysis yields very full data not only of devices of ornamentation but also of speech and sentence structure. Accordingly, therefore, eleven early plays of Shakespeare were analysed into one hundred and thirty rhetorical figures, based closely upon the scheme given by George Puttenham in the *Arte of English Poesie*. The plays selected were those, according to orthodox chronology, written between 1590 and 1596; i.e. *Henry VI*, parts two and three,[8] *Richard III*, *The Comedy of Errors*, *Titus Andronicus*, *The Taming of the Shrew*, *The Two Gentlemen of Verona*, *Love's Labour's Lost*, *Romeo and Juliet*, *Richard II*, and *A Midsummer Night's Dream*. This spread and variety of kinds, in embracing a good deal of experimentalism, seemed sufficient to allow of generalizations about Shakespeare's early dramatic style. The tabulated results of analysis are not given here because I wish to avoid the impression that one can reach scientific exactness in literary matters. In any case, it is only the wide divergencies and close similarities which can have any significance, not the difference between one or two decimal places.

Alliteration as an habitual verse ornament was gradually abandoned by Shakespeare, particularly in comedy during the first period of his writing. Naturally the frequency of alliteration is relatively high in *Romeo and Juliet* and *Richard II*, where a mounting and emphatic diction is sought, and Shakespeare continued to use it for special effects throughout his dramatic career, but what he thought of it as a mere mechanical device may be judged from Holofernes' "pricket" jingle and Bottom's "Ercles' vein". Like Sir Philip Sidney, he delighted in poetical flourish but he was equally critical of pedantry and excess. Shakespeare laughed at Holofernes; Sidney gave us Rombus, the schoolmaster of *The Lady of May*, with his "sojorned in the surging sulkes of the sandiferous seas". There is some difference between

> Clear up, fair queen, that cloudy countenance:
> Though chance of war hath wrought this change of cheer,
>
> (*Titus*, I, i, 263–4)

and

> For God's sake, let us sit upon the ground
> And tell sad stories of the death of kings. (*Richard II*, III, ii, 155–6)

Setting aside the general *naïveté* of alliteration in *Titus*, a conservative count shows that this play has an average of one example in eighteen lines, and is approached only by *2 Henry VI* and *Richard III* which have averages of one in twenty-four and one in twenty-eight lines, respectively. In general, the rest of the plays examined contain only half as much alliteration as *Titus*. If the play is wholly Shakespearian, then its excessive and tuneless playing on the letter seems to suggest that it must be a first play, written when the dramatist was less critical of style. It is, I suppose, just possible to argue that it was used deliberately for some special purpose as, for example, to give the verse a ring and emphasis in keeping with the Roman theme.

A study of Shakespeare's use of tropes in his early period discloses the curious fact that whereas *Titus* has a far higher average of simple metaphors than the *Henry VI* plays, it contains only half the number of continued metaphors usual in the early tragedies and histories. The richness of Shakespeare's diction owes much to his liking for continued metaphor, and one's impression of the un-Shakespearian quality of *Titus* derives in part from a general simplicity in metaphor. The point is illustrated by a comparison of the following passages:

> the good Andronicus,...
> With honour and with fortune is return'd
> From where he circumscribed with his sword,
> And brought to yoke, the enemies of Rome. (*Titus*, I, i, 64–9)

> If not, I'll use the advantage of my power
> And lay the summer's dust with showers of blood
> Rain'd from the wounds of slaughter'd Englishmen:
> The which, how far off from the mind of Bolingbroke
> It is, such crimson tempest should bedrench
> The fresh green lap of fair King Richard's land,
> My stooping duty tenderly shall show. (*Richard II*, III, iii, 42–8)

Not all of Shakespeare's continuous images are as elaborate as this one from *Richard II*, but the type is characteristic. The separate metaphors of the first example typify the empty diction which prevails through much of *Titus*, and while the play of course contains some continued metaphors, few are noticeably ornate. However, what needs to be emphasized is that a play which ought to be straining after the height of Seneca's style uses roughly only half the number of complex metaphors found in the other early tragedies and histories.

Shakespeare's early predilection for iterative word-play, found alike in his dramatic and non-dramatic verse, is patent to all. Now *Titus* is just the sort of play in which one would expect to find an abundance of the figures of repetition, and yet, with the exception of *2 Henry VI*, this play has the lowest average. Since the tendency in the early period is a regular increase in the frequency of their occurrence, the first play theory again suggests itself. But the matter is not quite so simple. Explanation will require the use of a few sesquipedalian terms from the rhetorical manuals. It is remarkable that *Titus* contains only one example of *antimetabole* (e.g. "his noble hand Did win what he did spend and spent not that Which his triumphant father's hand had won") for this figure was a favourite with Shakespeare and there is a steady increase in his tragic writing from two examples in *2 Henry VI* to seventeen in *Richard II*. Another complicated figure of repetition, *epanodis* (e.g. John of Gaunt's extended play on his name) is conspicuously infrequent in *Titus*. Its single occurrence in this play must be set against two in *2 Henry VI* and five and eight in *Richard III* and *Romeo and Juliet*, respectively. Titus provides only one example of *symploche* (e.g. "What stay had we but Clarence? and he's gone. What stays had I but they? and they are gone") compared with at least two and as many as nineteen in the other plays. Finally, the figure *epanalepsis* (e.g. "I will not budge for no man's pleasure, I.") is represented by an average which is only one-third of that usual in the early plays. These four figures comprise the more complex of the repetitive devices and may reasonably be considered together as providing an index to Shakespeare's mannered style. The results of such grouping shows the eccentricity of *Titus*. The sum total of these devices in *Titus* is six; figures for the other plays are: *2 Henry VI*, fourteen; *2 Henry VI*, twenty-two; *Richard III*, forty-seven; *Errors*, twenty-three; *The Shrew*, twenty; *Two Gentlemen*, twenty-three; *Love's Labour's Lost*, forty; *Romeo*, thirty-eight; *Richard II*, thirty-nine; *The Dream*, eighteen. In freedom from these mannerisms, constants in Shakespeare's early style, *Titus* stands alone. If the play is wholly from his hand, then one can only assume that it was his earliest, written when his penchant for word-play was scarcely realized.

Such a view is supported by an analysis of the various kinds of antithesis and pun, forms of word-play markedly apparent in both comedy and tragedy subsequent to the *Henry VI* plays. Generalizing broadly from the counts arrived at for these figures, *Titus* and the *Henry VI* plays are sharply distinguished from the eight remaining plays; the second group has averages two, three, and four times as great as those of the first in respect of antithesis and pun. The same is true of the incidence of *asyndeton* and *brachiologia* (a form of asyndeton). The effect of these two figures of speech is to loosen syntax, to speed up the verse, and generally to vary the smooth flow of the pentameters. Analysis again demonstrates the same sharp division between the *Titus-Henry VI* group and the other plays considered; the average occurrence of asyndeton in every one of the latter group is at least three times as great as that for *Titus* and the *Henry VI* plays whose averages are practically the same.

The deepest impression left by a close study of the early plays is that Shakespeare, from the very beginning, is never naïve in his use of language. In *Love's Labour's Lost* he is not only its master but also its severest critic, ranging from the open ridicule of the pedantries and bombast of Holofernes and Armado to the sly exposure of Berowne's subtler follies. Where in the early plays he seems to overwrite, careful scrutiny always shows the language to be decorously related to character and situation. Titus's involved play on "hands", like John of Gaunt's on his own name, is an emotional safety-valve, a rhetorical, formalized expression of mental anguish; the conceited speeches of Benvolio and Romeo in the opening scenes of the play create the mood of imagined love which has not yet awakened to real passion; and the fanciful amplification of slight themes by Berowne and Mercutio is intended to set the seal upon them as men of wit. Even the notorious lines in *2 Henry VI* beginning, "The gaudy, blabbing and remorseful day Is crept into the bosom of the sea" arise out of a need to elevate the style in preparation for the murder of Suffolk. Though less skilful, they are as decorous as the lines which herald a more famous murder, that of Banquo:

> Light thickens; and the crow
> Makes wing to the rooky wood.   (*Macbeth*, III, ii, 50 ff.)

Now the stylistic solecisms pilloried by Shakespeare in *Love's Labour's Lost* and *A Midsummer Night's Dream*—inkhorn terms, malapropisms, bombast, the synonym disease, tautology and excessive alliteration—were all catalogued by the rhetoricians in a group called the vices of language. Analysis shows that in his undoubted plays Shakespeare, with very few exceptions, is guilty of these vices only with deliberate intent, where he has some comic purpose in hand. Tautology and culpable wordiness are difficult to isolate in his writing because early and late he was accustomed to drive home the same point with several more or less parallel phrases. For example, from *Richard II*:

> Disclaiming here the kindred of the king,
> And lay aside my high blood's royalty.   (*Richard II*, I, i, 70–1)

And from *Macbeth*:

> For Banquo's issue have I filled my mind;
> For them the gracious Duncan have I murder'd;
> Put rancours in the vessel of my peace.   (*Macbeth*, III, i, 65–7)

However, with due regard to this and to associated characteristics of amplification, the attempt was made, with interesting results. In tautology Titus topped the list with twelve examples, followed by *2 Henry VI* with eight; no other play yielded more than three. In wordiness *Titus*, in my judgment, lapsed eighteen times, no other play more than six. When the two faults are taken together, *Titus* wins with thirty examples, the nearest contender for notoriety being *2 Henry VI* with eleven. (It is worth recording that there are twenty-four such lapses in *1 Henry VI*.)

So far care has been taken to ascertain what is *different* in the style of *Titus*, not what is *inferior*, for critics have been too prone to discountenance the play because they would not sully Shakespeare's gloss with its blemishes. Now, it is obvious that a writer of his swift and lively invention would glide over imperfections which a moment's consideration would have rectified, but in the matter of tautology I must make one with the critics. Except in *1 Henry VI*, nowhere does one find lines so grievously tautological as these from Titus:

> That ever eye with sight made heart lament!...
> Hath hurt me more than had he kill'd me dead....
> By working wreakful vengeance on thy foes....
> O, why should wrath be mute, and fury dumb?...
> That ever ear did hear to such effect.

"He hears with ears" is the rhetoricians' stock illustration of tautology (or *pleonasmus*, as they called it) which makes the last example so ridiculous that it is difficult to believe that any educated Elizabethan could have written it seriously. It is certainly of the same vintage as Pyramus's

O night, which ever art when day is not!

These faults alone should make one doubt the authenticity of *Titus*, especially when considered together with the abundance of empty, unmusical lines which are not susceptible of statistical treatment. *Love's Labour's Lost* is generally dated 1594–5, which makes one thing certain; to contend for sole Shakespearian authorship of *Titus* and composition in 1593–4 is nonsense.

In addition to a full rhetorical analysis note should obviously be made of any peculiarities of style not classified by the rhetoricians; these possess great evidential value since, falling just outside the well-known speech patterns, they may constitute the special 'tricks' of a writer. Thus, in counting the figure *epizeuxis* (simple repetition, e.g. "come, come") it was observed that a vocative was sometimes set between the repeated words in this manner: "Help, grandsire, help." Moreover, of the forty-five examples of *epizeuxis* in *Titus* sixteen take this peculiar form, whereas all the other plays contain only two to six examples each, and in none does the iteration have the woodenness found in *Titus*. There it has the aid of a cliché, a fault of which Shakespeare is seldom guilty. Oddly enough the trick is most apparent in the often suspected Act I,[9] where it occurs five times in one hundred and sixty-eight lines. A second unusual feature noted was the repetition of a clause with an inversion in the order of its grammatical parts. For example,

Hear me, grave fathers! noble tribunes, stay!

My lord, look here: look here, Lavinia.

Although not classified by the English rhetoricians, it is a figure certainly used by Seneca in his tragedies. Doubtless it could add to the music of poetry, but the mechanism in *Titus* is palpable; it is only the stiffness which attracts attention. There are at least eleven examples in *Titus*; the trick was noticed no more than twice in any one of the remaining plays studied. One cannot avoid the question: could Shakespeare's love of honeyed speech ever have betrayed him into a succession of vain repetitions? The music of words was his birthright and his faults those of excess, never the poverty of invention witnessed by these jejune phrases. Prompted by this thought I glanced through *The Battle of Alcazar* and found five examples at random—but now I am out of my text.

Without a doubt there is much in the style of the play which appears to have Shakespeare's stamp upon it, but our knowledge of other writers is too imprecise to allow us to dogmatize. Thus Shakespeare seems to me to show his hand in his methods of amplification, especially through the various kinds of comparison and proverbial, or quasi-proverbial, illustration. One is, for example, immediately disposed to take as Shakespearian the speech of Marcus to the mutilated Lavinia (II, iv, 11–57) where effortless invention spins out the sense through seven similes and a classical *exemplum* in the story of Philomel and Tereus. Shakespeare's work seems beyond doubt in the dialogue which begins,

But when ye have the honey ye desire,
Let not this wasp outlive, us both to sting—

and ends,

> 'Tis true; the raven doth not hatch a lark:
> Yet have I heard,—O, could I find it now!—
> The lion moved with pity did endure
> To have his princely paws par'd all away:
> Some say that ravens foster forlorn children,
> The whilst their own birds famish in their nests:
> O, be to me, though thy hard heart say no,
> Nothing so kind, but something pitiful!   (II, iii, 131–56)

Equally so appears the play on "hands", and the allegorical cast of Demetrius's speech (II, i, 82–9) proposing the rape of Lavinia, which ends in the triumphant incision of,

> Better than he have worn Vulcan's badge.

Yet such means of amplification, though characteristically Shakespearian, may not be peculiarly so. Thomas Wilson in his *Arte of Rhetorique* recommends precisely this use of proverb, simile and classical *exemplum* to achieve persuasive discourse; Pettie, Lyly and the emblem writers among others gave the method currency. We still need to be shown in detail the extent and nature of such amplification in Peele, Greene and Marlowe.

The study of Shakespeare's early manner and stylistic development forces me to the conclusion that if *Titus* is entirely Shakespearian it must have been written before the *Henry VI* plays (dated by Chambers 1590–1) as we have them in the First Folio. Such an early date is supported, one remembers, by Jonson's Induction to *Bartholomew Fair* (1614), which brackets *Titus* with *Jeronimo* as plays some twenty-five or thirty years old. Thus could one reasonably account for the infrequent occurrence of the devices of repetition, antithesis and pun, asyndeton and continued metaphor; in the same way it would be *just* possible to justify the presence of the excessive and mechanical alliteration, the tautology and the two odd clichés discussed above. A critical estimate of structure, characterization and theme corroborates this view in revealing a parallel *naïveté* and uncertain grasp of method such as one might expect in a dramatist of five-and-twenty. Chambers dates the play 1593–4 but, as J. C. Maxwell argues,[10] there appears to be no evidence which flatly contradicts a pre-1590 date. According to Henslowe's Diary the play was performed by the Earl of Sussex's men on 23 January 1594 and Henslowe describes it as "ne", but this may perhaps mean that the play was new to that company since, according to the title-page of the 1594 quarto, it had already been performed by the "Seruants" of the Earls of Derby and Pembroke. Other evidence of early composition is debatable.[11] Alternatively, if "ne" means revised, why not a revision at the end of 1593 by Shakespeare of his own earlier play? This would account for certain parallels, some convincing, with *Venus and Adonis* and *The Rape of Lucrece*,[12] although I see no reason why, when writing these poems, Shakespeare should not have recalled phrases and images from a play, written several years before, on a similar theme and under the same Ovidian influence.

The external evidence for Shakespearian authorship is, of course, Francis Meres' attribution in *Palladis Tamia* and the play's inclusion in the First Folio. A close study of the various kinds of internal evidence does not preclude acceptance of this orthodoxy if we hold that at least the bulk of the play as we now have it was written before 1590. Candour compels me to admit, however, that this is an interim conclusion, since certain elements in the style, characterization and moral position seem uncharacteristic and even unworthy of Shakespeare at any period in his writing. Collaboration might still be an explanation and the play's stylistic links with *Henry VI* plays, themselves of doubtful authenticity, throw weight in that scale. Only a similar full-scale investigation of the style and method of Shakespeare's contemporary dramatists can possibly solve the problem; not tell us which parts he or they wrote—that I believe incapable of demonstrable proof—but whether or not he wrote it alone. Success with *Titus Andronicus* would encourage a like attempt with other disputed and anonymous plays.

NOTES

1. See E. K. Chambers, *Shakespearean Gleanings* (1944), p. 26.

2. M. St Clare Byrne, 'Bibliographical Clues in Collaborate Plays', *The Library*, XIII (1932–3), 21–48.

3. See, for example, Alice Walker, 'The Reading of an Elizabethan: Some Sources of the Prose Pamphlets of Lodge', *Review of English Studies*, VIII (1932), 264–81, and the section on Nashe's reading in vol. v of R. B. McKerrow's edition of the collected works.

4. A. M. Sampley, '"Verbal Tests" for Peele's Plays', *Studies in Philology*, XXX (1933), 473–96.

5. Cf. Chambers, *op. cit.* p. 11.

6. See Moody E. Prior, 'Imagery as a Test of Authorship', *Shakespeare Quarterly*, VI (Autumn 1955), 381–6.

7. Edward Ravenscroft's remarks, found in the Address to the Reader prefaced to his adaptation of the play in 1687, are partial. To escape the censure of having "rob(bed) the dead of their praise" he describes *Titus* as a "heap of rubbish", and questions Shakespearian authorship on the sole authority of "some anciently conversant with the stage".

8. The authenticity of the *Henry VI* plays is, of course, still questioned. However, so much of Parts 2 and 3 is manifestly Shakespearian that their inclusion is essential to any consideration of his early "grand style".

9. So Dover Wilson, *Titus Andronicus*, New Cambridge Edition (1948), Introduction, pp. xxv–xxxii, and J. C. Maxwell, 'Peele and Shakespeare: A Stylometric Test', *Journal of English and Germanic Philology*, XLIX (1950), 557–61. Maxwell's stylistic evidence for Peele's authorship of Act I deserves attention because it has been subjected to, and in the main survived, the essential negative check against other Elizabethan dramatists.

10. *Titus Andronicus*, New Arden Edition (1953), Introduction, p. xxix.

11. The alleged reference to *Titus* in *A Knack to Know a Knave* (performed 10 June 1592) has recently been strongly challenged by Paul E. Bennett in 'An Apparent Allusion to "Titus Andronicus"', *Notes and Queries* (October 1955), pp. 422–4. Maxwell (*op. cit.* Introduction, pp. xxvi–xxvii) thinks there may be verbal echoes of *Titus* in *The Troublesome Reign of King John* (1591).

12. See T. M. Parrott, 'Shakespeare's Revision of "Titus Andronicus"', *Modern Language Review*, XIV (1919), 16–37.

CLASSICAL COSTUME IN
SHAKESPEARIAN PRODUCTIONS

BY

W. M. MERCHANT

We are fortunate in having precise knowledge of early seventeenth-century conceptions of classical costume for the stage, in the attempts made at recollecting ancient examples, and the equally important theatrical variations in masque costume *à la romaine*. The interplay of these two factors—the recurring attempts to return to original sources and the enduring conservatism of the masque tradition—constitutes the chief visual interest of the Roman plays in the theatre. Even when conscientious archaeological research was at its greatest, in the age of Kemble and again in E. W. Godwin's contribution to the late nineteenth-century stage, remembrances of Inigo Jones still remained.

Renaissance art had established its attitude to the antique in the generations before Shakespeare. Mantegna, more than a century earlier, had looked with profit at classical monuments and triumphal arches. The aim, fidelity to ancient models, is best summarized in Cesare Vecellio's *Habiti Antichi et Moderni di Tutto il Mondo*, first published in 1598, with engravings by Titian.[1] This comprehensive work opens with Roman costume, and like all succeeding scholars, Vecellio goes to sculpture and bas-relief for his main material, beginning with "quelle quattro figure di porfido di relievo pieno, armate, le quali sono dinanzi alla porta del palazzo di S. Marco". From these first examples, he traces the origins of Roman costume from the Greek by way of sculptures brought to Venice in her trading hey-day, and concludes: "io ritrovo essere quest'habito antichissimo usato da Troiani et da Romani, et anco in tempo d'Alessandro Magno". This similarity of Greek and Roman costume in origin and general form is echoed in the history of classical costume in the theatre. Neither in book illustration nor in stage performance has there been much difference between the presentation of the greater Roman plays and of *Titus Andronicus*, *Pericles*, *Timon of Athens*, *The Winter's Tale* and the Athenians in *A Midsummer Night's Dream*. This is basically the costume of Renaissance classicism in painting and sculpture.

The tradition of theatrical elaboration begins early; through the masque designs of Inigo Jones male costume became established for over a century: the Roman breastplate, shaped to the figure and modelling the torso muscles (a manner taken up and greatly exaggerated by Fuseli nearly two centuries later), the military skirt or kilt, the draped scarf and plumed helmet.[2] There are traces of this elaboration in our earliest Shakespeare drawing, the *Titus Andronicus* of 1595 (Plate I, 1). We are fortunately not concerned here with the disputations, whether Henry Peacham drew it, and its relation to the accompanying manuscript text;[3] of more importance is its evidence for contemporary theatre practice, which Dover Wilson summarizes:

It may tell them...something of the costumes adopted in the production of Roman plays; the lower classes being played apparently in "modern dress", whereas every effort was obviously made, contrary to the assumptions of our theatrical historians, to attain accuracy in the attire worn by patricians.

Moreover, since the actors shown in the drawing were probably members of Shakespeare's company—does that black profile belong to Burbage?—or at any rate of some London troupe like the Earl of Sussex's men, we may suspect that Julius Caesar, Brutus and Antony were so dressed on Shakespeare's stage, despite Casca's reference to the dictator's 'doublet'.[4]

Our next piece of illustrative material is the poor and derivative engraving in Quarles' 1655 edition of *The Rape of Lucrece* (Plate I, 2), sometimes attributed, on very slight evidence, to William Faithorne. Lucrece is swathed in the indeterminate garment which has clothed generations of Roman matrons on the stage, but Collatine wears a simplified version of classical military costume.

Meanwhile the baroque elaboration of masque costume had continued in France and Italy, to be reintroduced to England at the Restoration, both directly in the theatre and by way of book illustration. Its growth may be seen from Parigi's *Guerra di Bellezza* (produced in Florence in 1616) to the great Torelli's *Noces de Thétis et de Pélée* (in 1654 at the Petit-Bourbon);[5] the engravings by Callot and Silvestre of these performances and the later seventeenth-century book illustrations, particularly the later editions of Corneille and Racine,[6] constitute a direct line of development to the first illustrated *Shakespeare*, published by Tonson in 1709. Figures from two of the frontispieces (Plate I, 3 and 4) show the two main tendencies in the classical costume: the figures in the *Titus Andronicus* (like the overcrowded *Julius Caesar* frontispiece) wear the simple toga; Troilus and Cressida, on the other hand, come forward together to take a curtain call, dressed in full *costume à la romaine*. The frontispiece to *Coriolanus* is especially important;[7] here the engraver, Elisha Kirkall, has taken Poussin's painting of Coriolanus and adapted it to illustrate the scene of Coriolanus's encounter with his wife and mother; it is, therefore, doubtful whether the figures in Plate I, 5, taken from this engraving, truly represent stage costume in Cibber's age. Still greater doubts are raised by Plate I, 6 and 7. In 1749 James Thomson's classical rewriting of *Coriolanus* was produced by Quin at Covent Garden. The figures in Plate I, 6, are taken from an engraving in the *Universal Magazine*, which shows in a curious 'simultaneous setting'[8] both the meeting of Coriolanus and his mother and his later murder; both costumes are in a normal classical form. Plate I, 7, shows Quin in the role of Coriolanus, a costume which has caused amusement to our own day; the engraving is a poor thing and makes ridiculous what was in fact a rococo development of masque or operatic costume. James Laver demonstrates a parallel between this ballet-skirt effect and the kind of designs developed by Louis René Boquet at the Opéra and the Menus-Plaisirs;[9] indeed, a reasonable version of the costume may be found among Hogarth's drawings for *The Analysis of Beauty*.[10] But Quin's costume, like his acting technique, belonged to an outmoded tradition. In the winter of 1754/55 Covent Garden and Drury Lane put on two versions of the play: the former was Sheridan's rehash of the Thomson-Shakespeare text, while Garrick produced a version nearer Shakespeare's at Drury Lane, with a good deal of money and trouble spent on costume and setting and with an acting technique strikingly different from Quin's. It is possible in fact that Plate I, 6 and 7, fairly truly represent the contrast between the two approaches to the play.

Garrick was not of the heroic stature which inclined him to perform the Roman plays (though he produced *Antony and Cleopatra* in 1759 with heroic expenditure on costume), but three engravings from the Garrick period are of interest. The drawing of William Smith ("Gentleman"

PLATE I

1. *Titus Andronicus*: part of the 'Peacham
Drawing', 1595

2. *Rape of Lucrece*:
frontispiece 1655

3. *Julius Caesar*:
frontispiece 1709

4. *Troilus and Cressida*:
frontispiece 1709

5. *Coriolanus*: from the
frontispiece 1709

6. *Coriolanus*: from the *Universal
Magazine*, 1749

7. Quin as Coriolanus

CLASSICAL COSTUMES IN SHAKESPEARIAN PRODUCTIONS

PLATE II

8. Smith as Antony   9. Bensley as Antony   10. Sheridan as Brutus

11. Westall's *Julius Caesar*,
Boydell Shakespeare

12. Kemble as Coriolanus

13. Kean as Brutus   14. Warde as Brutus

CLASSICAL COSTUMES IN SHAKESPEARIAN PRODUCTIONS

PLATE III

15. Tailpiece from Knight's
Shakspere

16. Macready's *Coriolanus* drawn by Scharf, 1838

17. Phelps' 'Penny Plain'

18. Saxe-Meiningen Company's
Julius Caesar, 1881

19 'Death of Antony', *Illustrated
London News*, 1873

20. Beerbohm Tree, *Julius Caesar*, 1898

21. *Julius Caesar*, Old Vic, 1932

CLASSICAL COSTUMES IN SHAKESPEARIAN PRODUCTIONS

PLATE IV

'THE TWO GENTLEMEN OF VERONA', TRINITY COLLEGE, TORONTO, 1955.
THE EARLE GREY SHAKESPEARE COMPANY

Smith) as Antony (Plate II, 8) dated 28 January 1755, records the performance of *Julius Caesar* at Covent Garden. Of more importance is the drawing of Bensley as Antony (Plate II, 9); though the drawing was not published until November 1780, the performance was in October 1765 at Drury Lane. The quotation in the caption, "Look! in this place ran Cassius' dagger through", is illustrated by his actually wearing Caesar's cloak to show the dagger rents. Finally, Sheridan as Brutus (Plate II, 10) is from Bell's 'Dramatick Character' plates and, like so many of them, is drawn from life ("Roberts ad vivam del. White sc. Jan. 9 1776"). These three plates together indicate the degree of authenticity which costume had reached towards the end of this period.

The transition from Garrick's age to Kemble's, with the intensified search for fidelity to classical forms, is provided by the paintings and engravings prepared for Josiah Boydell's Shakespeare Gallery. Its origin and history are sufficiently well known;[11] its interest for us lies in the union of the heroic manner in history-painting (the first object of Boydell's venture) with the growing romantic concern for classical antiquities. Romney's "Cassandra Raving", the Hon. Anne Seymour Damer's "basso-relievo" of a scene from *Coriolanus*, and Westall's "Brutus and the Ghost of Caesar" (Plate II, 11) are in the same tradition that the painter David had established in France; we find no change of tone or manner in passing from these works to Meadows' stipple engraving, after the painting by Sir Thomas Lawrence, of J. P. Kemble as Coriolanus (Plate II, 12).

For Kemble was the characteristic romantic exponent of the classical manner. In the years 1811/13 he produced most of the Roman plays and others with similar costume and setting: *Coriolanus*, *Julius Caesar*, *Antony and Cleopatra*, *A Midsummer Night's Dream* and *A Winter's Tale*. To Kemble's bent towards the classical roles (Hazlitt described it as excellence in "one solitary sentiment or exclusive passion"), was added Mrs Siddon's use of the female roles in these plays to reform both the manner and costume of tragic acting. Boaden summarizes her contribution to Kemble's handling of the classical tragedies:

Conspiring with the larger stage to produce some change in her style was her delight in statuary, which directed her attention to the antique, and made a remarkable impression upon her as to simplicity of style and severity of attitude.[12]

This quality of the statuesque in their appearance, particularly as we see them in portrait painting and engraving, is the visual equivalent of Hazlitt's complaint that "Mr Kemble's manner...had always something dry, hard, and pedantic in it". Kean, on the other hand, made up for the "want of dignity of form, by the violence and contrast of his attitudes",[13] though this is not apparent in the admirable S. W. Reynolds mezzotint of Northcote's portrait (Plate II, 13).[14] Edmund Kean here compares in dignity with any of the classical players, while the distinction of the painter and engraver enhance the value of the print as evidence for both costume and setting. It may be compared with the series of prints which show the productions of *Julius Caesar* with Charles Kemble and Warde (one of which is here reproduced, Plate II, 14). Warde played Brutus for the first time at Covent Garden in September 1825 and Thurston's drawing records what must have been, visually, a notable production. Ten years later, Warde was playing Cassius at Covent Garden and a drawing by Mitchel shows him in an almost identical costume with the earlier Brutus, but with a more elaborate breastplate.

Two further pieces of evidence enable us to assess the attitude towards antique costume up to the middle of the century. Charles Kemble continued his brother's interest in the exact historical setting of the plays. An undistinguished actor, he deserves well of theatre historians by his patronage of J. R. Planché the omnicompetent, librettist, antiquarian and historian of costume. Much has been made of Planché's costumes for Kemble's *King John* in January 1824; they were notable, but they were the apprentice work of a young man and he had the assistance (which he acknowledges) of Samuel Meyricke and Francis Douce. His more mature scholarship is found in the costume notes which he contributed to Knight's *Pictorial Shakspere*. His note for *Julius Caesar*,[15] on the form of the Roman toga, is typical of his work:

The form of the toga has been a hotly-contested point; Dionysius of Halicarnassus says it was semi-circular; and an ingenious foreigner...has practically demonstrated that, though not perfectly semi-circular, its shape was such as to be better described by that term than any other.

His footnote on the "ingenious foreigner" has especial interest; he was

The late Mons. Combre, costumier to the Théâtre Français, Paris. This intelligent person, at the recommendation of Talma and Mr Charles Young, was engaged by Mr Charles Kemble...for the revival of Julius Caesar, and made the beautiful togas which have since been worn in all the Roman plays at that theatre [Covent Garden].

The engraving from Knight's *Shakspere* (Plate III, 15) accompanies the notes. Planché gives also a very detailed account of military costume and notes of the *lorica* that "it seems to have been impressed whilst wet with forms corresponding to those of the human body, and this peculiarity was preserved in its appearance when it was afterwards made of metal".

Planché's concern for accuracy is reflected in the 1837/38 season of William Macready, who produced first an indifferent *Julius Caesar* and then, in March 1838, a notable and elaborate *Coriolanus*, the décor and costume of which may be seen in the plate from Scharf's *Recollections of the Scenic Effects of Covent Garden Theatre*, 1838–9 (Plate III, 16). He, like Kemble, was concerned with dignity of posture, so far as his somewhat ungainly person permitted, and in his *Reminiscences*[16] he says: "To add dignity and grace to my deportment, I studied under D'Egville attitudes from the antique, and practised the more stately walk which was enforced by the peculiarity of their dress on the *gens togata*." But this was not the main visual concern of his productions; with an implied contrast to the aims of Kemble the critic in *John Bull* (19 March 1838) pointed out that Macready reduced "the brilliant light hitherto concentrated on the figure of Coriolanus" and by a more comprehensive production, brought out "statelier proportions and severer beauties". Samuel Phelps brought a like attitude to the more popular atmosphere of Sadler's Wells, properly represented here by the Redington Toy Theatre 'Penny Plain' portrait (Plate III, 17).

On all this learning applied to Roman costume until the days of Charles Kean (whose pedantically archaeological mind was turned to no production of the Roman plays) a note by Hazlitt some thirty years earlier forms a summary comment:

Though the preservation of the ancient costume is a good thing, it is of more importance not to shock our present prejudices. The managers of Covent-Garden are not the Society of Antiquaries. The attention to costume is only necessary to preserve probability.[17]

This comment reads strangely in view of the contributions made by the Meininger Players and of E. W. Godwin in the second half of the century. *The Illustrated London News* for 4 June 1881 depicts the *Julius Caesar* of the Saxe-Meiningen Company at Drury Lane (Plate III, 18). These players are now chiefly remembered for their ensemble effects, but the programme published by Augustus Harris to celebrate their visit claims the approbation of the "many learned antiquaries who have witnessed the performance".

Godwin's articles contributed during 1875 to *The Architect* were reprinted by his son Gordon Craig in *The Mask,* 1909–11 and show the sensitive, exploratory intelligence one would expect of the friend of William Morris, Burne-Jones and Whistler. His examination of period style in costume and architecture is at its best in analysing the appropriate settings for the Roman plays:

From the Rome of Coriolanus to the Rome of Julius Caesar we leap over four centuries...crowded with every kind of energy but with very little fine art....We must be careful...not to confound the distinctively Roman style of the fullblown empire, as shown on sculptured column and triumphal arch, with the transitional style of the later days of the Commonwealth. People are far too much in the habit of looking on the styles of art in Greece and Rome as stagnant, the one represented by the Parthenon, the other by the Colosseum.

Though his articles influenced the Bancroft production of *The Merchant of Venice*, unhappily no illustration of a production of a Roman play according to his ideas exists. Discriminating taste of this order in theatre design has been rare and the history of the Roman plays after Godwin's day and until 1914 was largely one of half-hearted archaeology in *décor* and somewhat indeterminate draping in costume.

Antony and Cleopatra, however, provided regular spectacle. In September 1873 it was adapted by Halliday with "new and magnificent scenery by William Beverley. The costumes designed by Mr E. C. Barnes from the Splendid Collection of Roman and Egyptian Antiquities at the British Museum".[18] Plate III, 19, is taken from "The Death of Antony" in the *Illustrated London News*, and the *Times* (27 September 1873) makes what was for that journal the surprising admission that "the stage architect and poet are brought into competition and the rivalry of the cognate arts gives birth to a picture worthy of the Shakespearean text". But on the whole, informed criticism was moving away from *décor* for its own sake—though there was still Beerbohm Tree to come at Her Majesty's with Alma-Tadema's "plastic hand" directing the *décor* for *Julius Caesar* in 1898 (Plate III, 20).

There have been many good productions of the Roman plays in our own day, mainly depending on accurate research for the costume, though sometimes illuminated by the personal manner of the artist. One experiment, the Old Vic production of *Julius Caesar* at Sadler's Wells in 1930, was outstanding. Harcourt Williams writes of his production: "I decided to abandon realism and, hanging on the coat-tails of Harley Granville-Barker and William Poel, and with the help of Paul Smyth, we achieved a rapid sequence of events almost kaleidoscopic in effect. For costumes we went to the pictures of Paul Veronese and Tiepolo." (Plate III, 21.) A shrewd criticism by James Agate on the dressing of this production adequately comments in retrospect on much of the work here discussed.

Obviously Shakespeare was familiar with the wardrobe [of the Globe] and must have known that to the playgoer of his day there would be little to show between the nobility of Verona and the gentry of

Eastcheap—and only a helmet or two between antique Roman and the Dane. But Shakespeare had as many consciousnesses as the rest of us and I will not believe that he refused to let his mind's eye see the characters in their habits as they lived....When Shakespeare wrote the line about Caesar's mantle and the rent in it the envious Casca made, are we to suppose he saw in his mind's eye a breach in one of Paul Veronese's Cramoisi velvets, though he knew quite well that this is what the spectator would in effect see?

NOTES

1. The author was Titian's nephew. I quote from the Italian-French edition of 1859. Vecellio had written an earlier work, *Degli abiti antichi et moderni di diverse parti del mondo* (Venice, 1590), the material of which is incorporated in the later volumes.

2. Walpole and Malone Societies, 1924, "Designs by Inigo Jones".

3. *Shakespeare Survey* 1, (1948), 17–22.

4. *Ibid.* p. 21.

5. See *Il Secolo dell' Invenzione Teatrale*, section 5, 30–1, a detailed exhibition catalogue, issued by the Centro di Richerche Teatrale (Rome, 1951). Joseph Gregor's *Weltgeschichte des Theaters* (Vienna, 1933) is a convenient source for reproductions of designs by Torelli, Parigi and Burnacini.

6. The plates in *Horace* and *Cinna* are well known; later editions of Molière had similar plates in the baroque manner; e.g. the Amsterdam edition of 1725, in which the frontispiece to *Les Plaisirs de l'Isle Enchantée* might have illustrated a Tonson *Tempest*.

7. See The *Bulletin* of the *John Rylands Library* (September 1954), 13–16, where I discuss this plate in greater detail.

8. 'Simultaneous setting' may be seen in some forms as late as the early seventeenth-century theatre but I know of no other example than this in the eighteenth century and even this is not likely to represent stage practice.

9. See James Laver, 'Costume', *Oxford Companion to the Theatre*, 160b.

10. Adolf Paul Oppé, *The Drawings of Hogarth* (1948), fig. 27, p. 51. The catalogue note 81f describes it as "A Roman General in a Peruque" with the comment "traditionally regarded as Quin in the character of Brutus"; it is almost certainly Quin as Coriolanus.

11. It is especially well and fully treated by T. S. R. Boase, *Journal of the Warburg and Courtauld Institutes*, x (1947), 83–108.

12. Cited G. C. D. Odell, *Shakespeare from Betterton to Irving* (New York, 1921), xi, 93.

13. Hazlitt, *View of the English Stage* (ed. Spencer Jackson, 1906), p. 330.

14. This engraving of Edmund Kean from the Enthoven collection, Victoria and Albert Museum, shows a scene from *Brutus, or The Fall of Tarquin* by "Cumberland and others" (Genest). Though dealing with a very different period of Roman history from Shakespeare's *Julius Caesar*, no distinction is made in costuming. It was performed at Drury Lane, 3 December 1818.

15. Knight, *Pictorial Shakspere*, Tragedies, xi, 219ff.

16. Macready, *Reminiscences* (ed. Pollock, 1876), p. 153.

17. *Op. cit.* p. 253 where he discusses the costumes for Ambrose Phillips' *Distressed Mother*, in which Macready played Orestes and Charles Kemble Pyrrhus.

18. The playbill for the first performance, in the Enthoven collection, Victoria and Albert Museum.

ACKNOWLEDGMENTS

Figures 3 and 4 are reproduced by courtesy of the Librarian, Birmingham Public Library; figures 8, 9, 10, 13, 14, 18 and 20 by courtesy of the Department of Prints and Drawings, the Victoria and Albert Museum (Enthoven Collection); figure 21 by courtesy of Mr J. W. Debenham.

SHAKESPEARE'S USE OF A GALLERY OVER THE STAGE

BY

RICHARD HOSLEY

One of the distinguishing characteristics of Elizabethan drama is the requirement of numerous plays that action be performed in a production-area somewhere above the stage. I believe we shall not be far from the mark if, without denying the possibility of alternative arrangements, we take this raised production-area to have been, at least in the public theatres of Shakespeare's time, a gallery over the stage generally similar to the one depicted by Arend van Buchell in his well-known drawing of the interior of the Swan Playhouse, based on an original made by Johannes de Witt around 1596.[1] It must be emphasized, however, that the gallery shown in the Swan drawing is not an "upper stage" in the usual sense of that rather inappropriate and in some respects misleading term, for it has neither curtains nor balustrade and is probably divided into boxes each about seven feet wide. Although it is impossible to say exactly how many public theatres of Shakespeare's time had a gallery over the stage comparable to the one at the Swan, there is minimal evidence that some of them, notably the Rose, the first Globe, and the Red Bull, probably had a generally similar gallery. Moreover, it is at least possible that they all had such a gallery, those at any rate that had two-storey tiring-houses, for the apparently widespread and certainly long-lived custom of sitting "over the stage i' the Lords roome" (as Jonson refers to it in 1599) suggests that it would have been an act of economic *naïveté* on the part of house-keepers (because of the consequent loss of revenue) to use the upper storey of a public-theatre tiring-house for any other general purpose than as a spectators' gallery which, when occasionally required, might function secondarily and simultaneously as a raised production-area.[2] In order, therefore, to formulate a theory of production that shall keep as close as possible to the few architectural facts definitely known about the Elizabethan public-theatre stage, I shall here adopt as a working hypothesis the assumption that each of Shakespeare's plays was designed for production in a theatre having a gallery over the stage essentially similar to the Lords' room shown in the Swan drawing.

I

At the outset I must beg the reader's indulgence for some necessary statistics. It seems clear that eighteen of Shakespeare's thirty-eight plays (47%) do not require the use of a gallery over the stage.[3] Of the twenty plays that require a gallery, twelve (32% of the total thirty-eight) do so only once per play: *Richard III* (III, vii), *Richard II* (III, iii), *The Merchant of Venice* (II, vi), *Henry V* (III, iii), *Julius Caesar* (v, iii), *Othello* (I, i), *Antony and Cleopatra* (IV, xv), *Coriolanus* (I, iv), *Timon of Athens* (v, iv), *The Tempest* (III, iii), *Henry VIII* (v, ii), and *The Two Noble Kinsmen* (II, i–ii). Four plays (10% of the total) require a gallery twice per play: *3 Henry VI* (IV, vii; v, i), *The Two Gentlemen of Verona* (IV, ii, iii), *Romeo and Juliet* (II, ii; III, v), and *King John* (II, i; IV, iii). Three plays (8%) require a gallery three times per play: *2 Henry VI* (I, iv;

IV, v, ix), *Titus Andronicus* (I, i, 1–63, 169–233, 296–337), and *The Taming of the Shrew* (Induction ii; I, i; v, i). And one play (3%) requires a gallery six times: *1 Henry VI* (I, vi; II, i, 38; III, ii, 26–35, 41–74; IV, ii; v, iii). Thus Shakespeare uses a gallery over the stage thirty-five times, or on an average just under once per play.[4]

More specifically, in Shakespeare's plays the gallery is used sixteen times as the "walls" of a town or castle, nine times as an upper-storey "window", seven times as miscellaneous elevated localities, and thrice as an undescribed place of observation.[5] In a large majority of cases (twenty-eight out of thirty-five) the gallery is in use for less than a hundred lines, the average length of such actions aloft being thirty-seven lines. In the remaining seven cases the gallery is in use for over a hundred lines, and in these the average length of action aloft is 194 lines.[6] The average length of all thirty-five actions aloft is sixty-eight lines. In thirteen instances only one player appears aloft, in one as many as nine. The average number of players aloft in all thirty-five actions is three.[7]

Seventeen uses of the gallery are designated in early stage-directions by what may be regarded as technical "theatrical" terms, fourteen by *aloft* or *above*, two (probably) by the admittedly ambiguous *on the top*, and one by *within*, this last use, like some others indicated by theatrical terms, being also designated by a "fictional" (or "dramatic" or "literary") term, in this case *on the Walls*. One use is implied by the theatrical term *below*, calling for use of the stage by a second group of players.[8] Twelve uses are designated by fictional terms only, ten by *on the Walls*, one by *out of the window*, and one by *on the Tarras*. One use is implied by the fictional term *before the Gates*, designating use of the stage by a second group of players. One use of the gallery is implied by dialogue and by a direction for descent from a fictional upper level. Three uses are not designated by directions of any sort but are implied by dialogue.[9]

Thirteen actions require "descents" from gallery to stage, these being of three kinds. One descent is effected by a rope ladder, two by jumping from gallery to stage, and ten by use of a stairway that may be postulated within the tiring-house.[10] The amount of dialogue provided to "cover" a stairway descent ranges from none to sixteen lines, the average being four; and the time required for such a descent, as determined by experimental productions on replica Elizabethan stages, must have been around eight or ten seconds.[11] Presumably, in those few cases where dialogue is insufficient to "bridge" this period, stage business by players remaining on the stage was employed to help cover descents; and evidently a *Flourish* of trumpets was also, where appropriate, occasionally used for this purpose. Five actions require "ascents" from stage to gallery, and these are also of three kinds. One is effected by a player's being *heaved aloft* in a manner that remains conjectural, one by *scaling Ladders*, and three by mounting the tiring-house stairs. Two of the stairway ascents are covered by three lines of dialogue, the third by forty.[12]

Five actions aloft require "hand" properties: a *burning torch* (thrust out), a "prayer book", a "casket" of money (thrown down), a "glove" (thrown up), and *apparel, Bason and Ewer, & other appurtenances*. One action aloft requires the property of a rope ladder, another *scaling Ladders*, and two others (in a single play) stools or a bench on which *Presenters* sit in order to view a "Comedie" upon the stage below.[13] No action aloft requires a large stage property such as a throne or bed, nor does any action aloft require a curtain for a discovery.[14]

II

In his use of a gallery over the stage Shakespeare generally introduces a secondary action aloft in support of an original action upon the stage below: Juliet appears at a window overlooking the orchard in which Romeo is awaiting her appearance (*Romeo and Juliet*, II, ii), Richard is summoned to the walls of Flint Castle by Northumberland and Bolingbroke below the walls (*Richard II*, III, iii), or Brabantio is called to the window of his house by Iago and Roderigo in the street below (*Othello*, I, i). But this basic pattern is often varied. For instance, the actions aloft and below may begin simultaneously: the Governor and Citizens of Harfleur come to the walls of that town at the same time that Henry and his besieging forces arrive below the walls (*Henry V*, III, iii). Or the action may begin in the gallery and afterwards be "supported" by an action upon the stage: Warwick, the Mayor, and others come to the walls of Coventry, and only fifteen lines later Edward, Richard, and their Soldiers appear below the walls to parley (*3 Henry VI*, v, i).[15] Thus although the stage is at first empty, its scene is nevertheless localized from the beginning of the action aloft. This is true also of two further variations in use of the gallery, each occurring once in Shakespeare. An action may begin aloft and then partly shift below: Romeo and Juliet converse at her window, he climbs down a rope ladder to the orchard, and from the window she then continues her dialogue with him below (*Romeo and Juliet*, III, v, 1–68). Or an action may begin aloft and then shift completely below: young Arthur appears for a moment upon the walls of a castle, jumps down, is killed by his fall, and subsequently is discovered by Salisbury, who arrives below the walls immediately after Arthur's death (*King John*, IV, iii). Another use of the gallery is also unique in Shakespeare. An action may be produced completely aloft, without a related action upon the stage below: Joan, the Dauphin, Reignier, Alençon, and Soldiers appear upon the walls of Orleans, the stage below remaining empty; but throughout the action the stage is nevertheless localized as a place below the walls (*1 Henry VI*, I, vi).

Still another use of the gallery, essentially similar (in that the stage is at first empty) to the uses just illustrated from *3 Henry VI*, *Romeo and Juliet*, and *King John*, is also represented by a unique example in Shakespeare. This occurs in the second action of the Induction to *The Taming of the Shrew*, in which Sly, having awakened from a drunken sleep, is beguiled into believing himself a "lord" and the victim of amnesia. Throughout most of the action the scene of the gallery is a "goodlie chamber" (ii, 86) and the stage is not only empty but also unlocalized, this action thus providing the only example in Shakespeare of use of the gallery without localization of the stage below. But towards the end of Induction ii the scene of the gallery changes to an undescribed place of observation from which the performance of a "Comedie" may be viewed (not even a lord may watch a play from a chamber), and the stage comes into use as a locality where such a performance may be presented. That is to say, the players remain within view of the audience but the scene changes after the fluid manner of Elizabethan staging. Thus Induction ii and I, i are from the theatrical point of view but a single action, and they are, of course, so printed in the First Folio. Exactly what the new scenes are we do not know—perhaps a fictional "gallery" in a Tudor house and the hall below, or perhaps even the Lords' room and stage of an Elizabethan public playhouse, the fictional situation thus coinciding with the theatrical. But no matter what localization we assign to the general scene, toward the end of Induction ii the gallery and stage are being used in conjunction to represent two scenically related localities, as they are in the subsequent use of the gallery for comment by the *Presenters* of the Shrew play (I, i).

Thus we may say that in Shakespeare's plays the scene of the gallery is generally related to that of the stage below; or, to put the matter somewhat differently, that the gallery and stage are generally used in conjunction to represent a single theatrical scene on two levels.[16] It follows, accordingly, that Shakespeare generally used the gallery and stage to represent any scene in which an actor on a fictional upper level might conceivably be seen talking with (or spying upon) another actor on a fictional lower level. It is for this reason that actions requiring the gallery are almost always localized on an "exterior" scene like the upper-storey window of a house and the street below. However, what I shall for convenience call the "exterior" theory of use of the gallery should not be understood as implying that interior localities "open" to a lower level were not occasionally represented by gallery and stage. Shakespeare's plays provide no example of such use of the gallery, but one is afforded by Marlowe's *Jew of Malta* (Act V), where Barabas appears aloft in a fictional "gallery" overlooking "a hall in the citadel"—to quote the localization footnoted in the Oxford World's Classics edition. But in general Shakespeare seems not to have used a gallery over the stage to represent a "closed" domestic interior like a chamber. Capulet's upbraiding of Juliet (*Romeo and Juliet*, III, v, 69–242) is no exception to this practice, for immediately after the lovers' "farewell" (1–68), Juliet, in accordance with the First Quarto stage-direction *She goeth downe from the window*, descends from gallery to stage, where the balance of III, v is then played.[17]

To be sure, an exception must immediately be noted in Induction ii of *The Taming of the Shrew*. It would appear, however, that this unique use of the gallery as a chamber was dictated by two special requirements of the production to which our text of *The Shrew* is related. (1) The Presenters must sit aloft, thus clearing the stage for the play proper,[18] and (2) the action must be uninterrupted by a pause toward the end of the Induction while the Presenters ascend from stage to gallery. Were it not for the first requirement, we should expect the whole of the Induction to have been played upon the stage, as it is in *The Taming of a Shrew*, where Sly and the others, as usually in plays calling for Presenters,[19] do not use the gallery but sit upon the stage continuously during the play proper. Or were it not for the second requirement, we should also expect the whole of the Induction to have been played upon the stage, the Presenters ascending to the gallery toward the end of Induction ii, shortly before the beginning of the Shrew play.

A corollary to Shakespeare's use of gallery and stage as parts of a single two-level scene is that action aloft consists generally of an actor's conversing with (or observing) another actor upon a place below the upper level. Therefore the player aloft, being as it were "anchored" to a player below, usually stands at the front of the gallery and, if the fiction or production requires such a movement perhaps as *walking* along the walls of a fortress (as in *2 Henry VI*, IV, v), passes laterally across the front of the gallery or (if the gallery is compartmented) of one of its boxes, remaining approximately within the vertical plane defined by the front opening of the gallery. (If the Swan stage was as wide as that at the Fortune—forty-three feet—each of the presumptive boxes of the Swan gallery would have been about seven feet wide.) That is to say, the player aloft continually maintains contact with a player below; and thus the typical action aloft does not involve a player or players in a dynamic flow of movement toward or away from the audience upon the horizontal plane of the gallery floor. Induction ii of *The Shrew* is only a partial exception to this stage practice, for the demands of the action will be satisfied if Sly sits in the front opening of the gallery or of one of its boxes (without question the action requires the property of a seat), with the Lord and Servingmen clustered about him making use of various hand properties. (If necessary, as occasionally also in actions occurring on the "walls" of a town or on the upper level of a "senate house", a second and even a third box may have been pressed into service on either side of the first, for although lateral access from one box to another was presumably impossible, players appearing in the openings of adjacent boxes would have appeared to the audience to be "together".)[20] No bed is required by the action or called for in stage-directions, and although in one instance the dialogue suggests possible use of a bed ("Madam undresse you, and come now to bed", ii, 117), in another instance it argues strongly against use of one, for it seems quite unlikely that if Sly were already in a bed the Lord would suggest moving him to another ("Or wilt thou sleepe? Wee'l have thee to a Couch, Softer and sweeter then the lustfull bed On purpose trim'd up for Semiramis", ii, 39–41). It may be added that although the directions call for an unusually large number of players aloft (nine, though only seven speak, the average in Shakespeare being three), no more than four actors are ever in direct conversation with Sly during the same sequence of dialogue, first the Lord and three Servingmen later the Lord, the "Lady", and a Messenger. Another partial exception occurs in the first "monument" action of *Antony and Cleopatra* (IV, xv). Certainly the business of "heaving Antony aloft" poses a difficult problem in historical reconstruction (which I hope to discuss in detail elsewhere), but regardless of the exact agency by which he was raised we shall be on pretty fair grounds (because of the two stage-directions calling for action *aloft*) in supposing that what he was raised to was a gallery over the stage. Thus the action demands hardly more than that Antony, once aloft, sit in the front opening of the gallery or of one of its boxes, clustered about by Cleopatra, Charmian, and Iras, that Cleopatra perhaps "swoon" against the parapet of the gallery after Antony's death, and that these actions aloft be watched by Diomedes and the Guard from the stage below.

Noting these two partial exceptions, we may conclude that, in general, action aloft in Shakespeare is a relatively static "tableau" (though not a "discovered" one), involving speech rather than movement and framed in the front opening of the gallery in conjunction with action upon the stage below.[21] The point is of some importance, for it would seem to answer an otherwise well-taken objection to a theory of use of the gallery for theatrical production, namely that action performed within a recessed area like the gallery shown in the Swan drawing would not have been generally visible because of limitations of sight-lines from the theatre yard and galleries round about. Certainly it would *not* have been generally visible if action aloft required much movement in two dimensions upon a horizontal plane, and not because of impossible sight-lines only, for in *The Gull's Hornbook*, in a passage that is perhaps all the more reliable for being satiric since if the charge were untrue the satire would have failed to achieve its effect, Dekker alludes to the "darknesse" of the Lords' room. However, since the typical Shakespearian action aloft, being anchored to the stage below, was necessarily produced in the front opening of the gallery with actors in most cases leaning out of "windows" or over the edges of "parapets", we may suppose that action aloft would have been pretty generally visible throughout the playhouse, both from the yard below and from its surrounding galleries.

Thus in Shakespeare the gallery is generally linked to the stage not only by the scene that the two production-areas combine to represent but also by conjunctive action between players aloft and below. In a majority of cases, furthermore, gallery and stage are also linked by a dramatic conflict between actors on different fictional levels. In actions involving windows and walls, actors upon one fictional level are often forcibly prevented from joining actors upon the other fictional level by locked doors or gates and the temporarily insurmountable drop between the two levels. That is to say, the vertical distance between gallery and stage is theatrically "practicable" in the sense that it is accepted by the audience as fictionally impassable. A lover wishes to climb to his beloved's window, or besiegers below the walls of a town wish to attack the besieged above them; but in each case locks and gravity conspire to keep the actors apart. Thus since the dramatic forces of the conflict are momentarily in balance, use of the gallery frequently poses a situation involving suspense: the audience wonders how the lover or besiegers will overcome the physical obstacles separating them from the actors on the other level.

Occasionally Shakespeare does not dramatize the resolution of this suspense: when Romeo leaves Juliet in the first "window" action the physical obstacles of locked doors and the vertical drop have not yet been overcome (*Romeo and Juliet*, II, ii), and we are not shown his later ascent to her window by a rope ladder. Often, however, resolution of the suspense is dramatized by an actor's ascent or descent from one level to the other, these shifts of action being of two general kinds. In some cases the physical obstacles are overcome by agreement between the actors aloft and below: Jessica at her window agrees to run away with Lorenzo and therefore descends to the street, to do so before our eyes (*The Merchant of Venice*, II, vi), or the Mayor of York consents to welcome Edward to his city and therefore descends from the walls to a place outside its gates, where we see him do so (*3 Henry VI*, IV, vii). Of course these resolutions of the suspense by agreement usually involve movements in the fiction from one level to the other by stairs not visible outside the house or town or castle; and therefore, since the shifts of action are effected in the theatre by use of the tiring-house stairs, the descents or ascents proper are not witnessed by the audience but only their beginnings and ends, which are produced on the exterior scene represented by gallery and stage. But in some cases the physical obstacles of locks and the vertical drop are overcome by movements in the fiction from one level to the other outside the house or town or castle; and here the theatrical ascents or descents are effected not by use of the tiring-house stairs but by the player's climbing or jumping from one level to the other within view of the audience. Thus the resolution of suspense is accomplished by a stunt of considerable theatrical effect: English soldiers scale the walls of Orleans (*1 Henry VI*, II, i), Romeo climbs down a rope ladder from Juliet's window (*Romeo and Juliet*, III, v), Arthur jumps down from the walls of a castle (*King John*, IV, iii), or Antony is "heaved aloft" to Cleopatra in her monument (*Antony and Cleopatra*, IV, xv). It is, incidentally, for the sake of a comparable theatrical effect that hand properties are in two cases thrown from one level to the other: a Senator upon the walls of Athens catches a glove thrown aloft as a token by the besieging Alcibiades (*Timon of Athens*, V, iv), and Lorenzo catches a casket full of Shylock's ducats, thrown down to him by Jessica from the window of her house (*The Merchant of Venice*, II, vi).

It must be added, however, that in a few cases there is no dramatic conflict between actors aloft and below, and here the gallery seems to have been used merely for theatrical "variety" or perhaps in order to achieve a more convenient disposition of players upon the stage. Pindarus, for example, could report to Cassius what he sees from the "hill" almost as effectively from the stage as from the gallery (*Julius Caesar*, v, iii); or the Presenters of *The Taming of the Shrew* could be placed almost as effectively upon the stage (as indeed they are in *The Taming of a Shrew*) as in the gallery. There is, to be sure, a convention behind use of the gallery in a "spying" action like Prospero's (*The Tempest*, III, iii), for the observer's entrance aloft seems often to have indicated that he is (as in this case) *invisible* through magic or divinity, or at least so well hidden by natural means as to make it impossible for the actors below to become aware of him. But generally observation can be staged without loss of dramatic suspense or even of much theatrical effect by the observer's "hiding" on the same level as the actors he is spying upon; and for this reason it is impossible conclusively to infer use of the gallery for observation in actions where it is likely but where dialogue and stage-directions afford no evidence of its use, as for instance in Othello's observation of Roderigo and the wounded Cassio, directly after the attempted murder of Cassio (*Othello*, v, i).

III

It remains to consider the theory held by John Cranford Adams that in addition to its "exterior" scenic functions the gallery over the stage (or "chamber", as he terms it) represented domestic interiors such as would in reality have been located on the upper storeys of Elizabethan houses.[22] A serious initial difficulty about this "interior" or "chamber" theory is that it must deny use of the gallery as a Lords' room, for spectators could hardly have sat in the gallery if the whole of that area was devoted to production some five times during the performance of the average Elizabethan play. Yet that the gallery over the stage was a Lords' room is a well-authenticated fact, albeit perhaps a difficult one for us of the twentieth century to understand, accustomed as we are to placing spectators only on one side of a proscenium-arch and players only on the other. Moreover, the chamber theory is based on surprisingly little evidence. In Shakespeare's thirty-eight plays, for example, only one action may be cited in its support. This is Induction ii of *The Taming of the Shrew*, where the scene is indeed localized as a "goodlie chamber". However, it seems clear (as we have seen) that the gallery was here used not because Sly's chamber is on an upper storey in the fiction but because the scene must change without a break in the action from the chamber where Sly wakes up to an elevated locality overlooking the place where a "Comedie" will be performed. Since Adams cites only one example doubtfully dating from around 1641 of a "chamber" action clearly designated aloft by a theatrical stage-direction,[23] we may suppose that Induction ii of *The Shrew* is extremely exceptional in its preliminary use of the gallery to represent a chamber.

It may be further pointed out that evidence for the chamber theory of use of the gallery is absent from Shakespearian plays having two or three variant texts, one at least of which might reasonably be expected to supply a hint of use of the gallery. Adams suggests, for example, that III, iii and III, iv of *Hamlet* were produced respectively in the "study" and on the "upper stage", these production-areas representing lower- and upper-level localities in the same building: a hall in the castle and the Queen's closet.[24] Now there are three texts of *Hamlet* deriving completely or in the main from independent manuscript authorities—the First and Second Quartos as well as the First Folio; yet in none of these three "collateral" texts is there any indication that the "closet" action was produced aloft.[25] Again, Adams suggests that the gallery was used six times in *King Lear* to represent a room on an upper storey of Gloucester's castle: in I, ii; II, i; III, iii,

83

v, vii; and IV, v.[26] Yet in neither of the two collateral texts of *King Lear* (the "Pied Bull" Quarto or the First Folio) is there a hint of use of the gallery for any of these six actions.[27] Moreover, the full significance of this lack of evidence for the chamber theory becomes apparent when one reflects upon how complete the evidence is for use of the gallery in its exterior scenic functions described on preceding pages. Of thirty-five generally accepted uses of the gallery in Shakespeare, only three are not indicated by a stage-direction of one sort or another; and two of these three uses, namely those occurring in *The Two Gentlemen of Verona* (IV, ii, iii), we should not in any case expect to be so indicated because of the peculiar nature of the "copy" for the Folio text, which contains "no directions whatever beyond bare entrances and exits".[28] Thus in order to accept Adams' theory one must assume that a direction for staging chamber action aloft occurs only once in thirty-eight plays (in Induction ii of *The Shrew*) or, since Adams suggests about five uses of the "upper stage" per play as a "normal" ratio,[29] in considerably less than 1% of possible cases (around 190);[30] whereas directions for staging exterior action aloft occur in thirty-two out of thirty-five uses or in just over 90% of generally accepted cases.

Furthermore, it should be noticed that chamber action aloft causes the gallery to develop at least three practical disadvantages that it does not have when used for "exterior" action performed in conjunction with the stage below. One is a poor view of the action on the part of a large portion of the audience. In exterior action aloft, players are necessarily in the front opening of the gallery where they can converse with (or observe) other players upon the stage below, and as a result most of the audience will have good visibility of the players aloft. However, chamber action aloft, being unrelated to action upon the stage, will generally move back and forth in depth within the gallery; and as the players move back away from the solid paling at the front of the Swan gallery or even from the generously spaced balusters that Adams postulates at the front of the Globe gallery, the audience will increasingly lose sight of the action because of limitations of sight-lines from the playhouse yard and its surrounding galleries (not to mention Dekker's "darknesse" once again). A second disadvantage is the limited playing-area of the gallery. This is of no concern in staging exterior action aloft, for such action is usually performed in the vertical plane defined by the front opening of the gallery, the players being "in contact" with other players upon the stage below. But the limited area of the gallery is of considerable importance in staging chamber action aloft, for in such action the players are usually involved in movement in two dimensions upon a horizontal plane. It seems reasonable to suppose that their movements would have been hampered within a gallery even as large as the "upper stage" or "chamber" in Adams' reconstruction of the Globe, and this handicap would have been much greater if not insuperable in a gallery that was partitioned into boxes, as the galleries in some public theatres of Shakespeare's time certainly were and as the galleries in all of them may have been. A third disadvantage is loss of audience contact because of excessive distance between the gallery and a majority of spectators. In the case of exterior action aloft this distance does not appreciably diminish audience contact, for the spectators' attention is focussed, so to speak, along a "line of contact" joining the player below with the player aloft. That is to say, the conjunctive action between the two levels tends to make the gallery an extension of the stage, with the player below directing the attention of the audience up and back to the player aloft. Or, to put the matter somewhat differently, the player below tends to "draw" the player aloft forward and down within the ambient of the spectators' easy attention. Also, in a large majority of cases in

Shakespeare (twenty-eight out of thirty-five), the average length of exterior action aloft is only thirty-seven lines. However, in the case of chamber action aloft, where there is necessarily no connexion with the stage below, the players in the gallery are isolated up in the air. The attention of the audience is not naturally directed up and back to them by the attention of a player upon the stage, and the players aloft must also overcome the distracting effect upon the audience of an empty and unlocalized stage stretching wide between them. It may be added that some of these theoretical objections to the chamber theory are borne out by comments of modern producers apropos of recent experimental productions on replica Elizabethan stages.[31]

An insight into the nature of the chamber theory has been suggested by George F. Reynolds, who in his review of *The Globe Playhouse* points out that one of Adams' basic assumptions is "that all scenes with large properties and all interior scenes of any kind used the curtained space either above or below. In this, of course, he is only reviving in exaggerated form the long discredited alternation theory which placed a front stage scene between every differently set rear stage scene. By this use of the 'chamber' along with the 'study' he thinks he avoids the 'clashes' that disproved the old theory."[32] When viewed in this light, the chamber theory would appear to be essentially an attempt to apply the "fourth-wall" convention of the proscenium-arch stage to the Elizabethan public-theatre gallery. Moreover, the weakness of the position becomes further apparent when one recognizes that the fourth-wall convention is equally inapplicable to an Elizabethan "discovery-space" on the level of the stage, for it seems probable, as Richard Southern persuasively suggests, that the proscenium-arch evolved not through gradual enlargement of a hypothetical "inner stage" but through enclosure of the stage itself (the "proscænium").[33] Furthermore, as Reynolds again points out, the "literal realism" of the chamber theory binds the Elizabethan stage more strictly than our most realistic modern drama, for even this "does not place on an upper stage all scenes conceived of as in second storey rooms."[34] Surely, as Dr Johnson might have said, he that imagines a gallery to be a chamber may imagine a stage to be one.

An additional word is perhaps in order concerning the psychological situation of the producer who works with a replica Elizabethan stage. It takes a great deal of effort to build such a stage, whether temporary or permanent, and once it is built the producer has a pretty toy to play with. He will naturally wish to give his audience a production in what he conceives to be the authentic Elizabethan manner. But suppose he is producing one of the eighteen Shakespearian plays that does not require use of a gallery? In such a case our producer might nevertheless decide to make use of his gallery rather than possibly undergo criticism for needless expenditure of time, labour, and funds. For such a producer, obviously, the chamber theory will have special attractions. It may well be, however, that he would do better to abandon his replica Elizabethan stage and build instead an original and possibly less expensive stage-structure that will equally well (or better) encourage such distinctively Elizabethan theatrical virtues as close audience contact, continuity of action, and fluidity of scene. An admirable example is the "open" stage used in productions of the annual Shakespeare Festival at Stratford, Ontario, designed by Tyrone Guthrie and Tanya Moiseiwitsch.[35] Or if a producer must build a replica Elizabethan stage, perhaps he should seat part of his audience aloft, as the Elizabethans evidently did and as was recently done by Bernard Miles in a production of the opening action of *Hamlet* upon the Mermaid Theatre stage, designed by Michael Stringer and C. Walter Hodges.[36] For the gallery over the stage seems also to have been a Lords' room.

NOTES

1. On the provenance of the Swan drawing compare E. K. Chambers, *The Elizabethan Stage* (1923), II, 526, and J. Q. Adams, *Shakespearean Playhouses* (1917), p. 166, n. 2.

2. The nature of the gallery over the stage, its simultaneous function as a raised production-area and as a Lords' room, and the problem of its terminology are discussed in my article, 'The Gallery over the Stage in the Public Playhouse of Shakespeare's Time', *Shakespeare Quarterly*, VIII (1957).

3. No evident use of the gallery: *Comedy of Errors*, *Love's Labour's Lost*, *Midsummer Night's Dream*, *1* and *2 Henry IV*, *Much Ado*, *As You Like It*, *Twelfth Night*, *Hamlet*, *Merry Wives*, *Troilus*, *All's Well*, *Measure for Measure*, *King Lear*, *Macbeth*, *Pericles*, *Cymbeline*, *Winter's Tale*.

4. Because of a higher incidence in the histories (1·7 uses per play), the gallery is rather more used in the earlier plays than in the later. I consider II, ii of *Romeo* as involving but a single action aloft, although Juliet momentarily leaves the scene at two points (ll. 139–41 and 156–8); and I consider Induction ii and I, i of *The Shrew* as involving two actions aloft, although the "Presenters" presumably remain within view of the audience during the interval between the beginning of I, i and l. 253.—I reject ten variously supposed uses of the gallery, in five plays cited for other uses: *1 Henry VI* (3: I, iv, 1–22, 23–111; II, i, 1–37), *3 Henry VI* (2: I, i; v, vi), *Titus* (2: v, ii, iii), *Caesar* (2: III, i, ii), *Antony* (v, ii). Although arguments against these uses of the gallery cannot be presented here, I may point out that in rejecting them I have the support of at least one modern editor in all but one case (*Titus*, v, ii).

5. Uses of the gallery: As "walls" (16); *1 Henry VI* (6: I, vi; II, i, 38; III, ii, 26–35, 41–74; IV, ii; v, iii), *2 Henry VI* (2: IV, v, ix), *3 Henry VI* (2: IV, vii; v, i), *Richard II* (III, iii), *King John* (2: II, i; IV, iii), *Henry V* (III, iii), *Coriolanus* (I, iv), *Timon* (v, iv).—As a "window" (9): *Two Gentlemen* (2: IV, ii, iii), *Shrew* (v, i), *Romeo* (2: II, ii; III, v), *Merchant* (II, vi), *Othello* (I, i), *Henry VIII* (v, II), *Kinsmen* (II, i–ii).—As miscellaneous elevated localities (7): *2 Henry VI* (I, iv, a place overlooking an "Orchard", Q), *Titus* (3: I, i, 1–63, 169–233, 296–337, the upper storey of a *Senat house*, seen from outside the building), *Richard III* (III, vii, the "leads" of a castle), *Caesar* (v, iii, a "hill"), *Antony* (IV, xv, the upper storey of a "Monument", seen from outside the building).—As an undescribed place of observation (3): *Shrew* (2: Induction ii; I, i), *Tempest* (III, iii).

6. Actions aloft of over a hundred lines (7): *3 Henry VI* (v, i: 113 lines), *Richard II* (III, iii: 122), *Shrew* (Induction ii: 147), *Richard III* (III, vii: 153), *Romeo* (II, ii: 178), *Kinsmen* (II, i–ii: 286), *King John* (II, i: 360).

7. Number of players aloft: one (13 instances), two (5), three (6), four (2), five (4), six (3), seven (1), nine (1).

8. "Theatrical" evidence: *Aloft* or *above* (14 uses): *1 Henry VI* (IV, ii), *2 Henry VI* (I, iv), *Richard III* (III, vii), *Titus* (2: I, i, 1–63, 296–337), *Shrew* (2: Induction ii: I, i), *Romeo* (III, v), *Merchant* (II, vi), *Caesar* (v, iii), *Othello* (I, i), *Antony* (IV, xv), *Henry VIII* (v, ii), *Kinsmen* (II, i–ii).—On *the top* (2): *1 Henry VI* (III, ii, 26–35), *Tempest* (III, iii). (This unusual term has been interpreted as referring to the "hut" on top of the "cover" over the stage—but the difficulty of visibility seems forbidding; and to a "music room" on the third level of the tiring-house—but for such a room in the public theatres of Shakespeare's time there seems to be no clear evidence. Presumably it does not designate the cover itself (apparently referred to as *the top of the Stage* in Greene's *Alphonsus, King of Aragon*), for it is difficult to imagine a player appearing there and in any case Joan is directed to thrust *out* a burning torch. I do not think it refers to the "top" of a structure upon the stage, for *1 Henry VI* was demonstrably produced without a "discovery-space", which such a structure would presumably have provided. I therefore interpret *on the top* as probably referring to the gallery, conceived of as the "top" of the tiring-house.)—*Within...on the walls* (1): *1 Henry VI* (III, ii, 41–74). (This direction is of special interest in that it suggests use of a recessed area like the gallery shown in the Swan drawing.)—*Below* (1): *2 Henry VI* (IV, v).

9. "Fictional" evidence only: *On the Walls* (10 uses, the preposition varying): *1 Henry VI* (3: I, vi; II, i, 38; v, iii), *3 Henry VI* (2: IV, vii; v, i), *Richard II* (III, iii), *King John* (2: II, i; IV, iii), *Coriolanus* (I, iv), *Timon* (v, iv). *Out of the window* (1): *Shrew* (v, i).—*On the Tarras* (1): *2 Henry VI* (IV, ix).—*Before the Gates* (1): *Henry V* (III, iii).—Dialogue and direction for descent only (1): *Titus* (I, i, 169–233, *A long Flourish till they come down*).—Dialogue only (3): *Two Gentlemen* (IV, ii, iii, "Now must we to her window"), *Romeo* (II, ii, "ore my head").

10. Descents (13 instances): By a rope ladder (1): *Romeo* (III, v, 42, *He goeth downe*, Q1).—By jumping (2): *1 Henry VI* (II, i, 38, *The French leape ore the walles*); *King John* (IV, iii, "The Wall is high, and yet will I leape downe"). (The difficulty of a player's jumping down from the gallery has been but should not be exaggerated. Young and

acrobatic players must obviously have been called upon to do the jumping, and if in any playhouse the altitude of the gallery was too great for a comfortable leap, the player could easily have hung by his hands and dropped, as the actor in the fiction presumably did.)—By a stairway within the tiring-house (10): *Timon* (v, iv, no lines of "covering" dialogue; "Descend"); *Titus* (I, i, 233, no lines but *A long Flourish till they come down*); *Romeo* (III, v, 68, no lines in Q2 but six in the variant Q1: *She goeth downe from the window*, Q1); *1 Henry VI* (v, iii, one line and a fanfare of *Trumpets*; direction for re-entrance); *Shrew* (v, i, two lines; direction for re-entrance); *Richard II* (III, iii, three lines; "Downe I come"); *Caesar* (v, iii, three lines; direction for re-entrance); *3 Henry VI* (IV, vii, five lines; *He descends*, F); *Merchant* (II, vi, seven lines; direction for re-entrance); *Othello* (I, i, sixteen lines; directions for exit and re-entrance).

11. The length of time required for a stairway descent (eight or ten seconds) is derived from the 1949 production of *Julius Caesar* by the Amherst College Masquers on the replica of the Fortune stage (modified) at the Folger Shakespeare Library; and from the 1954 production of *Romeo and Juliet* by the University of Virginia Players on a replica of the Globe stage as reconstructed by J. C. Adams in *The Globe Playhouse* (1942).

12. Ascents (5 instances): By "heaving aloft" (1): *Antony* (IV, xv, *They heave Anthony aloft to Cleopatra*).—By *scaling Ladders* (1): *1 Henry VI* (II, i, 38, "Ascend").—By the tiring-house stairs (3): *2 Henry VI* (I, iv, three lines of covering dialogue; *She goes up to the Tower*, Q); *Richard III* (III, vii, forty lines; directions for exit and re-entrance; *Caesar* (v, iii, three lines; directions for exit and re-entrance). (In the Folio text of *2 Henry VI* the ascending actor is Hume, Eleanor entering directly to the gallery; whereas in the variant Quarto text (*The Contention betwixt the Two Famous Houses of York and Lancaster*) it is Eleanor who ascends.)

13. Hand properties: *1 Henry VI* (III, ii, torch), *Richard III* (III, vii, prayer book), *Merchant* (II, vi, casket of money), *Timon* (v, iv, glove), *Shrew* (Induction ii, apparel, etc.).—Properties: *Romeo* (III, v, rope ladder), *1 Henry VI* (II, i, scaling ladders), *Shrew* (Induction ii; I, i, bench or stools).

14. An exception may be the curtain mentioned in the dialogue of *Henry VIII* (v, ii), possibly written with the Blackfriars stage in mind. However, as no curtain is called for in a stage-direction or required by the action, this may be regarded as fictional colouring appropriate to the situation of spying from a window. The unreliability of dialogue as a source of information concerning practicable elements of production is amply illustrated by G. F. Reynolds, *The Staging of Elizabethan Plays at the Red Bull Theater* (1940), pp. 42–6.

15. Somerville's entrance at l. 6 may be below rather than aloft, but if so the use of the gallery being illustrated remains essentially unchanged.

16. In two cases the scene of the stage changes locality after a stairway descent, once from an "orchard" beneath a window to a room inside the house (*Romeo*, III, v, 69), and once from a place outside the walls of a castle to the "base court" within them (*Richard II*, III, iii, 187).

17. I develop this interpretation in 'The Use of the Upper Stage in *Romeo and Juliet*', *Shakespeare Quarterly*, v (1954), to which J. C. Adams replies in 'Shakespeare's Use of the Upper Stage in *Romeo and Juliet*, III, v', *ibid.* VII (1956). Adams' argument is based on two questionable assumptions, namely that the tiring-house at the Curtain Theatre was equipped with "window-stages" and that its gallery was not used as a Lords' room. More important, however, his argument places a forced interpretation upon the Q1 stage-direction *She goeth downe from the window*. On the evidence of the earlier Q1 direction for Romeo's descent (*He goeth downe*), this direction, regardless of whether the pronoun *She* refers to Juliet or the Nurse, clearly calls for transfer of the action from gallery to stage immediately after the lovers' farewell.

18. Another possible reason for staging the Presenters aloft would be to permit them later to leave the scene unnoticed by the audience in order to "double" in the parts of actors subsequently appearing in the play proper, an hypothesis that would partly account for the incompleteness of the "enveloping" action in *The Shrew*. In *A Shrew* (where the enveloping action is completed) Sly re-enters not to the gallery but to the stage, carried by Servants in a chair: *Enter two with a table and a banquet on it, and two other, with Slie asleepe in a chaire, richlie apparelled.*

19. Although Chambers gives the impression that Presenters appear aloft fairly frequently (*The Elizabethan Stage*, III, 91–2), only two of the several plays he mentions clearly place a Presenter or Presenters in the gallery, Shakespeare's *Taming of the Shrew* and Lodge and Greene's *Looking Glass for London and England*.

20. The openings of adjacent boxes in a gallery like the Swan's may also have represented windows in adjacent houses, as in Jonson's *Devil is an Ass* (II, ii); see G. F. Reynolds, 'What We Know of the Elizabethan Stage', *Modern Philology*, IX (1911).

21. This conclusion accords in general with the views of Harley Granville-Barker, *Prefaces to Shakespeare* (1927–47); G. F. Reynolds, *The Staging of Elizabethan Plays*; C. Walter Hodges, *The Globe Restored* (1953); Alfred Harbage, *Theatre for Shakespeare* (1955); and W. F. Rothwell, *Methods of Production in the English Theater from 1550 to 1598* (unpublished Yale dissertation, 1953).

22. *The Globe Playhouse*, p. 275: "...an upper stage similar to the study below first made its appearance early in the last decade of the sixteenth century. This was the last major unit to be added to the Elizabethan multiple stage. Prior to its introduction all interior scenes had to be laid in the study, despite the fact that most London citizens utilized the ground floor of their houses for shops and had their living quarters above. The development, therefore, on the second level of the tiring-house of a sizable curtained stage which could be prepared in advance as a living room, a bed- or dressing room, a private room in a tavern, and so forth, enabled dramatists to reflect London life with greater fidelity. In general after 1595 such scenes as would in reality have taken place in some room on the second level of an Elizabethan dwelling, tavern, prison, or palace were presented above."

23. *The Globe Playhouse*, p. 278. The example is from Killigrew's *Parson's Wedding* (IV, vi): *The Tyring-Room, Curtains drawn, and they discourse, his Chamber, two Beds, two Tables, Looking-glasses, Night-cloathes, Waste-coats, Sweet-bags, Sweet-meats and Wine*, Wanton *drest like a Chamber-maid; all above if the Scene can be so order'd*. However, one may question the relevance of this evidence to stage practice in the public theatres during Shakespeare's time. *The Parson's Wedding* ("written at Basil in Switzerland") may have been designed for production at the Cockpit or Blackfriars just before the closing of the theatres, but this is by no means certain. Moreover, it was not printed until 1664, when it was also produced at Drury Lane; and as W. J. Lawrence points out (*The Elizabethan Playhouse* (1912), p. 94, note), the evidence of Sir Henry Herbert's Office Book that this was the play's first performance is conclusive. See also Montague Summers, *Restoration Comedies* (1921), p. xxix.

24. *The Globe Playhouse*, p. 276.

25. The initial stage-direction of III, iv reads as follows in the three collateral texts of *Hamlet*: *Enter Queene and Corambis* (Q1); *Enter Gertrard and Polonius* (Q2); *Enter Queene and Polonius* (F). The "substantive" variation among the three readings suggests that the three texts are indeed independent witnesses in their omission of an *aloft* or *above* from this direction.

26. 'The Original Staging of *King Lear*' in *J. Q. Adams Memorial Studies*, ed. J. G. McManaway *et al.* (1948).

27. The initial stage-directions of the six actions read as follows in the two collateral texts of *King Lear*. I, ii: *Enter Bastard Solus* (Q); *Enter Bastard* (F). II, i: *Enter Bast. and Curan meeting* (Q); *Enter Bastard, and Curan, severally* (F). III, iii: *Enter Gloster and the Bastard with lights* (Q); *Enter Gloster, and Edmund* (F). III, vi: *Enter Cornewell and Bastard* (Q); *Enter Cornwall, and Edmund* (F). III, vii: *Enter Cornwell, and Regan, and Gonorill, and Bastard* (Q); *Enter Cornwall, Regan, Gonerill, Bastard, and Servants* (F). IV, v: *Enter Regan and Steward* (Q): *Enter Regan, and Steward* (F). The substantive variation in the first five pairs of readings suggests that the two texts are indeed independent witnesses in their omission of an *aloft* or *above* from these directions.

28. W. W. Greg, *The Editorial Problem in Shakespeare* (1942), p. 141.

29. 'The Original Staging of *King Lear*', p. 316 (but for "five" should we not read "six"?). In *The Globe Playhouse* Adams suggests that approximately every fourth action was produced aloft: "lower-stage scenes outnumber upper-stage scenes by at least three to one" (p. 294).

30. $5 \times 38 = 190$. According to Adams' reconstruction of the Globe tiring-house and his theories of the use of its elements in production, most of the thirty-five exterior actions aloft in Shakespeare would have been produced not in the "upper-stage" or "chamber" but on the "tarras" before it or in one of two "window-stages" flanking it.

31. For example, Bernard Beckermann, in writing of his Shakespeare productions on a replica of the Globe stage as reconstructed by Adams, remarks that the "remoteness" of the "chamber" from the audience is even "more emphatic" than that of the "study", accordingly requiring of the player aloft "a broad and lively manner of playing" in order to bridge "The enormous gulf which separates him from the audience" ('The Globe Playhouse at Hofstra College', *Educational Theatre Journal*, V, 1953). Again, Frank McMullan writes as follows of Beckermann's production of *Macbeth* on this same replica stage. "The Lady Macbeth sleep-walking scene was played on the upper stage evidently because it connoted her apartment. Even though it was technically well acted and directed, the greater part of its effectiveness was lost because of the height of the acting area and the physical distance between the actors and the audience. Surely the use of the forestage for the scene would have better projected the nightmare aberrations of Lady Macbeth's mind" ('Producing Shakespeare', in *Shakespeare: Of an Age and for All Time*, ed. C. T.

Prouty, 1954). And Margaret Webster has this to say of chamber action aloft. "Were I to play Portia...or Lady Macbeth [on a replica Elizabethan stage], I would diffidently suggest that to put every one of my intimate scenes up in that wretched 'Chamber' was to rob me of all the vaunted intimacy which the [Elizabethan] theatre afforded, and to cramp me on a skied-up little 'picture stage' from which the delicate comedy of my 'Portia' would be as hard to handle as the electricity of Lady Macbeth's invocation or the terrible urgency of her Sleep-walking. 'Take me back,' I would say, 'to my nice intimate proscenium and let me, for Heaven's sake, walk down to it'" (review of Ronald Watkins' *On Producing Shakespeare*, in *Shakespeare Quarterly*, III, 1952).

32. *Journal of English and Germanic Philology*, XLII (1943). Reynolds' point, which is well illustrated in Adams' article on *King Lear*, explains the ratio of three actions below to one aloft cited in note 29 above, for the normal "cycle" of alternation would presumably involve two uses of the "platform", one of the "study", and one of the "chamber". Compare also R. Crompton Rhodes, *The Stagery of Shakespeare* (1922): "The theory—'of the triple stage'—may be considered a development of the theory of 'alternative scenes' as transformed by a recognition of the vast importance of the balcony as a scenic resource."

33. Richard Southern, *The Open Stage* (1953).

34. Reynolds, 'Was There a 'Tarras' in Shakespeare's Globe?' *Shakespeare Survey*, 4 (1951).

35. See Tyrone Guthrie 'Shakespeare at Stratford, Ontario', *Shakespeare Survey*, 8 (1955).

36. Bernard Miles and Josephine Wilson, 'Three Festivals at the Mermaid Theatre', *Shakespeare Quarterly*, V (1954).

LEAR'S QUESTIONS

BY

WINIFRED M. T. NOWOTTNY

The greatness of *King Lear* is of a kind that almost disables criticism: in it, Shakespeare has so reconciled opposites as to make it difficult to frame any valid statement about the nature of the play as a whole. The total impression is one of primitive simplicity, of solid rock unfretted by the artist's tool, but whenever, in studying it, the mind is visited by some small insight into its pattern (for of course it is patterned), further reflexion swiftly brings about a rush of critical excitement over the widening significances of what seemed at first a detail of the design, and this not once but many times; life is not long enough fully to explore *King Lear*. These repeated experiences of the play should inure the critic to the idea that whatever element of its design seems at any given moment most fascinating it is none the less merely one element among many, and the critic will do well to think of himself as the groping speleologist who traverses, astonished, one only of the many levels of that rock whose hidden intricacies are no more impressive than its simple mass. It is the purpose of this article to consider Lear's habit of asking questions, and though this (at the moment) seems to me of fundamental importance in the play, it must be stressed that commentary on them is made in mindfulness of the fact that the play is inexhaustibly patterned, and any act of critical consideration of its patterns must be at best limited and in the last resort less true to the play as a whole than a perception of the final unified simplicity of its effect—or, one should perhaps say, of the powerful illusion of simplicity which the play's patterns promote and subserve.

King Lear, as far as his outward fortunes are concerned, is a passive hero, but at the same time he is himself the active cause of what is tragic (as distinct from pathetic) in his experience, and is indeed more truly the maker of his own tragedy, by virtue of the questions he himself raises, than any other Shakespearian tragic hero. The play opens with the *locus classicus* of Lear's questioning: "Which of you shall we say doth love us most?" Goneril's comment that Lear has "put himself from rest" is applicable to this and to almost every subsequent question he asks. It is applicable too, to the essential condition of man, and what in Lear's questioning is wilful is also what (being autonomous) lifts him clear of the particular circumstances of plot and personality and makes him that Everyman that Macbeth with his Witches, Othello with his Iago, even Hamlet with his Ghost, cannot be. In the light of Lear's subsequent questions the first question is seen to be no mere device to get the play started, for his subsequent questions are in a sense as wilful as the first, going beyond the immediate provocation of the moment in which he formulates them. In Act I, sc. iv, when Goneril is insolent, Lear instantly flies at the questions:

> Doth any here know me? This is not Lear:
> Doth Lear walk thus? speak thus? Where are his eyes?
> Either his notion weakens, his discernings
> Are lethargied—Ha! waking? 'tis not so.
> Who is it that can tell me who I am?

The Fool interjects, "Lear's shadow", to which Lear ironically assents:

> I would learn that; for, by the marks of sovereignty, knowledge, and reason, I should be false per-
> suaded I had daughters.

Thus upon the goad of Goneril's insolence he has immediately involved himself in two questions which run through the play: whether or not he possesses sovereignty and whether or not he truly knows anything. When (in Act II, sc. iv) Regan and Goneril deny him his "additions", Lear takes in a serious sense the canting "What need one?" of Regan, and argues with real concern the problem of "true need":

> Allow not nature more than nature needs,
> Man's life's as cheap as beast's: thou art a lady;
> If only to go warm were gorgeous,
> Why, nature needs not what thou gorgeous wear'st,
> Which scarcely keeps thee warm—

and though in the course of the play he comes to condemn as sophistication what he here defends, this passage is the beginning of his involvement with the question of "unaccommodated man". In this same speech he goes on to question the gods themselves:

> If it be you that stir these daughters' hearts
> Against their father, fool me not so much
> To bear it tamely;

—this is a problem which comes to the fore in the speeches he hurls against the storm. When, conducted to the hovel, he encounters Poor Tom, he demands "Is man no more than this?" Such questions, however strong the personal feelings that underlie them, are more searching than the situation itself necessitates. Similarly, at the very last, over the body of Cordelia, Lear will ask,

> Why should a dog, a horse, a rat, have life,
> And thou no breath at all?

These are the questions of a Prometheus, even though they begin in a family quarrel, and Shakespeare meant it so: Lear himself uses the Promethean image,

> she hath tied
> Sharp-toothed unkindness, like a vulture, here.

Before the end of Act II, all the problems that dominate the dialogue of Lear's scenes in Acts III and IV have been posed, and posed by Lear himself: the nature of his own status and identity, the nature of knowing, the nature of need, the nature of the gods; and Lear has also raised, though not as a direct question, the problem of the inherent guilt of the flesh:

> thou art my flesh, my blood, my daughter;
> Or rather a disease that's in my flesh,
> Which I must needs call mine: thou art a boil,
> A plague-sore, an embossed carbuncle,
> In my corrupted blood.

It is the grand achievement of Act III to connect these problems so closely that each increases another's momentum. Lear's own experiences in the storm provide the emotional and logical connexions. The dialogue with the storm is, clearly, a battle with the gods. Pitting himself against the heavens, Lear challenges them to reveal their nature and his own: is he their slave? or is it they who are servile ministers? But this speech, the climax of Lear's resistance to the evil directed against himself by Goneril and Regan, is at the same time but the prelude to deeper issues between the gods and men: are they in their wrath the punishers of covert guilt? and what of the "poor naked wretches" who are involved in "seasons such as these"? Here, though Lear defiantly asserts his own innocence,

> I am a man
> More sinn'd against than sinning—

this assertion is of short duration, giving place at once to his recognition that he himself has taken too little thought of needy man, and destined to give place again to a deepening of his insight into that "disease that's in my flesh, which I must needs call mine". In this apparently inconclusive struggle with the gods, he does find answers to questions he himself has already raised: that of the nature of man's knowing, and that of his own status. He finds out (as we are told later) that he had been deceived about himself and he finds out also (as we are told immediately) that true knowledge is born of what is felt in the flesh:

> Take physic, pomp;
> Expose thy self to feel what wretches feel.

From this it is a short step to the notion that the man who must "answer with [his] uncovered body this extremity of the skies" is at the heart of truth; Poor Tom because he is most exposed must feel most and so know most, and so he becomes Lear's "philosopher", of whom Lear asks, "What is the cause of thunder?" Through the impact of the storm Shakespeare has effected one of the most difficult acts of communication necessary to the subsequent development of the play: he has brought home to us Lear's belief that all a man can know is what he knows through the flesh. Further, in Lear's defiance of the storm, his involvement with the problem of guilt has been brought to the fore. By a master-stroke, Shakespeare now establishes an intimate relation between Lear's several preoccupations, by using for them all the one symbol of the flesh: the flesh that suffers, knows, begets, is punished for its guilt. This is strikingly done when Lear first encounters Poor Tom. His first speech connects the idea of punishing the flesh with the idea of begetting:

> Is it the fashion, that discarded fathers
> Should have thus little mercy on their flesh?
> Judicious punishment! 'twas this flesh begot
> Those pelican daughters.

His next speech connects the idea of the exposed and suffering flesh with the idea of real truth:

Why, thou wert better in thy grave than to answer with thy uncovered body this extremity of the skies. Is man no more than this?...here's three on's are sophisticated! Thou art the thing itself....Off, off, you lendings! come, unbutton here.

Gloucester in the same scene furthers the power of the symbol with his words,

> Our flesh and blood is grown so vile, my lord,
> That it doth hate what gets it.

Henceforward the language takes on the function of binding more closely and exploring more deeply the connexions set up by Lear's experiences in the storm. It is the discovery of the metonymy, "the flesh", wherewith to advert to all the problems vital to the play which gives the language of the latter part of the tragedy its characteristic mark of simplicity charged with power, for within the metonymic structure made possible by the use of this common term, Shakespeare is able to sweep the strings of feeling whilst seeming to make no gesture at all.

The language of the play is further shaped for Shakespeare's purposes by a deliberate exploitation of the ambivalence of this term and of the aptness of the symbol for development through cognate terms such as "heart", "hand", "eyes", "brains", which also, in common usage, have both abstract and concrete significance. Much of the sombre power of the most memorable utterances in the mad scenes is due to the subtle interplay between the flesh as mere flesh and the qualities the flesh embodies, and to the interplay between the different members of that whole complex of ideas of which the flesh has been made the symbol. For instance, Lear's sudden demand,

> Then let them anatomize Regan; see what breeds about her heart. Is there any cause in nature that makes these hard hearts?

is macabre, not merely gruesome, because of the interplay between abstract and concrete, coupled with the interplay between the multiple references of the symbol: the flesh itself when dissected will reveal the truth, but an *intellectual* truth ("anatomize" meant not only to dissect but also to give a reasoned analysis or enumeration of qualities); this flesh is also the flesh in which evil things "breed" and the flesh subject to Nature's laws, the flesh in which the physical and spiritual are, according to Lear, so wholly united that the "heart" that breeds wickedness is also the "heart" that can be dissected and its hardness probed to seek the final cause. And the form of this sudden demand is such that we can simultaneously accept it as natural to Lear's way of thinking, and reject it as unnatural to our own. This is but one example of the way in which the language of the mad scenes achieves metaphysical subtlety without breaking the illusion of naturalistic presentation. In the mad scenes Lear again and again has sombre utterances whose power to strike directly at the heart is due to the peculiar dexterity with which they walk the precipice between the figurative and the true, as in Lear's,

> Give me an ounce of civet, good apothecary, to sweeten my imagination:

or in his,

> Let me have surgeons;
> I am cut to the brains.

This technique is, I am convinced, deliberate, and it does much to produce that sense of inexplicable power which we feel in attending a performance of the play. This is of course tricky ground for the critic; Shakespeare here is using means which outstrip our analytical terms. But the belief that the sense of shifting relations between true and false given by these utterances is of definable importance to the total effect of these scenes is strengthened by the evident fact that the mad scene with Gloucester (IV, vi) is a sustained exercise in the deployment of multiple uncertainties, so consistent in this aspect of its technique as to leave no doubt of what is being done.

In the mad scene with Gloucester the dialogue deliberately inhabits a no-man's-land between truth and falsehood; it is this ("matter and impertinency mixed") that makes it the pregnant "reason in madness" it is. Lear's first remark sets the tone:

No, they cannot touch me for coining; I am the king himself. Nature's above art in that respect.

This speech, whose immediate reference, no doubt, is to the imaginary press-money he is about to hand out, at once strikes the note of an uncertain relation between the true and the false, a note with many overtones: Lear is coining money, but is no coiner, since he is the King himself (and this phrase recalls his uncertainty about whether and in what sense he may be called king) and being by nature a king (if he is a king at all) his creations are true, unlike the feignings of art— but at the same time what he is now creating (the press-money) *is* a figment, with which he "pays" the other figments of his brain. (It has been well said that the play "disables the reflective reason of the reader"; dialogue such as this, which moves between the real and the unreal, is one of the means by which that effect is produced). Then Lear in his fantasy asks for the password. A voice from the real world offers one at random. "Pass". Unnervingly, it is the right password. And, as Lear accepts Edgar as part of his fantasy, his voice reaches the dark world of the blind and deluded Gloucester:

I know that voice.

Lear wheels upon him, not seeing him—"Goneril"—yet somehow seeing him—"with a white beard!"—and at once the white beard suggests white hairs as a figure of wisdom, and he recalls the deception of his daughters:

They flattered me like a dog; and told me I had white hairs in my beard ere the black ones were there.

With mad shrewdness he reflects that their "'Ay' and 'no' too, was no good divinity", and the word "divinity" takes his mind to that battle of his own with the gods in which he found out about the gods and himself and, like a dog, smelt out Regan and Goneril too. "They told me I was every thing; 'tis a lie, I am not ague-proof." This summing-up of his experiences and problems, which makes excellent sense to Lear and sense enough to us (who have been made to understand how Lear has put the tests of the senses in the place of ordinary reason) means nothing to Gloucester, but the voice that delivers it does:

The trick of that voice I do well remember:
Is't not the king?

When Lear replies, "Ay, every inch a king", we feel that claim to be true, though the Lear who makes it is mad and destitute, and childish too, for he proves his kingship by his power to terrify:

When I do stare, see how the subject quakes,

thus taking us back beyond the kingly Lear of the storm to the Lear of the opening scenes. But immediately upon this, as he turns to interrogate another phantom of his brain, it is as a king who pardons where he might have condemned:

> I pardon that man's life. What was thy cause?
> Adultery?
> Thou shalt not die: die for adultery! No.

Yet it is a wry and immoral compassion, a compassion for man which is possible only when man is seen as no different from the animals ("The wren goes to't, and the small gilded fly Does lecher in my sight") and his copulation useful ("To't, luxury, pell-mell! for I lack soldiers"). Suddenly the sense of man's difference from the animals (moral responsibility) returns, and with it a sense of sin and a revulsion from the animality of the sinful flesh, the compassion giving way to "There's hell, there's darkness, there's the sulphurous pit, Burning, scalding, stench, consumption." The grotesque picture of woman's sexuality (the extremest point of Lear's sense of the sinfulness of the flesh) is not only in itself a tale of false appearances, of monstrosity in nature and of a grotesque conjunction of gods and devils, but also it is in the end rejected as the vapour of an imagination itself in need of something to disguise its own stench. Hard upon this passage, both full of revulsion and provocative of revulsion in the hearer, come the words of Gloucester, charged with reverence and love:

> O, let me kiss that hand!

and, at this, Lear achieves the most sombre and powerful of those utterances in which the flesh and the spirit mingle in bewildering relations:

> Let me wipe it first; it smells of mortality.

It seems to me that, except for the last scene of all, there is no greater moment in the play than this. Here Lear is seen with that profound humanism which recognizes man as being at once wondrous and frail: supreme object of love and reverence, to whom one says, "O, let me kiss that hand!" and yet by his very condition, one who "smells of mortality"; in brief, the "ruined [master]piece of nature". This is a moment of complete truth, the more powerful because it comes as the climax of a dialogue fraught with ambiguities, with reason in madness, with lightning traversings and inversions of the familiar categories of the true and the false. This interchange between Lear and Gloucester is an epiphany of that idea of man by which the whole tragedy is informed. Immediately, the dialogue veers off into ambiguities more fantastic than before. For instance, when Gloucester asks, "Dost thou know me?" Lear's reply, "I remember thine eyes well enough" is as wildly untrue as it could be and yet true in the sense that Lear understands well enough the cruelty that brought about Gloucester's blindness, and he goes on to the paradoxically true statement, "A man may see how this world goes with no eyes", which in turn introduces Lear's own "great image of authority", that of the rational creature who in this world must run from the cur, and the passage on social injustice which so clearly analyses the perversions of justice and yet is, in the very absoluteness of its condemnation, so falsified a picture (just as the passage on sexuality was part penetration and part extravagance) that Edgar is moved to comment,

> O, matter and impertinency mix'd!
> Reason in madness!

As suddenly the twisted truth of this passage gives place to lucidity—"I know thee well enough; thy name is Gloucester" and to a simple observation of real life, "Thou know'st, the first time that we smell the air, We wawl and cry" which is swiftly followed by the metaphysical gloss, "we cry that we are come To this great stage of fools", and then the scene dissolves in mad cunning: "Nay, if you get it, you shall get it by running" and is linked to normality (which must now follow) by the comment of the gentleman who stands by,

> A sight most pitiful in the meanest wretch,
> Past speaking of in a king!

This comment makes explicit another of the qualities of this scene. It is that scene in which Shakespeare brings to a maximum effect of dissonance all the problems of the play. The problem of suffering is at its rawest in this scene, where mad Lear confronts blinded Gloucester in a visible spectacle of which nothing can be said, save "it is, And my heart breaks at it", a scene in whose fragmented dialogue, which every now and then sharpens to a sliver that stabs the heart and brain, the problems that have brought Lear to this pass are restated in their extremest form. In complete destitution, he claims himself "every inch a king"; he recalls that Titanic struggle with the gods which taught him he had been flattered like a dog; his sense of the guilt of the flesh takes him down into the pit, and his sense of the guilt of "authority" lifts him to a height of compassion proper only to a suffering god ("None does offend, none, I say, none; I'll able 'em: Take that of me, my friend, who have the power To seal the accuser's lips"). This scene of maximum dissonance leads to that resolution of dissonance which in the reunion with Cordelia brings the play to a penultimate close of pure, still pathos. In that reunion, Lear's passion is over, "the great rage...is killed in him", and the plot comes full circle when he is restored to comfort, love and majesty—accepted, humbly, as undeserved gifts, by one claiming no more for himself than

> I am a very foolish fond old man....Pray you now, forget and forgive: I am old and foolish.

These simple harmonies could not be as effective without the whirling dissonances of the mad scene with Gloucester. The simplicity of Lear's words in this scene could not be so moving were it not instinct with the memory of his long struggle to know the truth. The shifting relations between the false and the true, and between the physical 'real' and the non-physical 'real' now come to rest in such simple physical certainties as "I feel this pin prick"—certainties the more moving because they are now, to Lear, the only way he knows of settling those searching questions whose racking complexity has been revealed in the course of the play. We have come a long way from "Doth Lear walk thus? talk thus? where are his eyes?" to "I will not swear these are my hands", from "But goes thy heart with this?" to "Be your tears wet?"; all the wildness of the long journey is felt, quiescent now, in these questions and the simple physical tests by reference to which Lear finds some sort of answer. Similarly the simplicity of attitude, as in his hesitant,

"As I am a man, I think this lady To be my child Cordelia" is powerful because of all Lear has left behind him; he is no longer the wrathful dragon, the outraged king, the impotent revenger, the defiant Titan, the stoic, or the madman, but simply, now, a man. The daring of this is terrible. Shakespeare has made Lear, who has yet to face the worst, exhaust in advance every known tragic attitude (except that of self-destruction, but Gloucester has attempted and rejected that), leaving them all behind him. It is as though Shakespeare sought to write a tragedy which sets itself to present the bitterest experience of all without help of the trappings of tragic style or attitude. It is as man, not as tragic hero, that Lear is to meet the death of Cordelia—as man who has already of his own volition asked all the deepest metaphysical questions about man's condition, suffered all he could suffer because of them, and now, when "nature in [him] stands on the very verge Of her confine", confronts the one question he has so far escaped:

> Why should a dog, a horse, a rat, have life,
> And thou no breath at all?

And here the style, now in "a condition of complete simplicity, costing no less than everything" performs the final miracle of hardening from humble pathos to tragic rock by an intensification of its own simplicity: those same elements of which simple pathos was compounded, are compounded anew. Lear, so recently content to know so little, is now certain of the simplest, sharpest distinction of all: "I know when one is dead, and when one lives." A simple physical test, again, will settle the only question that matters: "Lend me a looking-glass; If that her breath will mist or stain the stone, Why then she lives." And if she lives, life even as he has known it makes sense:

> if it be so,
> It is a chance which does redeem all sorrows
> That ever I have felt.

And at the last, she seems to him to live.

The whole play is a dramatic answer to the one question in which all Lear's questions are subsumed: the question, What is Man? Man is that creature whose inherent nature is such as to raise the questions Lear asks; he is at once no more and no less than this, the creature at once vulnerable and tenacious, who must, but can, "answer with [his] uncovered body this extremity of the skies", the "ruined piece of nature" whose hand, smelling of mortality, is august, the creature whose mere life is so perfectly a value in itself that it redeems even those sorrows Lear has felt. This conception, explicit at the tragic peaks of the play, tacitly governs its whole structure. The sequence of Lear's deprivations is a sequence of revelations of his tenacity. It is to this end—revelation through suffering (rather than redemption through suffering)—that the whole play moves.

"EGREGIOUSLY AN ASS":
THE DARK SIDE OF THE MOOR.
A VIEW OF OTHELLO'S MIND

BY

ALBERT GERARD

It is through the malice of this earthly air, that only by being guilty of
Folly does mortal man in many cases arrive at the perception of sense.

HERMAN MELVILLE

There are three schools of *Othello* criticism. The most recent of these is the symbolic school, chiefly represented by G. Wilson Knight and J. I. M. Stewart, who have endeavoured to explain away the difficulties inherent in the traditional psychological interpretation of the Moor by turning the play into a mythic image of the eternal struggle between good and evil, embodied in the noble aspirations of Othello and the cunning cynicism of Iago.[1] This school arose in part as a reaction to an attitude mainly exemplified by Stoll, though already initiated by Rymer and Bridges, according to whom this tragedy ought to be treated as a purely dramatic phenomenon, created by Shakespeare for the sake of sensation and emotional effect.[2] The third school is the traditional school of naturalistic interpretation; it branches off into two main streams: the Romantic critics, from Coleridge to Bradley, take Othello at his own valuation, and seem to experience no difficulty in assuming that his greatness of mind should blind him to Iago's evil purposes; more recent students, however, tend to have a more realistic view of the Moor and to stress the flaws in his character: T. S. Eliot speaks of *bovarysme* and self-dramatization, while his homonym, G. R. Elliott, asserts that the main tragic fault in Othello is pride.[3]

One way to solve this crux of Shakespeare criticism is to use the inductive method recently advocated by R. S. Crane, and look for the "particular shaping principle (which) we must suppose to have governed Shakespeare's construction of the tragedy" through "a comparison of the material data of action, character, and motive supplied to Shakespeare by Cinthio's *novella* with what happened to these in the completed play".[4] By analysing the way Shakespeare used (or neglected) some of the data provided by Cinthio, the way he transmuted a vaudevillesque melodrama into one of the unforgettable tragedies in world literature, we may perhaps hope to gain a fresh insight into what he saw in it, why he was attracted by it and what he meant to do with it.

ERRING BARBARIAN AND CREDULOUS FOOL

This method is the one already applied by H. B. Charlton in his Clark Lectures at Cambridge, 1946–7.[5] According to Charlton, one of the most significant alterations made by Shakespeare to Cinthio's story consists in the strengthened emphasis upon the difference in manners and outlook between Desdemona and her husband. Though this motif is barely alluded to by Cinthio, Shakespeare seized on the hint and expanded it to meaningful proportions. The most conspicuous, though, admittedly, the most superficial, aspect of this difference is the complexion of the Moor. In the original tale, there is only one allusion to Othello's blackness. In the play, his black skin and thick lips are mentioned time and again. As it is obviously impossible to retain the Romantic view that Othello is not a real Negro,[6] we can safely assume that the blackness of the Moor, though it did not strike the Italian writer, appealed to the imagination of Shakespeare, who found it significant in a way that Cinthio, probably, could not even conceive.

Where is this significance to be found? I do not feel very happy about Charlton's suggestion that Shakespeare wanted to stress the physical and psychological antinomies between Othello and Desdemona because "the situation created by the marriage of a man and a woman who are widely different in race, in tradition and in customary way of life" was, at the time, "a particular problem of immediate contemporary interest". There does not seem to be any compelling evidence that such a problem was especially acute in the early seventeenth century, so that it may be worth while to try another line of interpretation.

In *The Dream of Learning*, D. G. James has made excellent use of the changes which Shakespeare introduced into the personality of Belleforest's Hamlet so as to make it plausible that this young Danish chieftain should appear to all ages as the embodiment of the man of thought, or, to use a more up-to-date expression, of the intellectual. Now, if Shakespeare turned Hamlet into an intellectual, it is equally true that he reversed the process in his handling of Othello. Not only does Iago call the Moor an "ass" and a "fool", not only does Othello concur with this unfavourable view in the last stages of the action, but the action itself is hinged upon Othello's obtuseness. This is quite palpable in III, iii, and we may be confident that if Partridge had seen *Othello* performed, he would have felt, at that moment, like jumping on to the stage and telling the Moor not to be an ass. Othello's muddle-headedness on this occasion is so extreme that critics like Rymer, Bridges and Stoll have indeed found it incredible and psychologically untrue. We might draw up a formidable list of Othello's glaring mistakes as exemplified in this scene. A few examples will suffice.

First, he must know that Iago wanted to become his lieutenant: he ought to be suspicious of his accusations against Cassio. Even though he believes, like everybody else, in Iago's honesty,[7] he must know that his Ancient has a vulgar mind, and he should not allow his imagination to be impressed by Iago's obscene pictures of Desdemona. It is also remarkable that he does not try to argue the matter with Iago; in the early stages of his evolution, he simply proclaims his faith in Desdemona's chastity, but he cannot find any sensible argument with which to counter Iago's charges. It is true that he asks for some material proof of his wife's treachery, but he never bothers to inquire about the value of the "evidence" produced by Iago. Finally, once he is convinced of Desdemona's unfaithfulness, surely the next step is to go and discuss things with her or with Cassio; this he never does. Few people would make such a hopeless mess of the situation.

Whereas Shakespeare had keyed Hamlet's intelligence to the highest possible pitch, he deliberately stressed Othello's lack of intellectual acumen, psychological insight, and even plain common sense. In the play, Othello's negroid physiognomy is simply the emblem of a difference that reaches down to the deepest levels of personality. If Hamlet is over-civilized, Othello is, in actual fact, what Iago says he is, a "barbarian" (I, iii, 363).

Othello's fundamental barbarousness becomes clear when we consider his religious beliefs. His superficial acceptance of Christianity should not blind us to his fundamental paganism. To quote again from Charlton's study, "when his innermost being is stirred to its depths", he has "gestures and phrases" which belong rather "to dim pagan cults than to any form of Christian worship". These primitive elements receive poetic and dramatic shape in the aura of black magic which at times surrounds Othello. Though Brabantio is wide of the mark when he charges the Moor with resorting to witchcraft in order to seduce his daughter, it is nevertheless true, as Mark Van Doren has said, that "an infusion of magic does tincture the play",[8] and it comes to the fore in the handkerchief episode. The magic in *Othello* results from his acquiescence in obscure savage beliefs. It is an elemental force at work in the soul of the hero. It helps to build up the Moor as a primitive type.

Here again, we wonder why Shakespeare was attracted by such a hero. A twentieth-century dramatist might be interested in the clash of two cultures, which occurs in the mind of Othello. But though this aspect of the situation is not altogether ignored by Shakespeare, his main concern lies in another direction. The fact is that this tragedy of deception, self-deception, unjustified jealousy and criminal revenge demanded such a hero.

The crime-columns of the newspapers teach us that the people who murder their wives out of jealousy are generally mental defectives. Ordinary sensible people simply cannot believe that such a crime should deserve such a punishment. It was impossible for Shakespeare to take a subnormal type as a hero for his tragedy. Tennessee Williams could do it, I suppose, but not Shakespeare, because the Renaissance tradition required that tragedy should chronicle the actions of aristocratic characters. He might have chosen as his hero some nobleman with an inflated sense of honour, but then he probably could not have made him gullible enough to swallow Iago's lies. *And it is precisely the gullibility that is essential.* Shakespeare was not intent on emulating Heywood's achievement of the year before in *A Woman Killed With Kindness*. *Othello* is not a tragedy of jealousy: it is a tragedy of *groundless* jealousy.

So, in Cinthio's tale, Shakespeare found reconciled with a maximum of credibility the requirements of Renaissance tragedy and the necessities of his own private purpose: a character with a high rank in society, with a noble heart, and with an under-developed mind. It seems therefore reasonable to suppose that if Shakespeare was interested in Othello, it was not primarily because he is a barbarian, but because this noble savage provided him with a plausible example, suitable for use within the framework of the Renaissance view of tragedy, of a psychological characteristic that makes Othello the very antithesis of Hamlet. Othello's intellectual shortcomings have not passed unnoticed by students of the play, but the importance of this feature for its total meaning has not received the attention it deserves. We may say without exaggeration that Othello's lack of intellectual power is the basic element in his character. It is a necessary pre-requisite for his predicament. It is essential to the development of the situation as Shakespeare intended it to develop. And it may also throw some light on the nature of Shakespeare's tragic inspiration.

STEPS TO SELF-KNOWLEDGE

At the beginning of the play, Othello appears as a noble figure, generous, composed, self-possessed. Besides, he is glamorously happy, both as a general and as a husband. He seems to be a fully integrated man, a great personality at peace with itself. But if we care to scrutinize this impressive and attractive façade, we find that there is a crack in it, which might be described as follows: it is the happiness of a spoilt child, not of a mature mind; it is the brittle wholeness of innocence; it is pre-conscious, pre-rational, pre-moral. Othello has not yet come to grips with the experience of inner crisis. He has had to overcome no moral obstacles. He has not yet left the chamber of maiden-thought, and is still blessedly unaware of the burden of the mystery.

Of course, the life of a general, with its tradition of obedience and authority, is never likely to give rise to acute moral crises—especially at a time when war crimes had not yet been invented. But even Othello's love affair with Desdemona, judging by his own report, seems to have developed smoothly, without painful moral searchings of any kind. Nor is there for him any heart-rending contradiction between his love and his career: Desdemona is even willing to share the austerity of his flinty couch, so that he has every reason to believe that he will be allowed to make the best of both worlds.

Yet, at the core of this monolithic content, there is at least one ominous contradiction which announces the final disintegration of his personality: the contradiction between his obvious openheartedness, honesty and self-approval, and the fact that he does not think it beneath his dignity to court and marry Desdemona secretly. This contradiction is part and parcel of Shakespeare's conscious purpose. As Allardyce Nicoll has observed, there is no such secrecy in Cinthio's tale, where, instead, the marriage occurs openly, though in the teeth of fierce parental opposition.[9]

Highly significant, too, is the fact that he does not seem to feel any remorse for this most peculiar procedure. When at last he has to face the irate Brabantio, he gives no explanation, offers no apology for his conduct. Everything in his attitude shows that he is completely unaware of infringing the *mores* of Venetian society, the ethical code of Christian behaviour, and the sophisticated conventions of polite morality. Othello quietly thinks of himself as a civilized Christian and a prominent citizen of Venice, certainly not as a barbarian (see II, iii, 170–2). He shares in Desdemona's illusion that his true visage is in his mind.

Beside the deficient understanding of the society into which he has made his way, the motif of the secret marriage then also suggests a definite lack of self-knowledge on Othello's part. His first step towards "perception of sense" about himself occurs in the middle of Act III. While still trying to resist Iago's innuendoes, Othello exclaims:

> Excellent wretch! Perdition catch my soul,
> But I do love thee! and when I love thee not,
> Chaos is come again. (III, iii, 90–2)

This word, "again", is perhaps the most unexpected word that Shakespeare could have used here. It is one of the most pregnant words in the whole tragedy. It indicates (a) Othello's dim sense that his life before he fell in love with Desdemona was in a state of chaos, in spite of the fact that he was at the time quite satisfied with it, and (b) his conviction that his love has redeemed him from chaos, has lifted him out of his former barbarousness. Such complacency shows his total obliviousness of the intricacies, the subtleties and the dangers of moral and spiritual growth. In this first anagnorisis, Othello realizes that he has lived so far in a sphere of spontaneous bravery and natural honesty, but he assumes without any further questionings that his love has gained him easy access to the sphere of moral awareness, of high spiritual existence.

In fact, he assumes that his super-ego has materialised, suddenly and without tears. Hence, of course, the impressive self-assurance of his demeanour in circumstances which would be most embarrassing to any man gifted with more accurate self-knowledge.

This first anagnorisis is soon followed by another one, in which Othello achieves some sort of recognition of what has become of him after his faith in Desdemona has been shattered. The short speech he utters then marks a new step forward in his progress to self-knowledge:

> I had been happy, if the general camp,
> Pioners and all, had tasted her sweet body,
> So I had nothing known. O, now, for ever
> Farewell the tranquil mind! farewell content!
> Farewell the plumed troop, and the big wars,
> That make ambition virtue! O, farewell!
>
> . . . .
>
> Farewell! Othello's occupation's gone! (III, iii, 345–57)

The spontaneous outcry of the first three lines results from Othello's disturbed awareness that the new world he has entered into is one of (to him) unmanageable complexity. He is now facing a new kind of chaos, and he wishes he could take refuge in an ignorance similar to his former condition of moral innocence. The pathetic childishness of this ostrich-like attitude is proportionate in its intensity to the apparent monolithic quality of his previous complacency.

What follows sounds like a *non sequitur*. Instead of this farewell to arms, we might have expected some denunciation of the deceitful aspirations that have led him to this quandary, coupled, maybe, with a resolution to seek oblivion in renewed military activity. But we may surmise that his allusion to "the general camp", reminding him of his "occupation", turns his mind away from his immediate preoccupations. The transition occurs in the line

> Farewell the tranquil mind! farewell content!

which carries ambivalent implications. The content he has now lost is not only the "absolute content" his soul enjoyed as a result of his love for Desdemona: it is also the content he had known previously, at the time when he could rejoice in his "unhoused free condition". This was the content of innocence and spontaneous adjustment to life. There is no recovering it, for, in this respect, he reached a point of no return when he glimpsed the truly chaotic nature of that state of innocence.

The fact that Othello starts talking about himself in the third person is of considerable significance. G. R. Elliott has noticed that the words have "a piercing primitive appeal: he is now simply a name".[10] Besides, in this sudden ejaculation, there is a note of childish self-pity that reminds one of the first lines of the speech. But the main point is that it marks the occurrence of a deep dichotomy in Othello's consciousness of himself. As he had discarded his former self as an emblem of "chaos", so now he discards the super-ego that he thought had emerged into actual existence as a result of his love. It is as if that man known by the name of Othello was different from the one who will be speaking henceforward. The Othello of whom he speaks is the happy husband of Desdemona, the civilized Christian, the worthy Venetian, the illusory super-ego; but he is also the noble-spirited soldier and the natural man who guesses at heaven. That man has now disappeared, and the "I" who speaks of him is truly the savage Othello, the barbarian stripped of his wishful thinking, who gives himself up to jealousy, black magic and cruelty, the man who coarsely announces that he will "chop" his wife "into messes", the man who debases his magnificent oratory by borrowing shamelessly from Iago's lecherous vocabulary.

Thus Othello, whom love had brought from pre-rational, pre-moral satisfaction and adjustment to life to moral awareness and a higher form of "content", is now taken from excessive complacency and illusory happiness to equally excessive despair and nihilism. These are his steps to self-knowledge. That they should drive him to such alternative excesses gives the measure of his lack of judgment.

No Marriage of True Minds

From the purely psychological point of view of character-analysis, critics have always found it difficult satisfactorily to account for Othello's steep downfall. That it would have been easy, as Robert Bridges wrote, for Shakespeare "to have provided a more reasonable ground for Othello's jealousy", is obvious to all reasonable readers.[11] The fact that Othello's destruction occurs through the agency of Iago has induced the critics in the Romantic tradition to make much of what Coleridge has called Iago's "superhuman art", which, of course, relieves the Moor of all responsibility and deprives the play of most of its interest on the ethical and psychological level. More searching analyses, however, have shown that Iago is far from being a devil in disguise.[12] And T. S. Eliot has exposed the Moor as a case of *bovarysme*, or "the human will to see things as they are not",[13] while Leo Kirschbaum has denounced him as "a romantic idealist, who considers human nature superior to what it actually is".[14]

For our examination of *Othello* as a study in the relationships between the intellect and the moral life, it is interesting to note that the ultimate responsibility for the fateful development of the plot rests with a flaw in Othello himself. There is no "reasonable ground" for his jealousy; or, to put it somewhat differently, Shakespeare did not chose to provide any "reasonable" ground for it. The true motive, we may safely deduce, must be unreasonable. Yet, I find it difficult to agree that the Moor "considers human nature superior to what it actually is": this may be true of his opinion of Iago, but Desdemona is really the emblem of purity and trustworthiness that he initially thought her to be. Nor can we justifiably speak of his "*will* to see things as they are not" (though these words might actually fit Desdemona); in his confusion and perplexity there is no opportunity for his will to exert itself in any direction. The basic element that permits Othello's destiny to evolve the way it does is his utter *inability* to grasp the actual. If we want to locate with any accuracy the psychological origin of what F. R. Leavis has called his "readiness to respond" to Iago's fiendish suggestions, we cannot escape the conclusion that his gullibility makes manifest his lack of rationality, of psychological insight and of mere common sense, and that it is a necessary product of his undeveloped mind.

Othello has to choose between trusting Iago and trusting Desdemona. This is the heart of the matter, put in the simplest possible terms. The question, then, is: why does he rate Iago's honesty higher than Desdemona's? If it is admitted that Iago is not a symbol of devilish skill in evil-doing, but a mere fallible villain, the true answer can only be that Othello does not know his own wife.

More than a century of sentimental criticism based on the Romantic view of Othello as the trustful, chivalrous and sublime lover, has blurred our perception of his feeling for Desdemona. The quality of his "love" has recently been gone into with unprecedented thoroughness by G. R. Elliott, who points out that the Moor's speech to the Duke and Senators (I, iii) shows that "his affection for her, though fixed and true, is comparatively superficial".[15] Othello sounds, indeed, curiously detached about Desdemona. His love is clearly subordinated, at that moment, to his soldierly pride. If he asks the Duke to let her go to Cyprus with him, it is because *she* wants it, it is "to be free and bounteous to her mind". In the juxtaposition of Desdemona's and Othello's speeches about this, there is an uncomfortable suggestion that his love is not at all equal to hers, who "did love the Moor to live with him", and that he is not interested in her as we feel he ought to be. At a later stage the same self-centredness colours his vision of Desdemona as the vital source of his soul's life and happiness: his main concern lies with the "joy" (II, i, 186), the "absolute content" (II, i, 193), the salvation (III, iii, 90–1) of his own soul, not with Desdemona as a woman in love, a human person. It lies with *his* love and the changes his love has wrought in him, rather than with the object of his love. It is not surprising, then, that he should know so little about his wife's inner life as to believe the charges raised by Iago.

On the other hand, his attitude to Desdemona is truly one of idealization, but in a very limited, one might even say philosophical, sense. Coleridge wrote that "Othello does not kill Desdemona in jealousy, but in the belief that she, his angel, had fallen from the heaven of her native innocence".[16] But Coleridge failed to stress the most important point, which is that this belief is mistaken. Desdemona is *not* "impure and worthless", she has *not* fallen from the heaven of her native innocence. Othello is unable to recognize this, and his failure is thus primarily an intellectual failure.

His attitude to Desdemona is different from that of the "romantic idealist" who endows his girl with qualities which she does not possess. Desdemona does have all the qualities that her husband expects to find in her. What matters to him, however, is not Desdemona as she is, but Desdemona as a symbol, or, in other words, it is his vision of Desdemona.

In his *Essay on Man*, Ernst Cassirer has the following remark about the working of the primitive mind:

In primitive thought, it is still very difficult to differentiate between the two spheres of being and meaning. They are constantly being confused: a symbol is looked upon as if it were endowed with magical or metaphysical powers.[17]

That is just what has happened to Othello: in Desdemona he has failed to differentiate between the human being and the angelic symbol. Or rather, he has overlooked the woman in his preoccupation with the angel. She is to him merely the emblem of his highest ideal, and their marriage is merely the ritual of his admission into her native world, into her spiritual sphere of values. Because he is identifying "the two spheres of being and meaning", he is possessed by the feeling that neither these values nor his accession to them have any actual existence outside her: his lack of psychological insight is only matched by his lack of rational power.

The Neo-Platonic conceit that the lover's heart and soul have their dwelling in the person of the beloved is used by Othello in a poignantly literal sense (IV, ii, 57–60). If she fails him, everything fails him. If she is not pure, then purity does not exist. If she is not true to his ideal, that means that his ideal is an illusion. If it can be established that she does not belong to that world in which he sees her enshrined, that means that there is no such world. She becomes completely and explicitly identified with all higher spiritual values when he says:

> If she be false, O! then heaven mocks itself!   (III, iii, 278)

Hence the apocalyptic quality of his nihilism and despair.

The fundamental tragic fault in the Moor can therefore be said to lie in the shortcomings of his intellect. His moral balance is without any rational foundation. He is entirely devoid of the capacity for abstraction. He fails to make the right distinction between the sphere of meaning, of the abstract, the ideal, the universal, and the sphere of being, of the concrete, the actual, the singular.

When Othello is finally made to see the truth, he recognizes the utter lack of wisdom (v, ii, 344) which is the mainspring of his tragedy, and, in the final anagnorisis, he sees himself for what he is: a "fool" (v, ii, 323). The full import of the story is made clear in Othello's last speech, which is so seldom given the attention it merits that it may be well to quote it at some length:

> I pray you, in your letters,
> When you shall these unlucky deeds relate,
> Speak of me as I am; nothing extenuate,
> Nor set down aught in malice: then, must you speak
> Of one that loved not wisely but too well;
> Of one not easily jealous, but being wrought
> Perplex'd in the extreme; of one whose hand,
> Like the base Indian, threw a pearl away
> Richer than all his tribe; of one whose subdued eyes,
> Albeit unused to the melting mood,
> Drop tears as fast as the Arabian trees
> Their medicinal gum. Set you down this;
> And say besides, that in Aleppo once,
> Where a malignant and a turban'd Turk
> Beat a Venetian and traduced the state,
> I took by the throat the circumcised dog,
> And smote him, thus.   (*Stabs himself*)   (v, ii, 340–56)

One may find it strange that Shakespeare should have introduced at the end of Othello's last speech this apparently irrelevant allusion to a trivial incident in the course of which the Moor killed a Turk who had insulted Venice. But if we care to investigate the allegorical potentialities of the speech, we find that it is not a mere fit of oratorical self-dramatization: it clarifies the meaning of the play as a whole. There is a link between the pearl, the Venetian and Desdemona: taken together, they are an emblem of beauty, moral virtue, spiritual richness and civilized refinement. And there is a link between the "base Indian", the "malignant Turk" and Othello himself: all three are barbarians: all three have shown themselves unaware of the true value and dignity of what lay within their reach. Othello has thrown his pearl away, like the Indian. In so doing, he has insulted, like the Turk, everything that Venice and Desdemona stand for. As the Turk "traduced the State", so did Othello misrepresent to himself that heaven of which Desdemona was the sensuous image.

S. L. Bethell has left us in no doubt that the manner of Othello's death was intended by Shakespeare as an indication that the hero is doomed to eternal damnation.[18] Such a view provides us with a suitable climax for this tragedy. Othello has attained full consciousness of his barbarian nature; yet, even that ultimate flash of awareness does not lift him up above his true self. He remains a barbarian to the very end, and condemns his own soul to the everlasting torments of hell in obeying the same primitive sense of rough-handed justice that had formerly prompted him to kill Desdemona: it is a natural culmination to what a Swiss critic has aptly called "eine Tragödie der Verirrung".[19]

NOTES

1. G. Wilson Knight, 'The *Othello* Music' in *The Wheel of Fire* (1930; fourth edition, 1949). J. I. M. Stewart, *Character and Motive in Shakespeare* (1949).

2. For a close discussion of the views of Rymer, Bridges and Stoll, cf. Stewart, *op. cit.*

3. T. S. Eliot, 'Shakespeare and the Stoicism of Seneca', in *Selected Essays* (1932); G. R. Elliott, *Flaming Minister. A Study of Othello* (Duke University Press, Durham, 1953).

4. R. S. Crane, *The Languages of Criticism and the Structure of Poetry* (Toronto, 1953), p. 147. The quotations are taken from a discussion of R. B. Heilman's method in his 'More Fair than Black: Light and Dark in *Othello*', *Essays in Criticism*, I (1951), 315–35.

5. H. B. Charlton, 'Othello', in *Shakespearian Tragedy* (Cambridge, 1948).

6. Cf. Coleridge, *Lectures and Notes on Shakespere and Other English Poets* (1904), p. 386.

7. Levin L. Schucking, in *Shakespeare und der Tragödienstil seiner Zeit* (Bern, 1947) considers Othello's belief in Iago's honesty as "eine der Hauptschwächen in der Konstruktion der Fabel", for, he says "es ist höchst unwahrscheinlich, dasz Othello nach so langem Zusammenleben im Kriegsdienst sich derart über den bösartigen Character seines Fahnrichs im unklaren geblieben sein sollte" (p. 68). The general consensus about Iago's honesty, carefully stressed by Shakespeare, should nullify this particular criticism.

8. Mark Van Doren, *Shakespeare* (New York, 1953), p. 196.

9. Allardyce Nicoll, *Shakespeare* (1952), p. 144.

10. G. R. Elliott, *op. cit.* p. 130, n. 30.

11. R. Bridges, 'The Influence of the Audience on Shakespeare's Drama' in *Collected Essays*, I (1927).

12. Cf. G. R. Elliott, *op. cit. passim*; J. I. M. Stewart, *op. cit.* p. 103; and F. R. Leavis, 'Diabolic Intellect and the Noble Hero', in *The Common Pursuit* (1952), p. 140.

13. T. S. Eliot, *op. cit.*

14. In *ELH*, December 1944 (quoted by J. I. M. Stewart, *op. cit.* p. 104).

15. G. R. Elliott, *op. cit.* p. 34.

16. Coleridge, *op. cit.* pp. 393 and 529.

17. E. Cassirer, *An Essay on Man* (New Haven, 1944), p. 57.

18. S. L. Bethell, 'Shakespeare's Imagery: The Diabolic Images in *Othello*', *Shakespeare Survey*, 5 (1952), 62–80.

19. R. Fricker, *Kontrast und Polarität in den Charakterbildern Shakespeares* (Bern, 1951).

SHAKESPEARE IN SCHOOLS

BY

J. H. WALTER

The teaching of Shakespeare's plays in the grammar school, particularly in forms taking courses leading to the General Certificate of Education Examination, Ordinary Level, has its critics: some allege unsympathetic, biased and insensitive treatment of the plays; others assert that the plays should not be in the curriculum at all, on the grounds that not only are the classroom methods used unsuitable, but that the language and conventions of the plays themselves are too difficult for immature minds to grasp. All contend that irreparable harm is being done.

Why, in fact, are Shakespeare's plays included in the curriculum?

Education, properly conceived, demands not only the acquiring of skills, the assimilation of knowledge, the training of thought processes, but the leading of pupils to respond to works of art and thereby to increase and refine their understanding and enjoyment of artistic achievement. English Literature is the only subject, in schools where there is no classics side, that can consistently give this particular training. Music, Painting and Drawing are normally treated in a different way, they are more dependent on special skills and so are less accessible to children. Drama, even more than poetry, has an intimate and immediate appeal to children: in their first years at school it can fulfil their instincts for make-believe; and later in the adolescent awareness of emotions it is complementary to their needs. Drama, then, is the most appropriate of all the arts to introduce into the classroom. Since Shakespeare in thought, feeling and language has range, form and texture beyond all other English writers, since he is the most comprehensive and universal of them all, and since he is in the centre of English literary tradition, it is reasonable to suppose that his plays would be included judiciously in any such curriculum.

Such a straightforward statement ignores the obstacles with which the English teacher is faced, and which, in a large measure, impose the limitations on his work which give rise to criticisms. Since candidates for the Certificate Examination can offer from one to eight (or nine) selected subjects, and since the pass mark is higher than that of the examination it displaced, the value of English Literature has become relative to the wishes or needs of the individual pupil: it is a subject chosen if one has a flair for that sort of thing, or if one wishes to specialize in Arts subjects. Consequently there has appeared a tendency on the part of some pupils to regard it as having only esoteric value. Some examiners consider there is evidence that this attitude, as far as Shakespeare's plays are concerned, is encouraged by teachers who are unduly influenced by the partial truths of particular theorists: the neo-rhetoricians, the imagists, the archetypists, the realists and the symbolists.

Again, the disposition of the timetable, the limited lesson time, the physical nature of the classroom, lead inevitably to the breaking down of a play into fragments. In the past teachers did not always avoid using the various portions of the play as exercises in paraphrase, etymology, grammar, or as poetry unrelated to the drama as a whole, so that at best the play was hardly equal to the sum of its parts. Some critics believe that this practice has not entirely disappeared. The difficulty, in short, is to see the play as a play and to see it whole.

Yet these difficulties have not proved insuperable. Many a grammar school pupil can testify to the rich field of pleasure opened for him by the study of Shakespeare at school. Moreover, the excellent support for professional Shakespeare productions comes in the main from present and past grammar school pupils. It is not to be supposed that these audiences would have been greater or more enthusiastic if Shakespeare's plays had been reserved for study at the university.

There is room for improvement. If the classroom is unavoidable, those responsible for building a school might well allow for, say, two rooms a little larger than the normal classroom, where a small apron stage or an amphitheatre space could be contrived. Allowances for flexibility in grouping have been embodied in new modern and primary schools, but nothing much in this kind has been made available to grammar schools.

The master himself needs to have his aims and methods clearly in view. Here, following the work of pioneers such as Caldwell Cook, there has been growing up a technique in which the master handles the play with its essential unity and the idea of production foremost in his mind. Pupils consistently trained in such methods through the school can use them with advantage in the examination year. Indeed, the intensive preliminary study of the text of a play necessary for production will admirably prepare a pupil for the General Certificate of Education Ordinary Level examination papers. An excellent little book *Shakespeare and the Classroom* (1954), compiled by A. K. Hudson for the Society for Teachers of English, describes the method in detail with practical examples, stressing always that the work on a play should be stage-centred.

It is necessary, however, that examiners also should see that the questions set are consistent with teaching practice; and it is pleasant to record that some papers set recently have shown a clear appreciation of these trends in schools. This may well lead to modification in the school editions of Shakespeare, to the shedding of many annotations and the introduction of dramatic pointers. Some attempts have already been made, but the rightly balanced edition has yet to appear.

The appropriate editions of the plays, it is sometimes alleged, are too costly, particularly with the variation in plays set for examinations. Difficulties of this kind could be reduced if the Examining Boards allowed schools a free choice of play or plays for examination, or, alternatively, prescribed permanently a large number of plays from which the selection could be made. This would also have the very great advantage of allowing a school to have a carefully planned, fixed and progressive course in Shakespeare's plays throughout its main forms with editions appropriate to the forms. There would be no necessity for stocks of plays not set to be in the stockroom, nor for them to be used unsuitably in lower forms.

These are general and material things; the teacher and the pupil are the essential particulars. The importance of the teacher is incalculable. He may by his personality, or by his prowess in sport, or by something quite irrelevant to teaching rouse a child's interest in the subject he teaches. There are the elements of blind discipleship in this, but clearly it is unpredictable, and should best be regarded as a chance emotional aid. Alternatively, dislike of a teacher can so easily lead to a dislike of his subject. Strictly the heart of the matter is expressed in a graceless playground comment on a member of staff, "He's a rotten twerp, but gosh, he knows his stuff!" In short, the teacher should overcome any defect in his personality, not only by sensitive perception and sheer intellection, but by keeping abreast of new information on his subject.

It is important, therefore, that he should have available the results of recent research and also that he should be stimulated by seeing experiments in classroom techniques. The latter can perhaps best be done by Ministry of Education courses, but it would seem preferable that the courses should be devised in co-operation with lecturers in post-graduate training departments and with practising teachers. Such a course might well include a symposium, later to be published and circulated possibly in summarized form. The presence of a professional producer of standing at such a meeting might be most helpful. At present few schools are equipped with television receiving sets, but in the future television programmes in which producers and critics demonstrate their methods with illustrative scenes from Shakespeare's plays could have great possibilities.

As far as recent Shakespearian research is concerned there are two aspects to be considered; the real value of any particular piece of research and access to it. The philosophies of art are many and confusing, and belief in the value of art ranges from the confidence of O'Shaughnessy's ode to Thomas Mann's fears that the writer may "enchant a lost world...and never give it even the shadow of a saving truth to grasp". Within a larger philosophy of art the clarification of dramatic theory is a necessary preliminary to the evaluation of new writing on Shakespeare. Thus the definition of art put forward by S. Langer, *Feeling and Form* (1953) and the stimulating and satisfying sections of the work devoted to drama could readily be the basis for authoritative lectures followed by discussion. A comprehensive survey of recent research work on Shakespeare in appropriate sections, and the reading of papers, with a forum for discussion, could be treated similarly, not simply as courses of lectures but as some kind of meetings more in the nature of seminars. Possibly the best way to arrange for this would be the organization of conferences at Stratford, or at University centres elsewhere, for teachers, lecturers in Training Departments, members of the Inspectorate, to meet university teachers qualified in the matters under consideration. Again, the publication in summary form of the matters raised would be helpful. Indeed, this might be included in a bulletin or news letter incorporating bibliographical notes, theatre and production notes and other more general Shakespearian topics than were touched on at the conference. Such conferences might be perhaps the more effective if held biennially, though the bulletin could be issued annually. The timing is also important, if they could be held at Stratford during the "season", that would be a further inducement to teachers to attend.

The possibility of conferences for VIth formers should not be overlooked. The conferences could be made perhaps more relevant to their studies, but they would encourage in schools a leavening body of informed opinion.

With all this there is yet a limit to what can be achieved in schools, the obstacles do impose restrictions beyond which it is unreasonable to expect progress. Very few schoolchildren will see the professional performance of a Shakespeare play more than once in their school life, and late on at that, and some will not see one at all, in spite of the endeavours of their teachers. Thus, the play as a whole will be conceived in the imagination unsupported by the theatre. It will be an inner vision, sometimes shadowy and imperfect, often fleeting and intermittent, yet a complex built up out of what the memory holds of persons and places linked together transcending space and time. Wholeness of view cannot be expected of all plays, for children, like adults, find difficulty in seeing things whole; but if one or two plays are thus observed, that is enough. Two such conceptions from schooldays have remained vividly in the mind of the present writer, of

Hamlet and the *Tempest*; they exist amiably alongside later interpretations of stage productions, and are at least as valid.

The difficulty of Shakespeare's plays has been raised as an objection. There is perhaps some confusion of thought here. *Richard II*, a play frequently set for Ordinary Level, is extremely difficult to comprehend as a work of art, though not as a narrative. *Hamlet*, although its verbal difficulties and metaphysical infusion are well known, has a striking appeal to adolescents. The point is that the wholeness of the impression is not absolute and can deepen and refine itself in later years; but it is worth while accepting the challenge of a play such as *Hamlet*, knowing that appreciation will be incomplete, in preference to a play like *Richard II*, with its remote symbolism.

Other rewards too may be expected. Interpretation for production needs concentrated study of the text. A child will begin to perceive whether a word is discursive, figurative, symbolic or incantatory, and will become aware of the purposive movement of the action. He will begin to distinguish between enjoyment and amusement in drama. He will also gain knowledge of some things that are adjuncts to the play as a whole; human motives, memorable poetry and unforgettable characters. And if on occasions he quotes the well-known words of a famous critic, it may charitably be granted that to him they have all the freshness of an original truth.

Much of the adverse comment springs from a wrong premise. Criticism, too, is an art and does not spring to birth fully armed, it grows, it is deceived; but the critics who shrink from its adolescent crudities are as bad as those who shrink like sensitive plants from the analysis of any work of art.

Most grammar school pupils leave at the age of sixteen; if the necessary groundwork to the appreciation of Shakespeare's plays has not been completed by then only rarely will an individual make the necessary effort subsequently. He will miss therefore some of the greatest works of art we possess; he will lose a significant part of his cultural heritage. On the other hand if he works in this way with Shakespeare's plays he will provide himself with armour against the cheap, the shoddy and the sensational posing everywhere as art; he will comprehend that a work of art contains, as Whistler said on a memorable occasion, "the experience of a lifetime", and, one might add, the experience of a civilization

SHAKESPEARE FESTIVAL, TORONTO, CANADA

BY

EARLE GREY

Some years ago an experiment in producing Shakespeare's plays was tried by the Earle Grey Shakespeare Company in the spacious grounds of Trinity College, University of Toronto. The completion of the first eight years of the annual open-air Shakespeare Festival in Toronto, Canada, seems to be as good a time as any to relate how this company came into being, what were its principles, and how far these latter have been followed.

It is a commonplace that chance plays a great part in any enterprise. So it was with the Festival. During the war years chance placed us in Toronto. Strangers in the city, my wife (Mary Godwin) and I spent one morning exploring its University grounds, which lie in its heart. Among the many fine buildings there we were especially attracted towards one in particular. Built of stone, in early Jacobean style, it closely resembled an English college. It was Trinity College, founded some ninety years before by Bishop Strachan, an Anglican.

Its very beautiful and impressive buildings were ranged around three sides of a noble quadrangle. The open side to the north, not yet built upon, was bounded by a broad terrace whose centre steps led down to a turfed lower level. It was a ready-made stage, ideal for open-air Shakespeare. Such was the thought which sprang into our minds. Some years were to pass before that thought could be put into action.

The conclusion of the war and the consequent possibility of resuming our usual theatrical activities made us resolve to try and materialize our thought. The Provost of Trinity College, R. S. K. Seeley, was whole-heartedly in favour of the project and some trial performances of several of the plays were arranged. These were so well received that in 1949 we resolved to launch our first Shakespeare Festival. It would be three weeks in length and three plays would be presented: *As You Like It*; *A Midsummer Night's Dream*; *Twelfth Night*.

A decision being made, it was plainly essential to go into ways and means. What were our assets and liabilities? Our assets were, first, the plays themselves; secondly, considerable enthusiasm tempered by caution; thirdly, some experience and knowledge in the acting and direction of the plays; and lastly, the fact that the field was at that time completely free for us to roam at will. And our liabilities? Limited financial resources, no scenery, costumes, properties or lighting. Most disquieting of all, hardly any suitable actors.

It was evident that we had to make up our minds on the two vital problems of artistic and financial policy. Convinced that art should always precede, not follow, finance, we sat down to decide fundamental artistic principles—that is to say, the manner in which we would try to act the plays. On this point we had no doubt. We would try to do them as they were done in Shakespeare's own day.

This did not mean any 'ye olde Elizabethan' nonsense. What it did mean—and still does—was that the plays would be interpreted as far as possible from the viewpoint of a man in Elizabethan times. The director and his actors would try to see the plays as they were seen by Shakespeare's own company. As far as possible twentieth-century notions would not be permitted. Stunts, fashionable slants, Freudian implications, and silly-clever ideas which are the bane of the contemporary Shakespeare theatre would be ruled out. Arrogant directors would not provide crutches to help the aged and halting playwright in his shamble to oblivion. The accumulation of varnish and the over-painting of centuries would be stripped off and the picture shown as Shakespeare's brush had left it. Our watchword would be 'Back to Shakespeare'.

We were not foolish enough to imagine that we could be completely successful in our aim. No living person knows *exactly* how audiences in Shakespeare's time thought or how his actors performed. At the best, all we could hope for would be a reasonable approximation. We also knew that inevitably modern thought would seep in and modify our productions, for no man can entirely escape his own day. But our resolution would be to try and give our audience what *Shakespeare* had in mind when he wrote, and not some distortion or misconception based on modern ideas.

So much for our basic principle. The next thing was how to put it into action. We took it for granted that the only sensible manner in which to play Shakespeare was simply and naturally, scene following scene without break in continuity except for an interval or two in deference to the frailty of present-day audiences. There would be no attempt at realistic scenery and we would try and get actors with good speaking voices and train them to speak their lines with real appreciation of their meaning, literally and emotionally. The necessity for these latter elementary requirements needs no explanation to anyone who has heard the careless and slipshod delivery of the average actor. We would assume that our audience was witnessing each play *for the first time* without any previous acquaintance. Therefore we would stress the plot structure and clearly identify each character upon its first appearance. We would encourage our actors to study the political and social background of Shakespeare's time to help them in the understanding of the characters they were to represent. Our author having brilliantly created real people in his plays, it would be our preoccupation to see that we presented real people on our stage.

We knew that there was nothing revolutionary or even particularly novel in our general approach. But we believed that if we put our theories into practice the result would be productions of honesty, vitality and quality.

We were now at the point where we had decided how to present the plays, and we had found a stage at Trinity College upon which to perform them. Our next task was to find actors—but where were they to come from? For a generation Toronto had been practically theatreless. Twenty years previously the double impact of the Talkies and the Great Depression of the paralysed 1930's had done to death all but one of Toronto's many live theatres. A generation had arisen which knew not footlights. The outlook was bleak, the situation desperate. Of course, that is always the moment in which solutions are found—simply because they must be found. We argued that in a city as large as Toronto there must be actors somewhere. We would organize a search party. So we combed the hedges, dredged the ditches, tramped the highways in pursuit of performers. Slowly they were assembled; a few old professional actors glad to smell greasepaint once more; reasonably experienced members of Little Theatre groups; and young persons who in unquenchable hope had used their post-war gratuities in studying the drama in London or New York and had come back home to Toronto.

We rehearsed by night, it being impossible to assemble the Company at any other time because so many of its members had bread and butter commitments by day. Except for ourselves, few had had any experience in playing Shakespeare, a handicap we accepted as an asset because there would be no preconceived notions to battle. There was a clean canvas upon which to work.

We now turned to the physical presentation of the plays—scenery, lights, costumes and properties. On our large and open stage some sort of scenery was required in order to focus the attention of the audience and hide actors awaiting entrance cues. But it would have to be of the barest possible nature and strictly a background. (Later we somewhat modified this rather austere creed.) And as we would play by night, there would have to be lighting. The idea of daytime playing was abandoned after one experiment. The fierce summer sun was too much for our patrons, who fled to the shade of distant trees from which little could be seen and nothing heard. Costumes would have to be hired until we could set up facilities to make them. Rich and colourful costumes, properly designed and executed, we regarded as very important. But it was some years before we found a satisfactory solution to our wardrobe problem. In the meantime we hired the best that could be obtained.

Having set all these considerations in train it was now time to deal with the question of money. How was the Festival to be financed? Our cash in hand was meagre, hardly more indeed than would serve to prime the pump. The question to be decided was: should we make that little do, or should we follow what seems to be the usual practice of making a splash with borrowed cash? Our decision was to make do with what we had. If we could not immediately pay for a thing we would do without it. We would be solvent right from the beginning—and solvent we have remained ever since. Maybe this was not in accordance with modern business methods, but it is what we did and we have never regretted it.

And so in 1949, the Festival was launched. It had many shortcomings, it was ill-equipped, but it floated. Something had been done, the banner of Shakespeare had been displayed, the cry of trumpets and the roll of drums, though muted, were heard distinctly. The march of the first Shakespeare Festival in Canada had begun.

Since that day, now eight years ago, the story is one of steady improvement. Artistically, technically and financially, the Festival has gone forward. It now runs five weeks, and could indeed run longer, if College commitments permitted longer tenancy. It has greatly helped to develop the playing of Elizabethan music in Toronto, for three concerts of the music which Shakespeare must have heard have been added to the annual programme. These are given in the open air and are free to playgoers. Musicians of international reputation play and sing to viol, lute and recorder.

We are particularly proud of our costumes, for the 'eye must be fed' and we have always been careful to dress our players as sumptuously as possible. For some years this was something of a problem, but eventually it was handsomely solved. Mabel Letchford, an experienced costumier from Hollywood, became interested in the Festival. From that moment our costume concerns disappeared. Dress after dress has come from under her hands and the Festival now owns a wardrobe second to none.

Two years ago we were compelled to move from the terrace which had long been our stage. The College wished to build there some badly needed residences. We had the alternative of suspending operations for at least a year or moving to a smaller and less convenient site on the west side of the quadrangle. A break in continuity being unthinkable we decided to transfer to the west terrace. At first view this did not seem possible. The terrace was shallow and was guarded by a heavy stone balustrade four feet high. For the moment our hearts sank. But, as usual, what seemed to be a handicap proved to be an advantage. We designed an entirely new stage, based upon that probably in use in Shakespeare's Globe Theatre. Built upon two levels, it has a forestage twenty feet wide by ten deep, with steps leading down to quadrangle level at both ends. Three broad shallow steps lead from this forestage to the upper stage, which has two long entrance ramps running from each side down to terrace level. The upper stage has a curtained 'study' eighteen feet wide and seven and a half feet deep with a wide archway at its back, and a trap-door centre. To right and left of the upper stage are practicable windows. Altogether there are ten entrances to our stage. A fortunately placed tree, growing in the centre of our audience, provides support for excellent frontal lighting. Our stage, which equals in almost all respects that for which Shakespeare designed his plays, is the only one of its kind in Canada.

Since its inception, the Festival Company has toured the schools and colleges of Ontario each autumn with one of its summer plays. Thousands of enthusiastic students benefit in their studies by these tours. We travel by car, bus or railway as circumstances require, set up our simple scenery on the local stage, play our show and depart to the next engagement. These tours are regarded as a most important adjunct to our work as they help to create the audience of the future.

There is, of course, still much to do. Mistakes have been made and opportunities not fully grasped, inevitable happenings in the dust and heat of the arena. But we are confident that our feet are upon the right road, and we are happy in the knowledge that we have a share in the revival of the living theatre in Canada.

INTERNATIONAL NOTES

A selection has been made from the reports received from our correspondents, those which present material of a particularly interesting kind being printed wholly or largely in their entirety. It should be emphasized that the choice of countries to be thus represented has depended on the nature of the information presented in the reports, not upon either the importance of the countries concerned or upon the character of the reports themselves.

Australia

There have been no notable professional productions of Shakespeare's plays by Australian companies since the disbanding of John Alden's company in 1953 (vol. 6), and Michael Langham's presentation of *Richard III* (vol. 7). This is not to disparage the work of the 'Little' Theatres in all the capital cities and the efforts of small towns such as Swan Hill, Victoria; yet it has to be understood that these are amateur productions with sometimes a professional producer and a professional radio actor in the lead, but always suffering from under-rehearsal and lack of stage equipment and of an adequate wardrobe.

To commemorate the visit of Her Majesty the Queen in 1954 an Australian Elizabethan Theatre Trust has been established to present annual sessions of drama, opera and ballet in Australia's six state capitals. Hugh Hunt, formerly of the Bristol and London Old Vic Companies, is the Executive Officer, and his first Australian Company will include *Twelfth Night* in its repertoire (1956).

ERNEST W. BURBRIDGE

Belgium

The 1955–6 Season (September–July) has offered very little in the field of Shakespearian productions.

For the Flemish part only one company, 'Het Reizend Volkstheater' (Popular Touring Theatre), has repeated its success of the previous seasons with *De Koopman van Venetie* (*The Merchant of Venice*) and *Driekoningenavond* (*Twelfth Night*) in the translation of L. A. J. Burgersdyk and produced by Rik Jacobs. A series of annual open-air performances in the courtyard of Rubens-house in Antwerp, will include *De Getemde Feeks* (*The Taming of the Shrew*), produced by Rik Jacobs.

The 'Théâtre National de Belgique' is responsible for the season's only contribution in the French-Belgian theatre, with the production of *Troilus and Cressida*, the first time this play has ever been produced in Belgium. The French adaptation was by Jean Le Paillot, production by Johan De Meester, known in Belgium for his work with 'Het Vlaamse Volkstoneel' (1924–7), settings and costumes by Denis Martin. The production, presented in 'Spacemen' and 'Martian' style, with a kind of 'concrete' music suggesting modern and future warfare, did not add to the beauty and dramatic integrity of the play.

The death of Robert De Smet (Romain Sanvic) is a great loss to Belgian theatre culture. Belgium has lost a true Shakespearian scholar, whose translations are probably the best renderings in French of the original text. His book *Le Théâtre Elisabethain* was published shortly after his death.   M. DE GRUYTER

Brazil

Pericles Eugenio da Silva Ramos has translated *Hamlet*, presented in a parallel text, with an introduction and elucidative notes. It is the most meticulous and complete translation of the play in the Portuguese language.

A start has been made with the publication of the complete works translated by Carlos Alberto Nunes.

EUGENIO GOMES

Bulgaria

The greatest success of the season has been *Romeo and Juliet* at the National Theatre in a new translation by the poet Nikolai Liliev. The performance was interesting mainly for an unusual interpretation of the Nurse by Olga Kircheva as a lively, energetic, sharp-witted little woman—a somewhat uneven performance, but extremely moving. A number of provincial theatres have followed suit with productions of their own, and *The Comedy of Errors* has also been given in Sofia. L. Ognyanov's new translation of *Hamlet*—the eighteenth version in Bulgarian—has just been published.

M. MINCOFF

Canada

In 1955 Canada decided to build a permanent theatre for the presentation of Shakespeare's plays. The Stratford (Ontario) Shakespeare Festival has, in three years, established itself so firmly that it at last can graduate from the elaborate tent where it was born.

The new theatre will be built according to the general principles of the Elizabethan stage, and will closely duplicate the stage already in use in the tent. Both Tyrone Guthrie and Tanya Moiseiwitsch, who designed the original, have been consulted about the new designs, and the building should be ready for the 1957 season.

The place which the Stratford Festival now takes in the life of Canada was shown this year by the disputes which ranged in newspapers and in the Canadian Broadcasting Corporation's various programmes over the choice of *The Merchant of Venice* as one of the two festival plays. The anti-Semitism of the play was decried by several vocal groups and was equally vigorously defended on artistic grounds by others no less vocal. For the morality of art to become a national question is indeed a step forward in this as yet pioneer country.

The performance of *The Merchant of Venice* was an interesting one, notable mainly for the tremendous acting of Frederick Valk in the part of Shylock. Playing it sincerely and straight he yet showed his connexion with the theatre of a nearly bygone age where the star actor swept all before him. A standing ovation on the first night showed the audience's delight. The rest of the production was good, as any production by Tyrone Guthrie is apt to be, though several critics lamented, and rightly, the lack of poetry in the piece, the Lorenzo-Jessica scene at Belmont being perfunctory and flat.

The second production of the Festival was *Julius Caesar*, directed by Michael Langham, who is to succeed Tyrone Guthrie as the director of the whole festival in 1956. This was a swirling, muscular production with waving banners, clamorous mobs and superb costumes by Tanya Moiseiwitsch. But Lorne Green as Brutus was dull, and Lloyd Bochner, who did a very good television performance of *Hamlet* during the winter, was too overwrought as Cassius. Robert Christie caricatured Caesar and the women were uniformly uninspired. This production brought a good deal of criticism of the festival director Tyrone Guthrie. Several critics maintained that the time had come for less *corps de ballet* performances and more productions which would concentrate on the characterization and on the poetry of Shakespeare.

Frederick Valk stayed on in Canada after the summer season to open the regular winter season of repertory at the Crest Theatre in Toronto as Othello. As was to be expected, the performance was a great success and it ran for six weeks to packed houses, despite some complaint that Valk was occasionally so moved in his passion as to be almost incoherent.

Another group of actors from the Stratford Festival went on tour through the mid-western United States and the west of Canada with *Macbeth*. Under the direction of Douglas Campbell, an English actor who now makes Canada his home, this troupe has had great success. Douglas Campbell plays Macbeth, and Frances Hyland, who has come home to Canada after her success in London's West End, played Lady Macbeth. Unfortunately, her health broke down, but the tour triumphantly continued with Anne Casson, Campbell's wife, in the role.

What with these delights and the Earle Grey players' offering in the quadrangle of Trinity College, Toronto, during the summer, Canada had a thoroughly successful Shakespeare year.

ARNOLD EDINBOROUGH

Czechoslovakia

Last year attention was drawn to Shakespeare almost officially: Erik Adolf Saudek, whose translations of Shakespeare are now widely played and are issued simultaneously by three publishing houses, was awarded the State Prize of Klement Gottwald, while the Budějovice production of *Hamlet* was selected for performance in Prague after a nation-wide competition. This production was enthusiastically welcomed by the Prague public; *Hamlet* had not been staged professionally in the capital for several years.

Recently Otakar Vočadlo, who is tireless in his efforts to spread knowledge of Shakespeare, has succeeded in discovering the long-lost translation of the *Sonnets* by one of the foremost Czech poets, Jaroslav Vrchlický (1853–1912). This, published in a limited edition, was sold out immediately upon its appearance. Another three Shakespearian books were also quickly sold out—Jaroslav Pokorný's Marxist manual *Shakespeare's Theatre and Shakespeare's Age*, Jan Vladislav's complete translation of the *Sonnets*, and the first volume of Shakespeare's selected works in E. A. Saudek's translations.

Professional productions included *Twelfth Night* (in 9 theatres), *A Midsummer Night's Dream* (8), *Romeo and Juliet* (6), *The Merry Wives of Windsor* (5), *The Taming of the Shrew* (4), *The Merchant of Venice* (4), *Othello* (3), *The Comedy of Errors* (2), *Two Gentlemen of Verona* (2), *Hamlet* (1), *As You Like It* (1), *Much Ado About Nothing* (1) and *Timon of Athens* (1). Plzeň produced this year *Much Ado* in a new translation by Aloys Skoumal.

BŘETISLAV HODEK

East Africa

The twenty-third anniversary of the establishment of the East African Shakespeare Festivals was marked by radio broadcasts and by a stage presentation of *Much Ado About Nothing* in the Kenya National Theatre.

A semi-permanent setting was used for the production. This occupied the full stage and had a rostrum with steps giving central, up-stage, entrances and exits. The rostrum was also used for small inset scenes when the permanent setting was screened with drapes: it also became the altar for the church scene. Scene to scene action was continuous with only one interval. The playing time, including a fifteen-minute interval, was roughly two hours and thirty-five minutes.

Special *matinée* performances were given for the English speaking African adults (arranged by various welfare officers) and for English speaking schoolchildren of all races (arranged by the Education Department). "House Full" notices were displayed at all *matinées*.

An African senior boys' school, a few miles from Nairobi, has been producing the Shakespeare play set for examination during the last four years. A remarkably good interpretation of *As You Like It* was their latest effort, given in English in their school hall with an all-male African cast drawn from various tribes. The more talented of these young tribesmen who have gained experience in such performances are being registered with the hope of forming an African Shakespearian company to perform the play set for school examinations each year. Further promise for extending the scope of the Festivals lies in the up-country districts where little theatres are being planned to house existing talented companies.

A. J. R. MASTER

Finland

The most remarkable production of 1955 was *The Tempest* at the National Theatre, with music composed by Sibelius in 1926. This was a festival production to mark the composer's ninetieth birthday. With Sibelius' music played by a large orchestra, the play was impressive. The producers, Arvi Kivimaa and Edvin Laine, had succeeded in welding word and music into a harmonious unity. Acting was simple, and so was also the stage design, by Leo Lehto. Prospero's part was played with distinction by Urho Somersalmi, an actor of the old school.

Another remarkable event was *King Lear* at the Tampere Theatre. The producer, Jouko Paavola, while emphasizing the individual qualities of Lear's character, achieved a tragical effect on a broad human basis. Kalle Kirjavainen's Lear was a fine performance.

The Merchant of Venice continues to be very popular; in 1955 it figured in the repertories of three theatres. The National Theatre production, by Vilho Ilmari, was a solid piece of work, though it lacked in inspiration. Portia's role was played by Mrs Ansa Ikonen. Vilho Ilmari also produced the play at the Tampere Workers' Theatre. At the Turku Theatre, Jorma Nortimo produced *The Merchant of Venice* during the spring season and Jouko Paavola *The Taming of the Shrew* in the autumn. *The Shrew* also figured in the open air repertory of the Helsinki Popular Theatre last summer, a vigorous production by Glory Leppänen. The Swedish Theatre in Helsinki produced *Julius Caesar* and the Kemi Town Theatre *Twelfth Night*. Kemi is a small town in northern Finland, not far from the Arctic Circle.

A new Finnish translation of seven plays of Shakespeare's, by Yrjö Jylhä, was published in 1955–6, with forewords by Eino Krohn.

RAFAEL KOSKIMIES

France

Last year's account of Shakespearian activities in France was largely devoted to Jean Vilar's *Macbeth*. It was maintained for a second season, with a major change in the cast, Alain Cuny replacing Vilar in the title part. The production was slightly rehandled in view of a simpler, more rapid and 'streamlined' performance. A new effect was introduced which I, for one, considered unfortunate. When Macbeth died, the stage was plunged for a moment into total darkness while a loud-speaker magnified the witches' laughter, recorded on tape. The cuckoo-clock effect of a raven cry, as a comment upon the imagery during one of Lady Macbeth's soliloquies, was kept, though Vilar should have left such tricks to Walt Disney. But these were occasional blemishes; on the whole the agency of evil was aptly suggested without resorting to the anecdotic.

Discussion in the press rightly centred on the respective merits of Vilar's and Cuny's interpretation of the leading part. The change of attitude in *Théâtre Populaire* is worthy of notice. This magazine is by no means an official publication of the T.N.P.; its contributors can be quite outspoken in their criticism though they stand for Vilar's general principles of production. A first reviewer, Roland Barthes—an admirer of Brecht—considered Vilar's acting as the nearest approach we ever had in France to the "V effect"; he never identified himself with the character but maintained a critical distance, thus enabling the spectator to become critical also, instead of remaining passively at an emotional level. So far so good, but in a second paper, Jean Duvignaud declared that Vilar had wisely taken into account adverse criticism of his conception, allowed Cuny to impersonate Macbeth as a creature of flesh and blood, and by doing so to bring his interpretation to the same plane as Maria Casarès who was all instinct and passion as Lady Macbeth. My own impression was that Vilar attached too much importance to critics determined to see far more eroticism in the play than the text allows. Phrases such as "obsession sexuelle", "envoûtement charnel" were repeatedly found in their reviews, with the implication that Macbeth committed murder lest his wife would refuse him access to her bed. Jacques Lemarchand (Figaro Littéraire), who had pulled Vilar's interpretation to pieces, was delighted with Cuny's; the latter, as Macbeth, was stronger, more brutal, and experienced "pleasures and terrors far more physical than spiritual", and made one feel that he was attached to his wife by unusually strong "carnal ties". In fact this carnal business is as irrelevant to the play as the number of children of Lady Macbeth.

Fortunately neither Casarès nor Cuny actually gave to their parts the erotic overtones which an unexpected number of critics seemed to discern—though it is true that at times Cuny unnecessarily clung to his partner in order to show his helplessness and dependence. Cuny revealed, in an interview with Marc Begbeider (Lettres Françaises) that he had set himself a very high standard of acting. Men must learn from the play, not to be led into temptation by the destructive aspect of their thoughts. Macbeth is moving because he has become his own victim, having lost sight of all rules of human conduct and been unable to resist the fulfilment of his destiny through evil. I am sorry to say that the acting was inferior to the intentions. Cuny looked more like a warrior than Vilar ever did. But while the latter reached far too early the 'tomorrow and tomorrow' stage, and gave too much the impression of thinking and analysing his part all the time instead of acting it, Cuny's Macbeth

remained so impulsive and brutish that he seemed unable to think at all and one regretted Vilar in his imaginative and introspective moods. Vilar succeeded somehow in conveying the message which Cuny also had in mind but failed to communicate.

Shakespeare has retained his popularity with the regional Centres Dramatiques and the organisers of summer festivals. Michel Saint-Denis' Romeo and Juliet (Comédie de l'Est), which I mentioned in last year's notes, was presented at the Paris Festival. So was Maurice Sarrasin's Much Ado About Nothing (Grenier de Toulouse), based on a somewhat modernized adaptation, with a strong emphasis on the comic elements, at the expense of the poetical and the witty. The representation of Hamlet in Château-gaillard might have proved an interesting experiment, but unfortunately the play began three hours late, while the night was unusually cold and comments on the weather in I, i, became extremely topical at "Elseneur sur Seine", as one of several sarcastic critics chose to call the place. The actors were members of the Madeleine Renaud–J. L. Barrault company, with the charming Simone Valère as Ophelia, and Jean Desailly, who was judged too simple and candid, in Hamlet's part. André Steiger (Comédie du Centre-Ouest was responsible for the production of J. L. Piachaud's version of The Merry Wives at Bellac. Performance of Julius Caesar and Coriolanus in the vast arena of Nîmes, which can hold up to 25,000 spectators, posed special problems to Jean Hermantier, who had to spread the action over a wide area and made much use of the evolution of warriors, messengers and torch-bearers. In consequence the best way of enjoying the show was to sit high up in order to have a plunging view of the stage.

Jean Dasté (Comédie de Saint-Etienne) took the part of Prospero in John Blatchey's production of The Tempest in a seventeenth-century castle near Saint-Etienne. The version used is due to the collaboration of S. Bing and Copeau, Dasté's master and father-in-law. The settings were by Jean Bazine, a painter of great originality and talent. I am sorry I can give only scanty information about the Festival of Sarlat, which was noticed only in the regional press. Cymbeline is so rarely presented that Maurice Jacquemont's enterprise deserved to have had more encouragement and a full discussion. Like most Festival performances this was given at night and in the open air, in front of an ancient building, in this case the Présidial of Sarlat. The play was 'adapted' by Jacques Tournier and the producer. JEAN JACQUOT

Germany

As in recent years, certain Shakespeare plays have come unexpectedly into the foreground simultaneously and independently staged at various places. Thus *Henry IV* was newly produced at three different theatres (Halle, Stuttgart, and Mainz) almost at the same time, and these were followed by productions at the famous Schiller-Theater, Berlin, at Hamburg and at Hanover. In each instance both parts were performed on one night. So, during the past season, *Antony and Cleopatra* was shown at two leading theatres, Bochum (under Hans Schalla's direction) and Göttingen, where Heinz Hilpert was the producer. The Ruhr festival at Recklinghausen saw a particularly distinguished performance of *Hamlet* produced by Karlheinz Stroux with Will Quadflieg as Hamlet. Another equally remarkable *Hamlet* production could be seen in quite unusual surroundings at the Hersfeld festival where the ruins of the old monastery served as background for an impressive performance with Albin Skoda of Vienna's Burgtheater as Hamlet. Also unusual, but on a less distinguished level, was a performance of *Macbeth* in Schiller's adaptation (1955 being the Schiller Year) in the romantic cloisters of Feuchtwangen (Franconia). Very different from this presentation in style, acting, and setting was the *Macbeth* at Darmstadt's theatre where G. Sellner, one of Germany's most progressive and modern producers, was the regisseur. Of equally high rank was *Julius Caesar* at the Residenztheater of Munich, produced by F. Kortner. At the same theatre *Troilus and Cressida*, not often played in Germany, attracted much attention, baffling the audience through its strange mixture of satire and tragedy. Of the comedies, *Measure for Measure*, *As You Like It* and *The Taming of the Shrew* were particularly successful, the two latter seen in excellent productions by H. Schalla at the Shakespeare festival in Bochum. Besides the classical translations of Schlegel-Tieck, Richard Flatter's translations have been most frequently used for stage performances during the last year.

WOLFGANG STROEDEL
WOLFGANG CLEMEN

Greece

1. *Hamlet*, translated by Basil Rotas. Produced in Salonica, Constantinople and Egypt by the Lambeti-Pappas-Horn Company.

2. *Macbeth*, translated by Cleandros Karthaios. Produced at the Kotopouli Theatre, Athens. Directed by Demetrios Myrat.

3. *The Merry Wives of Windsor*, translated by Cleandros Karthaios. National Theatre, Athens. Directed by Costis Michaelidis.

4. *The Merchant of Venice*, translated by Alex. Pallis. Produced in the suburban theatre 'Dionysia', Athens, by a young company named 'New Free Stage'.

5. *Othello*, translated by Cleandros Karthaios. Produced in an open air theatre in Salonica during the summer by the T. Carousos Company.

6. *Hamlet*, translated by B. Rotas. Produced and directed by Nicos Hatziskos in the National Gardens, Athens, during the summer.

7. *Hamlet*, translated by B. Rotas. National Theatre, Athens. Directed by Alexis Minotis.

GEORGE THEOTOKAS

Israel

The performance of *King Lear* by the Habimah players was a great event in our theatrical life in Israel. Julius Gellner's direction was carefully planned, bringing forth the primitive, villanous, and pathetic elements of the story most intelligently. With Joseph Carl's settings, praiseworthy for their primitiveness of colour and design and with Gari Bertini's music as accompaniment, Abraham Shlonsky's Hebrew version proved both powerful and grand. It is worthy of note that two of Habimah's outstanding players alternated in the lead. Aharon Meskin's Lear was both pathetic and passionate; in Simon Finkel's portrayal of the old king one could sense the crescendo from simplicity and old-age to final madness and despair. Shlomo Barshavit played the Fool and Shoshana Ravid played Cordelia on Meskin's nights, whereas Alvin Epstein and Miriam Zohar played the Fool and Cordelia, respectively, on Finkel's nights, both with different approaches and interpretations. The play ran over a period of several months and was welcomed by the press and the public. REUBEN AVINOAM

Italy

While Calvin Hoffman was hatching in America his presentation of Marlowe as the author of the works which go under the name of Shakespeare, an obscure Italian writer, whose list of publications includes a couple of novels as well as practical guides how to produce films and how to become cinema stars, published a long essay, *Un italiano autore delle opere shakespeariane* (Milan, Gastaldi, 1955). The name of the ambitious essayist is Santi Paladino, who already in 1929 had published in Reggio Calabria a pamphlet with the title *Shakespeare sarebbe il pseudonimo di un poeta italiano?*—which he claims to have caused a sensation all over the world ("l'ipotesi da me lanciata aveva trovato larga eco fin nelle steppe più remote e nelle lande più lontane").

Paladino's hypothesis is that "Shakespeare's" works (sonnets included) were written by Michelangelo Florio, and translated into English by his son Giovanni. Paladino (to whom a gipsy had predicted that he was destined to make an *importante rivelazione* to the world) does not place the ultimate test of his hypotheses in the profanation of a tomb, like Hoffman, but states that if we could know the contents of Giovanni Florio's will and consult the manuscripts which formed part of his library, perhaps we should have in our hand the key to the mystery. Apparently he ignores the fact that Florio's will (Somerset House P.C.C. 97 Hele) was printed by Comtesse de Longworth Chambrun and Arthur Acheson. This is enough to give the calibre of his scholarship; but his book is entertaining owing to the disarming quality of the author's absurdity.

The year's Shakespearian performances include *Coriolanus* (September 1955) in Domitian's Stadium on the Palatine, with Carlo Tamberlani as Coriolanus and Giovanna Scotto as Volumnia (translation by Cesare Vico Ludovici) and *King Lear* (February 1956) at the Teatro Quirino, Rome, with Renzo Ricci as Lear, Eva Magni as Cordelia and Anna Proclemer as Goneril. Verdi's opera *Macbeth* has been staged at the Roman Teatro dell'Opera, but there is little of Shakespeare's drama in this superficial, melodramatic travesty overladen with choreography (a whole interlude consisting of a witches' ballet). Gabriele Baldini, who has given a new translation of the three parts of *Henry VI* (published by Rizzoli of Milan), has edited a selection of Restoration plays (*Teatro inglese della Retaurazione e del Settecento*, Florence, Sansoni, 1955) with a valuable introduction in which Shakespeare's vicissitudes during the period are amply discussed. MARIO PRAZ

Norway

Four Shakespearian plays were staged in this country in 1955: *Twelfth Night* in January at the 'Riksteater' (The Travelling National Theatre); *Macbeth* in February at the National Theatre, Oslo; *Othello* at the People's Theatre, Oslo in April, and *The Taming of the Shrew* at the Open Air Theatre, Oslo, in June.

I saw neither *Twelfth Night* nor *The Shrew* myself; to judge from the reviews, it was the comical element in *Twelfth Night* that carried the day—represented by Per Gjersöe as Malvolio, William Nyrén as Sir Toby, and Adolf Bjerke as Andrew Aguecheek.

The Taming of the Shrew was given in the Frogner Park by a company of young actors who filled the play with exuberant high spirits. Both the Shrew and her conqueror were respectable and at times charming performances, but the one outstanding achievement was that of Willi Hoel, a very gifted comedian, as Petruchio's servant Grumio.

Börseth Rasmussen possesses neither the dimensions nor the rich register of voice required in a tragic hero, but—aided by the skilful direction of Knut Hergel—he brought his Macbeth down on a level where he could carry through the figure in a climax carefully planned, from the split personality of the first act—wavering wildly between loyalty and ambition—to the hardened tyrant and criminal of the end. Mrs Tore Segelcke's Lady Macbeth was a beautiful and thrilling performance.

Hans Jacob Nielsen wanted both the breadth and the weight necessary in the part of Othello, but I have never seen a better Iago than the one given by Ola Isene—a virtuoso of intelligence enjoying intensely his own devilish inventions. LORENTZ ECKHOFF

Poland

Two state publishing houses contributed some major features in the field of Shakespearian scholarship in Poland during the last year. The Państwowy Instytut Wydawniczy (Polish Publishing Institute) in Warsaw added a new volume to its Shakespeare Series, namely the tragedy of *Coriolanus*, rendered into Polish by Zofia Siwicka, a gifted and indefatigable translator of Shakespeare's plays.

Still more important is the splendid folio volume issued by the same publishing house under the title *Szekspir, pięć dramatów* (Shakespeare, Five Dramas). This brings to the Polish reading public *A Midsummer Night's Dream*, *Romeo and Juliet*, *The Merry Wives of Windsor*, *Hamlet*, and *Macbeth*, all in corrected and improved versions, by three eminent nineteenth century translators, Stanisław Koźmian, Józef Paszkowski and Leon Ulrich. A concise essay by Jan Parandowski, introduces this literary enterprise, of which 30,000 copies have been printed. The work is illustrated by Joanna Konarska, a well-known black-and-white artist.

The Biblioteka Narodowa (National Library) in Wroclaw has begun by issuing a set of ten plays most frequently staged in Poland, starting with *Hamlet* in a new translation by Władysław Tarnawski. The book has been hailed as most useful to the theatre, the student and the general reader. Stanisław Helsztyński, the editor, makes use of the results of Western, as well as of Polish, investigations. *King Lear*, also translated by Tarnawski, will be the next in the series. STANISŁAW HELSZTYŃSKI

INTERNATIONAL NOTES

South Africa

Children's Theatre, Johannesburg, an active organization for bringing drama to the younger generation, has been presenting a Shakespeare play in the open-air each year since 1953. Under expert professional guidance, the Theatre has produced *As You Like It*, *The Tempest* and *The Taming of the Shrew*, the last being the play of 1955. In the perfect setting of Rhodes Park, Kensington, the Society has sought to capture the pastoral atmosphere of the Regent's Park Theatre in London, and the performances have been of a standard high enough to attract considerable audiences. The Shakespeare play promises to be an annual event, and the Society gives other evidence of its vitality in the frequent provision of lectures. A. C. PARTRIDGE

Sweden

The production of Shakespeare in Swedish theatres during the last two years owes much to the deep interest of Karl Ragnar Gierow, the manager of our national stage, K. Dramatiska teatern. An experienced playwright, Gierow has now shown his capacity as a translator of Shakespeare both in the *Macbeth* at the Dramatiska teatern 1955 and later in *A Midsummer Night's Dream*, recently acted at the Opera, the performance being a joint work of the Royal theatres (Dramatiska teatern and Operan). *Macbeth* was produced by Bengt Ekeroth. The experienced veteran actor Lars Hansson created the title-role. The other important performance, *A Midsummer Night's Dream*, owes much to Alf Sjöberg, the well-known producer. Music by Dag Wiren and dancing carried the action forward through the play. The ballet was a prominent feature—some critics thought too prominent.

Much interest was aroused by the performance of *Hamlet* at Uppsala stadsteater (later continued in Gävle). The producer was Hans Dahlin, who seems to have been rather parsimonious with the scenery.

The popularity of the *Taming of the Shrew* was clearly manifested at the performance at the Norrköping municipal theatre in a production by John Zacharias and in a new translation by Allan Bergstrand.

Shakespeare is rapidly gaining ground in Swedish schools. This is in no small degree the result of the never tiring efforts of Margreta Söderwall, teacher at Umeå. A Shakespeare Society has been founded at the Umeå secondary school where also a theatrical company of enthusiastic youths has been active, travelling all over the north of Sweden. NILS MOLIN

Switzerland

Of Shakespeare performances, none was given in the French-speaking part of the country. In Bâle, Bern and Zurich, on the other hand, several plays in German translation scored their usual success: *Twelfth Night* at Bâle and Bern, *The Two Gentlemen of Verona* and *Macbeth* at Bern, *A Midsummer Night's Dream*, *As You Like It* and both parts of *Henry IV* in Zurich, but none of those productions seems to have offered any feature of outstanding interest. G. A. BONNARD

U.S.A.

In the United States, the Shakespeare boom continues. New festivals like the American Shakespeare Festival Theatre and Academy are opening up and older ones like that at Antioch College are expanding into other cities to offer their repertories to hundreds of thousands of others.

The programme notes of dozens of collegiate and community productions reveal that there is no lack of imagination or resource. There are Elizabethan, modern dress, and erewhon settings; arena, apron (Fortune and Globe), and proscenium stagings; one level and two level stages; stages with one or two rotating units; indoor and outdoor; all boys; traditional and imaginative renderings; a deaf-mute production of *Macbeth* with supplemental narrators; a *Winter's Tale* in which the "puppet" characters are brought to life by Father Time—with the griffin and rose used throughout as symbols of innocence and jealousy; a *Two Noble Kinsmen* where the symbolism is more direct—the schoolmaster wears a tremendous book as a neck ruff; the wooer, a huge pin-cushion heart.

New Yorkers have had opportunities to see at least half-a-dozen productions. At the City Centre, Orson Welles' *King Lear* was unfortunately forced to close down because its star broke an ankle just before the opening and sprained another immediately after the opening.

The perennial Shakespearewrights under the aegis of Donald L. Goldman offered a continuous repertory. They were praised for their *Macbeth* and *Romeo and Juliet*, but their *Dream* fared poorly. The Shakespearean Theatre Workshop presented only a fair *Romeo and Juliet* but deserves mention because in the 1956 season it will present twelve weeks of free open air Shakespeare in a 2000 seat amphitheatre.

Throughout the United States the numerous festivals entertained thousands. The Oregon Festival on its outdoor Fortune-type stage presented *All's Well*, *Timon*,

Macbeth, 3 Henry VI and *A Midsummer Night's Dream.* The Old Globe replica theatre in San Diego, California, offered *Measure for Measure* (directed by B. Iden Payne), and the *Shrew.* Antioch College for its fourth season continued with *Macbeth, Merry Wives, As You Like It, Twelfth Night, Cymbeline, Winter's Tale,* and *The Two Noble Kinsmen,* with seven more plays promised in 1956 to complete the thirty-eight play canon.

Latest and most spectacular entry into the festival parade was the American Shakespeare Festival Theatre Academy in Stratford, Connecticut. Critics were but slightly impressed by the conventional *Julius Caesar* starring Raymond Massey under the direction of Denis Carey. Direction, conception, casting, lack of preparation and rehearsal time, etc., were cited as causes for the censure. But here there is great promise: with new direction, construction of an apron stage, and more time,

the future is brighter. Its sponsors expect one day to rival the Memorial Theatre and establish an American school of Shakespearian acting.

There has been a flurry of excitement in the discussion of this new American 'style'. What is the objection to the English classic style? Is it just a matter of accent or gesture? When Orson Welles was refused permission to import English talent for his *King Lear,* Arnold Moss publicly remonstrated. Moss, a member of the teaching staff of the American Shakespeare Academy (the Connecticut Festival School to train classic actors), declared that Americans did *know how*: they merely needed *opportunities.* "We are different (from the English players) because we are Americans and we have a right to do it (Shakespeare) in our way." Will it be different from the English 'way'? We pause for time to give the answer.   LOUIS MARDER

SHAKESPEARE PRODUCTIONS IN THE UNITED KINGDOM: 1955

A List compiled from its Records by the
Shakespeare Memorial Library, Birmingham

JANUARY

11   *Macbeth:* Curtain Theatre Rochdale. *Producer:* David E. Ormerod.

17   *Richard II:* Theatre Workshop, at the Theatre Royal, Stratford, London. *Producer:* Joan Littlewood.

18   *Richard II:* The Old Vic Company, at the Old Vic Theatre, London. *Producer:* Michael Benthall.

24   *Othello:* The Sheffield Repertory Company, at The Playhouse, Sheffield.

28   *Hamlet:* The Elizabethan Theatre Company, under the auspices of the Arts Council (on tour). *Producer:* Peter Wood.

31   *Othello:* Oldham Repertory Theatre Club. *Producer:* Harry Lomax.

FEBRUARY

3   *Hamlet:* The Amateur Dramatic Company of the University of Cambridge, at the A.D.C. Theatre. *Producer:* Henry Burke.

22   *As You Like It:* The David Lewis Theatre, Liverpool. *Producer:* Thomas G. Read.

28   *Twelfth Night:* The Ipswich Theatre. *Producer:* Val May.

MARCH

1   *As You Like It:* The Old Vic Company, at the Old Vic Theatre, London. *Producer:* Robert Helpmann.

    The Merchant of Venice: Bristol Old Vic Company, at The Theatre Royal, Bristol. *Producer:* John Moody.

7   *Othello:* Leeds University Union Theatre Group, at Riley Smith Theatre, Leeds. *Producer:* A. Creedy.

8   *Richard II:* The Library Theatre, Manchester. *Producer:* Royston Morley.

15   *As You Like It:* Northampton Repertory Theatre. *Producer:* Alex Reeve.

16   *Troilus and Cressida:* Sloane School, London. *Producer:* Guy Boas.

APRIL

12   *Twelfth Night:* Shakespeare Memorial Theatre, Stratford-upon-Avon. *Director:* John Gielgud.

26   *All's Well That Ends Well:* Shakespeare Memorial Theatre, Stratford-upon-Avon. *Director:* Noel Willman.

27 and 28   *Henry IV.* Parts I and II: The Old Vic Theatre, London. *Director:* Douglas Seale.

MAY

2   *Richard III:* Arts Theatre, Salisbury. *Producer:* Richard Scott.

10   *The Winter's Tale:* Bristol Old Vic Company, at the Theatre Royal, Bristol. *Producer:* John Moody.

MAY

13 *Much Ado About Nothing:* The Maddermarket Theatre, Norwich. *Director:* JAMES ROOSE EVANS.

14 *The Merchant of Venice:* The Old Vic Theatre Company. Foreign tour opening at the Tivoli Theatre, Sydney. *Producer:* MICHAEL BENTHALL.

23 *The Taming of the Shrew:* The Old Vic Theatre Company. Foreign tour opening at the Tivoli Theatre, Sydney. *Producer:* MICHAEL BENTHALL.

30 *Measure for Measure:* The Old Vic Theatre Company. Foreign tour opening at the Tivoli Theatre, Sydney. *Producer:* MICHAEL BENTHALL.

JUNE

1 *The Tempest:* Regent's Park Open-Air Theatre, London. *Director:* DAVID WILLIAMS.

3 *As You Like It:* Harrow School. *Producer:* RONALD WATKINS.

6 *Much Ado About Nothing:* Theatre Royal, Brighton (Shakespeare Memorial Theatre Company). (Afterwards on tour abroad and at Shakespeare Memorial Theatre, Stratford-upon-Avon, 7–17 December.) *Producer:* JOHN GIELGUD.

7 *Macbeth:* Shakespeare Memorial Theatre, Stratford-upon-Avon. *Producer:* GLEN BYAM SHAW.

14 *King Lear:* Theatre Royal, Brighton (Shakespeare Memorial Theatre Company). (Afterwards on tour, abroad and at Shakespeare Memorial Theatre, Stratford-upon-Avon, 28 November–6 December.) *Producer:* GEORGE DEVINE.

15 *As You Like It:* Oxford University Dramatic Society, in Worcester College Gardens. *Producer:* NEVILL COGHILL.

21 *Richard II:* The Repertory Theatre, Birmingham. *Director:* DOUGLAS SEALE.

24 *A Midsummer Night's Dream:* Regent's Park Open-Air Theatre, London. *Producer:* ROBERT ATKINS.

25 *The Tempest:* Keighley Theatre Group, at the Little Theatre. *Producer:* ERIC B. BROSTER.

JULY

12 *The Merry Wives of Windsor:* Shakespeare Memorial Theatre, Stratford-upon-Avon. *Director:* GLEN BYAM SHAW.

AUGUST

3 *A Midsummer Night's Dream:* Windsor Theatre Guild. *Producer:* CHARLES HUNT.

8 *Julius Caesar:* The Old Vic Company at The Empire, Swansea. (Afterwards at the Edinburgh Festival and at the Old Vic Theatre, London, 7 September.) *Director:* MICHAEL BENTHALL.

16 *Titus Andronicus:* Shakespeare Memorial Theatre, Stratford-upon-Avon. *Director:* PETER BROOK.

SEPTEMBER

5 *The Two Noble Kinsmen:* Birmingham University Guild Theatre Group, in the Lauriston Hall Edinburgh. *Producer:* GEOFFREY MEREDITH.

27 *The Merry Wives of Windsor:* The Old Vic Company, at the Old Vic Theatre, London. *Producer:* DOUGLAS SEALE.

SHAKESPEARE PRODUCTIONS IN THE UNITED KINGDOM

OCTOBER

10   *As You Like It:* Guildford Theatre. *Producer:* ROGER WINTON.

      The Merchant of Venice: The Gateway Theatre, Edinburgh. *Producer:* LENNOX MILNE.

11   *Othello:* Liverpool Playhouse. *Producer:* WILLARD STOKER.

25   *Hamlet:* Theatre Royal, Brighton. (Afterwards on tour in Great Britain and U.S.S.R. At the Phoenix Theatre, London, 8 December 1955.) *Producer:* PETER BROOK.

29   *The Taming of the Shrew:* Bradford Civic Playhouse. *Producer:* RAY TAYLOR.

NOVEMBER

1   *The Winter's Tale:* The Old Vic Theatre, London. *Producer:* MICHAEL BENTHALL.

5   *Hamlet:* Questors Theatre, London. *Producer:* BARBARA HUTCHINS.

14   *The Comedy of Errors:* Midland Theatre Company at the College Theatre, Coventry. *Producer:* FRANK DUNLOP.

22   *Othello:* The Library Theatre, Manchester. *Producer:* ROYSTON MORLEY.

DECEMBER

9   *The Merry Wives of Windsor:* The Maddermarket Theatre, Norwich. *Producer:* FRANK HARWOOD.

13   *Henry V:* The Old Vic Theatre, London. *Producer:* MICHAEL BENTHALL.

DRAMS OF EALE

[*A review of recent productions, with special reference to* Titus Andronicus (*Stratford*, 1955), Hamlet
(*Phoenix*, 1955), Troilus and Cressida (*Old Vic*, 1956) *and* Othello (*Stratford*, 1956)]

BY

RICHARD DAVID

> Their virtues else—be they as pure as grace,
> As infinite as man may undergo—
> Shall in the general censure take corruption
> From that particular fault: the dram of evil
> Doth all the noble substance of a doubt
> To his own scandal.

Hamlet's analysis applies to productions of Shakespeare as well as to men. The 1955–6 season
promised marvels and in performance displayed an infinity of individual virtues. And yet the
total impression was one of disappointment. There was always a dram of evil that finally undermined the most notable production.

Peter Brook's *Titus Andronicus* at Stratford (which came too late for inclusion in my last
report) was certainly that. Brook had not only produced the play but had designed scenery,
costumes and musical accompaniment, and he achieved a quite extraordinary unity and con-
centration of effect. The staging was powerfully simple: three great squared pillars, set angle-on
to the audience, fluted, and bronzy-grey in colour (Plate VA). The two visible sides could be
swung back, revealing inner recesses that might be used as entrances or, in the central pillar, as
a two-storeyed inner stage. This was the tomb of the Andronici, sombre and shadowy against
the vivid green of the priests' robes and mushroom-hats; festooned with lianes it became the
murder-pit and the forest floor above it; stained a yellowish natural-wood colour it provided a
background of Roman frugality to the bereaved and brooding Titus at his family table; blood-
red, it made a macabre eyrie of the upper chamber from which the Revenger peers out upon his
victims, come in fantastic disguise to entrap him. In the court scenes the closed pillars, supported
by heavy side-gratings of the same colour and hangings of purple and green, richly suggested
the civilized barbarity of late imperial Rome.

Within this frame the whole phantasmagoria unrolled without hitch or hesitation—from the
opening, when the citizens, in ruffed gowns of shot satin and dark fustian, broke off their rival
acclamations to perform the obsequies for Titus' sons, marching and counter-marching with
obstinate purposefulness in a dirge-like quadrille; to the closing scene, when in the glare of the
torches the victims topple forward in succession across the dinner-table like a row of ninepins
skittled from behind. It was as if the actors were engaged in a ritual at once fluent from habitual
performance and yet still practised with concentrated attention. There was something puppet-
like about them; but puppets manipulated by a master whose genius for improvisation constantly
enlivened his expert routine.

The compulsive and incantatory nature of the production (which sent some spectators off into faints before ever a throat was cut) was reinforced by the musical effects, all of a marvellous directness. The overture was a roll of drum and cymbal, the dirge for the slain Andronici, so strange and powerful, no more than the first two bars of *Three Blind Mice*, in the minor and endlessly repeated. A slow see-saw of two bass notes, a semitone apart, wrought the tension of the final scene to an unbearable pitch, and ceased abruptly, with breath-taking effect, as the first morsel of son-pie passed Tamora's lips. Even more harrowing were the hurrying carillon of electronic bells that led up to the abduction of Lavinia and the slow plucking of harp-strings, like drops of blood falling into a pool, that accompanied her return to the stage.

In speaking of the actors as puppets of the producer's conception, I do not mean to imply that there were not performances of strong individuality but only that, like the dyer's hand, they were all loyally subdued to what they worked in. The freest, from the very nature of his part in the play, is Aaron the Moor, and to him Antony Quayle brought a rich gusto, as fetching in the creamy slyness that cheats Titus of his hand (Plate VA) as in the bounce and glory of the defence of his black baby. But Aaron is a nice fat part for anyone; that Laurence Olivier should succeed in giving equal richness to the stock Revenger, Titus, was a more unexpected feat. At his first entry one might almost have accused him of mugging, so hard did he work with swallowing and pursing, wrinkling and charming to build up, on the bare bones of the part, a Great Man, cantankerous, choleric and at the same time compelling (Plate VIA). Yet by making Titus a "character', in every sense, he was able not only to gloss over some of the play's awkwardnesses but to rise (when, all too seldom, the chance was there) into a freer air than that of Grand Guignol. We could accept the conqueror's, and patriot's, blazing rage, that with "Barr'st me my way in Rome?" sweeps his youngest son out of existence. And the great central scene, where Titus stands

> as one upon a rock
> Environ'd with a wilderness of sea,
> Who marks the waxing tide grow wave by wave,

so grew and proliferated in the astonishing variety of his reactions to disaster (the enormous physical agony of the severed hand was almost unbearable) that with the crowning frenzy of "I am the sea" Olivier seemed to break through the illusion and become, not old Hieronimo run mad again, but madness itself.

As with individual performances, so with individual scenes. Who could forget the return of the ravishers with Lavinia? They bring her through the leafy arch that was the central pillar and leave her standing there, right arm outstretched and head drooping away from it, left arm crooked with the wrist at her mouth. Her hair falls in disorder over face and shoulders, and from wrist and wrist-and-mouth trail scarlet streamers, symbols of her mutilation. The two assassins retreat from her, step by step, looking back at her, on either side of the stage. Their taunts fall softly, lingeringly, as if they themselves were in a daze at the horror of their deed; and the air tingles and reverberates with the slow plucking of harp-strings. Another peak was the scene in which Titus makes his followers shoot arrows into the sky with messages for the gods. Here Brook cheated, bringing on the yokel, who seems to come in answer to the prayers, in a basket from the flies, and writing in a line about "fetching down his pigeons from the walls" to make this plausible. It was certainly in keeping, and added a crowning touch of fantasy to a most fantastical invention.

It was the whole, however, the one extended conjuring-trick, that held the spectator spell-bound—spell-bound and yet quite unmoved. What was it that in the last analysis made the evening so unrewarding, the effect so cold beside that of the perhaps more run-of-the-mill *Macbeth*? It was the conviction, unsought but growing irresistibly as the play proceeded, that this piece on which so much labour and ingenuity had been lavished, and to which we had been invited to attend for two and a half hours, was—twaddle. Perhaps this would have been less apparent if producer and company had not worked so hard to persuade us that it was otherwise. The Cambridge Marlowe Society's production in 1954, a shortened version played with frank gusto and dash, had prepared me to find in the play itself a straightforward blood-and-thunder entertainment. In striving to make it more than this Brook made it less than nothing. The blood was, we have seen, turned to favours and to prettiness. Severed heads were not allowed to appear unless decently swathed in black velvet and enclosed in ornate funerary caskets. Titus' hand, so swaddled and coffered, was decorously cradled in Lavinia's arms, not carried off between her teeth as the text directs. The pig-killing of Chiron and Demetrius occurred off-stage and (perhaps to compensate the audience with one maiming in place of another) Titus' final cry of triumph,

Why, there they are both, baked in that pie,

was lopped of its last four words. But no amount of sand-papering and gilding can turn this old shocker into high tragedy à la Racine. Has Shakespeare's *Titus* really any life left in it? The question is not yet answered. Certainly Brook's romantic play of the same name was still-born.

That he had made so much of *Titus* nevertheless encouraged extravagant expectations of his *Hamlet*. Designed as a cultural export to Moscow, this production certainly achieved celebrity; but however much it may have excited the columnist and the politician it was a bitter disappointment to the rest of us.

Its fault was that which of all I should have thought most foreign to Brook—incoherence. A sort of unity was imposed by the setting (not this time by Brook himself but by Georges Wakhevitch), though its simplicity was no doubt primarily dictated by the necessity of transporting it to Russia and erecting it on unfamiliar stages. It was dominated by a construction of interlocking Gothic arches, forming a great lantern or skeleton dome that occupied most of the stage up-centre. Perhaps this cage was to emphasize that "Denmark's a prison"; certainly the stage became "a plot whereon the numbers cannot try the cause". The actors had scarcely elbow-room. The business on the battlements was a hole and corner affair, and the awkwardness of the ghost's exit and re-entry was magnified by the "more removed ground" being so palpably the same little patch of stage he had but lately left. The subsequent interview between father and son was denied all impressiveness because it had to be conducted either in flat profile across the width of the shallow stage or with Hamlet awkwardly jammed under the ghost's skirts. Even the duel was cramped, though one good point came out of this in-fighting: the rapier-blade caught as it passed above Hamlet's shoulder and held so that the light struck upon its unbated point and upon Hamlet's face turned to look on it aghast. Worst of all there was no room for Claudius in the play-scene except upon a little ledge in a back corner of the stage, from which at the climax he was ignominiously tipped off into the wings. This muddled away what is perhaps the most straightforwardly effective stroke in the play, when guilt is at last unkennelled and stands a moment exposed with bared fangs.

PLATE V

A. 'TITUS ANDRONICUS', SHAKESPEARE MEMORIAL THEATRE, STRATFORD–UPON–AVON,
1955. PRODUCED AND DESIGNED BY PETER BROOK. TITUS CHEATED OF HIS HAND

B. 'TROILUS AND CRESSIDA', OLD VIC THEATRE, 1956. PRODUCED BY TYRONE
GUTHRIE, DESIGNED BY FREDERICK CROOKE. GREEK G.H.Q.

PLATE VI

B. 'OTHELLO', SHAKESPEARE MEMORIAL THEATRE, STRATFORD–UPON–AVON, 1956. PRODUCED BY GLEN BYAM SHAW, DESIGNED BY MOTLEY. IAGO AND THE MOOR

A. 'TITUS ANDRONICUS.' THE HERO

PLATE VII

B. 'TROILUS AND CRESSIDA.' IN THE CONSERVATORY

A. 'TROILUS AND CRESSIDA.' IN THE PADDOCK

PLATE VIII

B. 'HAMLET', SHAKESPEARE MEMORIAL THEATRE, STRATFORD–UPON–AVON, 1956. PRODUCED BY MICHAEL LANGHAM, DE–SIGNED BY MICHAEL NORTHERN, COSTUMES BY DESMOND HEELEY. THE BREAD–BOARD

A. 'HAMLET', PHOENIX THEATRE, 1955. PRODUCED BY PETER BROOK, DESIGNED BY GEORGES WAKHEVITCH. LAERTES, CLAUDIUS, HAMLET, GERTRUDE, HORATIO

In the event, too, the setting imposed disunity rather than unity, for the ever-insistent keystone merely emphasized the disparity of the scenes enacted beneath it and the incongruity of the other scenic elements brought in to relieve its monotony. Sometimes these elements were realistic, as on the quayside where Polonius and Ophelia took leave of Laertes and (most unrealistically) voiced their private fears and instructions before a crowd of dock-hands; or in the armoury that, with its racks of bows and foils, provided a pertinent background to Claudius' and Laertes' plot of the fencing-match. Sometimes they were the opposite: above all the delicious little four-poster, symbolical, heraldic, and ridiculous, which was popped out of the back-curtains in two successive scenes and signified, dexter, the King's bedroom, sinister, the Queen's.

Acting styles were as varied as the furnishings. At one extreme was the Polonius of Ernest Thesiger, slowly built up in a series of deft and almost imperceptible touches (the spread hand wagging impatiently from the wrist as he describes the prince's feckless walking in the lobby); and yet so naturalistic that the Chamberlain was near to becoming a genuine bore. In the middle of the scale came Alec Clunes' Claudius, as firmly grounded as the Polonius and yet more strongly and deliberately varied: a beautiful performance this, that conveyed the baseness, and the charm, and the dangerous force of Hamlet's adversary (Plate VIIIA). At the further end was Paul Scofield's Hamlet, mannered in the extreme and yet markedly lacking in variation, so that melancholy, passion, feigned madness, and deeply-pondered philosophy all appeared in the same cranky disguise. The four great soliloquies received exactly similar treatment, an apparently ratiocinative deliberation that nevertheless quite overrode the logic both of meaning and of rhythm. The only difference of context or mood was that two of these speeches were introduced by forced gestures. "O, that this too too solid flesh" began with Hamlet, his back hitherto to the audience, making himself known by a sudden violent turning of his head over his shoulder. Before "O, what a rogue" he slowly climbed from stool to table and set himself in the exact posture in which the First Player had lately delivered the Hecuba speech—as if to get inside the very skin of the man's passion. I liked this (others didn't); but these devices were essentially stagy in a production that was predominantly naturalistic, and they stood out like sore thumbs. Scofield was at his best in prose and banter. The sudden check of "Saw who?" and the preoccupied urgency of his questioning of Horatio and Marcellus about the ghost, the baffling of Polonius, the wary testing of Rosencrantz and Guildenstern (the snap of the ink-well lid as he finally traps them was a stage-trick more in keeping)—all these gripped, as the set-pieces failed to do. And Scofield possesses in high degree the quality that is above all essential for a Hamlet: a stage-personality so compellingly sympathetic that every fault must be forgiven. Even the melodramatic tenor tremor on "I doubt some foul play" somehow just escaped a laugh.

It is interesting to compare with this, in parenthesis, the *Hamlet* with which the Stratford season opened. Justice has not been done to this production, for it possessed notable virtues, as well as faults, both in striking opposition to those of Brook's version. Michael Langham signally achieved the unity that had eluded Brook. The set was almost non-existent, and in this vacuum scene succeeded scene so rapidly that as the players of one left the stage their successors were already entering from the other side. This gave a great sense of fluidity and fluency, of destiny unrolling so steadily that the individual incidents coalesced as in a kaleidoscope, of the viewer viewing it, like some Spirit of the Pities, from a great distance. Two things, however, marred the effect. First Michael Northen's setting, for all its abstraction, was too particular. The playing-space too strongly recalled an octagonal bread-board (Plate VIIIB), with at its back a single silvery-blue drape, squared off at shoulder-height like a dressmaker's sample (a resemblance reinforced by the modern dinner dresses and hair-styles of Ophelia and the Queen). If the scene of the play is to be Everywhere and Nowhere it is essential that no property shall tie it to a particular locality, least of all to the shop-window of Messrs Debenham and Hollingsworth. (The same error planted Gielgud's last *Lear* in the Mars of the spacemen.) Secondly, the Hamlet of Alan Badel never really established itself. He is a highly accomplished and versatile actor; his reading of the part was deeply felt and intelligent; but he lacks precisely that magnetism that Scofield possesses, and was further hampered by the clogging costumes. Designers should beware lest in bagging and befrogging the play to make it authentically Danish they smother the Renaissance *élan* that is its essence. The final effect was over-earnest, plodding and monotonous.

At the Old Vic meanwhile Michael Benthall had given us *Julius Caesar*, forceful in a somewhat over-theatrical style, with lashings of gore, a hiss in every conspiracy, and spectacular falls for the suicides (Cassius certainly had the back-trick simply as strong as any man in Illyria); and Douglas Seale an extra light-weight *Merry Wives*. The designer of *The Winter's Tale*, Peter Rice, clearly knew what the play was about, for he gave it two perfect settings: a romanticized Grecian patio in strong and luminous colours, Veronese-style, for the court, and for the pastoral a group of Arcadian barns, all straw-plaits and dollies. The Leontes knew it too, for Paul Rogers' performance was exactly poised between reality and fairy-tale. Benthall, however, was so much at sea that he allowed Hermione, in defiance of Shakespeare's phrasing, to gasp and sob out her defence like any prospective divorcée about to break down in the witness-box; and he brought on Perdita and Florizel, the noble Innocents who are to redeem the follies of Experience, playing tig in a gale of giggles. His *Henry V* was so lacking in pointedness and coherence that the business of Williams and the glove must have been quite lost on anyone who did not already know the play, and so ill-regulated that the interval was allowed to break into the very middle of the Agincourt story. There was some compensation in Dudley Jones' adroit and winning Fluellen, and it was interesting to see how four years had added weight to Richard Burton's King (for which he received a special award) at the expense, I thought, of the boyish camaraderie that had warmed his 1951 performance. Of the twin *Othello*, with Neville and Burton alternating Iago and the Moor, there will be something to say when we get to Stratford.

Tyrone Guthrie's *Troilus and Cressida* was, as expected, lively, gay and shrewd. Frederick Crooke's Edwardian *décor* certainly pointed up some characteristics of the play. Morning-coat and top-hat of Ascot grey were fair enough for the smart worldliness of a Pandarus who was, nevertheless, more Chaucerian than Shakespearian, and his dialogue with the riding-habited Cressida, as they took turns with his field-glasses to view the returning army, appeared in its proper perspective as small-talk in the paddock (Plate VIIA). The Prussian severity of the Greeks contrasted aptly with the Ruritanian Trojans, and the solemn absurdity of the council of war came nearer home with Ulysses in admiral's frock-coat and Menelaus as a be-monocled Staff Officer Operations (Plate VB). And I have never seen a happier Nestor (Dudley Jones again) than this fiery little old man, whom even the vast military great-coat, the profusion of whisker, and the peaked cap many sizes too big, could not extinguish. Helen's conservatory was a model of decadent silliness (Plate VIIB). Cassandra, as a half-crazy devotee of séances, in sack tunic, much embroidered, and waist-long strings of beads, was essentially right, though not royal; and Thersites as war-correspondent, in cloth cap, knickerbockers, and brown boots, if not right was at least more definite than the nothing of most productions. Yet there were disadvantages. It was a pity to place this play, of which a main subject is war, in a period that emphasized only war's glamour and never its reality. Ceremonial uniforms filled the scene, and the battles, including the killing of Hector, were perfunctory. The producer, indeed, had not really come to grips with the play. A programme-note read: "Shakespeare, we believe, was concerned to shew that the causes of the war, so far as causes of any event can ever be determined, were utterly confused and unreasonable.... The Trojans are shewn to be undermined by frivolity; the Greeks by faction." Even if we accept this as far as it goes (and "frivolity" is not the right word for the Trojans' fault) it leaves out too much—notably the hero and heroine. They were indeed shabbily treated, reduced to a mere sub-plot of thoughtless undergraduate seduced by bitch. Their first meeting was trifled away, for as Pandarus Paul Rogers was unforgiveably allowed to distract the audience with foolery and a shawl. Their parting was a little better, though the violence of Cressida's sobs and Troilus' hasty pinning of her into her dress added a stronger dash of the comic than the moment can rightly stand. Even then the lovers were not allowed to claim undivided attention, for the scene was played on a double set, bedroom above, hall below, with the impatient escort quite as prominent as the protagonists. Another expressionist trick destroyed the end of the affair. The audience, tittering at the elegant game of blind man's buff played, in full light, by Cressida, her wooer, and the two parties of eavesdroppers, could hardly spare a serious thought for Troilus' passion. In place of the play's advertised subject we were offered some curious decorations by the producer: a flirtation between Cressida and her groom, and a psychopathic enlargement of Patroclus. Though it was an amusing evening, it was also an infuriating one.

Stratford's second play, *The Merchant of Venice*, produced by Margaret Webster, was generally liked for the pretty and fantastic settings by Alan Tagg (how they thundered when on the move!), for the elaboration of business ("I *did* like those nuns" gushed an ingénue in the foyer), for the flesh-creeping squalor of Emlyn Williams' Shylock, and for the sprightly, too sprightly, Portia of Margaret Johnston. These seemed to me nearer vices than virtues. But since the key scenes of casket and trial (in which last Miss Johnston shed her giggles for sweet-reasonableness) were absorbing one really cannot complain.

Othello sets the producer the same two problems as *Macbeth*. The action is unusually rapid in both, and yet must be delicately controlled, in *Macbeth* because it is oddly fore-shortened, in *Othello* because for all its rapidity it proceeds irregularly by a series of quantum jumps. Again, in both plays Shakespeare seems to have deliberately handicapped himself by taking as his tragic hero a person likely to excite, at least initially, revulsion and not sympathy in the audience. Macbeth is a "butcher"; Othello is black—a full negro if we accept "thick-lips" in this sense. In *Othello* Shakespeare in effect makes one handicap cancel out the other. It is easier to make *something* of this play, which can be reasonably satisfying on a comparatively low level. But to touch the heights a further effort of a quite different order is needed, whereas in *Macbeth* it is the initial difficulties that are everything.

The speed of *Othello* is partly generated by the periodic injection, into a dialogue already tense, of sudden spirts of action: the entry of Brabantio and his followers to arrest Othello, the arrival in Cyprus, the brawl, Othello's half-throttling of Iago, the swoon, the striking of Desdemona. All this was brilliantly managed by Byam Shaw, who has made peculiarly his own a trick of suddenly filling the stage with a rapid swirl of motion: the banter flags between Iago and Desdemona, newly landed in Cyprus, there is a stir off-stage that grows almost instantaneously to a tumult, and there is Othello, victorious and radiant, at the centre of the stage, his soldiers about him and his standard flaunting above his head. The brawl was first-rate, exploding out of nowhere and convincingly violent. Othello's striking of his wife, too, generally a weak scene, was here a major climax, the producer cleverly exploiting the special qualities of Miss Johnston's gallant and spirited Desdemona. Five seconds of horror-struck stillness followed the blow, and then Desdemona's control cracked suddenly in outraged sobbing (the same trick that last year made the Lady Macduff scene); and her agony was unbearably prolonged by allowing her to climb to the top of the staircase before Othello, maliciously misinterpreting the ambassador's words, calls her back for further humiliation.

The sense of speed derives also from the famous 'double time' of the play. One reckoning hustles the whole of the action at Cyprus into twenty-four hours. A second suggests the lapse of a week or more. Now in this longer time Desdemona's misconduct is just conceivable, but Othello must still go through the whole gamut of behaviour, from highest nobility to the most abject barbarity and back to nobility again, in a period that, whether measured in terms of drama or of actuality, is too short to contain so large a process. Othello is accordingly shown only at certain points in his course, and between each appearance his state is liable to undergo an unexpected boosting. It is the business of the producer to give the illusion of a continuous and ordered progress, making these gear-changes silently.

The most violent occur between the first and second temptation scenes, and before Othello's final entry to kill Desdemona. In the first temptation scene Iago succeeds in putting the idea of betrayal into Othello's mind, but at the end of it as the Moor goes off to supper he can still say

> If she be false, O, then heaven mocks itself!
> I'll not believe 't.

Yet when he returns, only forty lines later, he does believe in Desdemona's guilt and in his own disgrace—"What sense had I of her stol'n hours of lust?" and "Farewell...Othello's occupation's gone." On this Iago comments "Is't possible?", and there is real danger that the audience will answer "No".

Here Byam Shaw and his Othello, Harry Andrews, courted danger by stressing the Moor's confidence. The encounter opened with Othello seating himself, back to the audience, at a central table to examine the map of the fortifications. Iago, standing at the head of a little staircase, stage right, had visibly to steel himself for the attempt, which he began by taking three steps, at once fateful and gingerly, down the staircase into the arena. His first gambit was a complete failure. Othello's "Why, why is this?" was spoken in exasperated amusement at Iago's riddling, not in fear of his insinuations; and Iago was compelled, with still greater effort, to screw up his courage again before launching the second attack. It is obvious that the scene is very much more exciting if Iago's victory is not a walk-over, and if his own danger is emphasized. Othello is a bomb that will certainly explode if the technician engaged on drawing its sting should fumble or be slow to change his tactics at the first whisper of trouble. So it was here:

the scene in itself was thrilling, and I am sure it should be played thus. Yet unless Othello shows, at the second attempt, a much greater acceleration of passion than Andrews achieved, the break between this scene and the next will gape all the more. This transition was one of two things better done at the Old Vic, for Burton, initially as unruffled as Andrews, produced a sudden flare in the second half of the scene that linked his exit naturally with his distraught re-entry.

"It is the cause" is simply one of the hardest of Shakespeare's speeches, and I have never yet heard it come off. We have just seen Othello gloating over the assassination (as he thinks) of Cassio. Now he comes to murder Desdemona; but the moods of the two killings are very different. One is revenge, the other execution. Cassio he hates; Desdemona he loves (he tells us so) even as he kills her, but he is heaven's instrument and must destroy that which has flouted heaven, whatever his personal feelings. The speech, then, must be hieratic, sublime. Indeed the whole scene must have sublimity, for we must not take Emilia's abuse too seriously and, after a moment of utter confusion and abasement, the Moor regains his full nobility. He has executed Desdemona in what he thought was justice. Now he finds it was not so, and for his injustice he executes himself. If Othello becomes a mere scarecrow of grief, the whole burden of the scene falls upon Emilia, and however hard she works to keep up the interest it is almost bound to flag, as it did both at Stratford and at the Old Vic. Uncle Gratiano and the other onlookers, who should lighten the tension, dissipate it altogether. Then the carpers have some excuse for finding Othello a fool and a posturing wind-bag, and the play a failure.

It is here that the choice of hero tells. He is a Moor, an alien, alien in colour, nature, upbringing. That he is foreign in every sense, not a civilized man as civilized men understand each other, is at once the point of the play, the germ of Iago's plot, and the solution of the playwright's technical problem. Othello's tragedy is the tragedy of Adam, natural nobility enmeshed by experience; upon the incalculability of the Moor Iago makes his calculations; and in a noble savage savagery, nobility, and the alternation between them are all explicable.

Othello, then, must never be a European, tastefully browned. Of the three actors who attempted the part, two at the Old Vic and one at Stratford, John Neville perhaps got nearest to the essential strangeness, but he lacked the magnificence, and became weaselish in affliction. Burton had more of the size, but his all-too-reasonable despair seemed mere self-pity. Andrews had the power, something of the glory and, at moments, a touch of exotic fascination. His narration to the senate was far and away the best of the three: no set oration but a rapt re-living of his adventures and of the wooing they set on. On the whole, however, this Othello, like so many others, remained too penny-plain. For this I partly blame Motley's clothes: a close-fitting scarlet guardee uniform, and for the bedroom a green smoking-jacket and black court smalls (the traditional dressing-gown appeared only momentarily, to quell the brawl). No doubt these styles were intended to exorcise the romantic view of Othello and make us focus on him anew. The process went too far. The uniform made of him at best an Emperor Jones, at worst an organ-grinder's monkey; and no one, black or white, can commit murder in jacket and knee-breeches and get away with it.

The Iago of Emlyn Williams was a pleasure to watch. Played with precision and control, every stroke telling, the worst that could be said of it was that it never really engaged with the Othello (Plate VIB). It was an exhibition of knife-throwing, the blades placed with exquisite neatness round the unconscious victim, never a duel. The cold deliberation of Iago's playing, besides providing no foothold for Othello's trust or the others' good-fellowship, petrified the opening of the play, which did not quicken until the splendid senate scene. Both Old Vic Iagos brought to this opening a sense of desperate malice straining to be unleashed, an immense imminence of evil. Iago's hoarse and intemperate imprecations, vaulting over Roderigo's more polite appeals, urged the scene quickly to a climax. Burton's Iago indeed (Neville's was no more than personified spite) was nearly a very great one. For once the revelation that Iago is no more than "four times seven years" did not come as a shock. Debonair, open-faced, as winning as Steerforth and as reliable as Claggart, he might have won any comrade's trust. The manipulation of Othello had just the right air of deft experiment; the humour a touch of lower-deck roughness, the sex-jokes a hint (no more) of over-emphasis. It was only in the soliloquies that Burton's Iago failed, for they must be explosive, revealing in a flash that the touch of roughness is innate brutality, the sex-jokes a symptom of pathological obsession. Emlyn Williams gave the soliloquies explosiveness, but what they revealed was no more than already appeared in his daily conversation. Neither actor gave us the whole of Iago.

The particular fault of the Stratford *Othello* was ultimately the actor's, who failed to build on the foundations laid by the producer; just as in Brook's *Hamlet*, it was the failure of the producer to co-ordinate individual performances, some of them substantial. *Titus*, on the other hand, and Guthrie's *Troilus and Cressida*, were magnificently all-of-a-piece, but their imposing façades covered in one a distortion, in the other a negation of Shakespeare's idea. The season's palm must go to no stage production, but to the film of *Richard III*. This (however 'lacking in real cinematic qualities') combined a continuous dramatic and stylistic tautness with loyalty to the author's intentions. But that is another story.

THE YEAR'S CONTRIBUTIONS TO
SHAKESPEARIAN STUDY

1. CRITICAL STUDIES

reviewed by KENNETH MUIR

John Lawlor tells us[1] that "the liberty of interpreting" resembles "other forms of liberty: we have it on the condition of vigilance". He is answering an essay by L. C. Knights, reviewed here last year, on the limitations of historical scholarship. Although he does not seriously differ from Knights' conclusions he takes issue with him and with Abercrombie on some of their arguments. He warns us, quite rightly, that "the present will not come to life in our studies when it is used to galvanize the past" and he refuses to make a distinction between "historical scholarship" and "the Shakespeare experience".

Some of the year's historical scholarship certainly assists our understanding of Shakespeare. Gladys D. Willcock, for example, devoted her British Academy lecture[2] to a study of the use of rhetoric in his early plays. She helps us to appreciate what Shakespeare was trying to do, though she realizes that though he might never have become a great poet without his rhetorical training, he had to transcend it before he could become great. Robert Hillis Goldsmith is another scholar who enables us to see one aspect of Shakespeare's work more plainly. Part of his book[3] on Shakespearian Fools covers much the same ground as Enid Welsford's, and some of it stems from the work of Oscar James Campbell who contributes an introduction; but there is no book on the subject which covers quite the same field. Goldsmith discusses fools and similar figures in different kinds of literature from Aristophanes onwards. He has, for example, a good account of the Vice with some unfamiliar quotations. He deals with Elizabethan fools and clowns; he discusses each of Shakespeare's fools in turn, taking issue with Hotson on "motley"; and in his last chapters he discusses satire and the dramatic function of the fool in comedy and tragedy. He concludes, as we might expect, that "Lear's Fool intensifies the pathos and at the same time humanizes the tragedy for us" while Feste "tempers the comedy of *Twelfth Night*, simultaneously rendering it gayer and more thoughtful".

M. D. H. Parker, setting out to discover Shakespeare's philosophy of life,[4] was astonished at her own conclusions. Her Shakespeare was "a Papist in sympathy and doctrine" whether he was a recusant or not. We cannot help suspecting that she finds what she brings, though examples of special pleading are rare and her direct discussions of the evidence decently objective. Most readers today would agree that Shakespeare exhibits knowledge of Christian doctrine, but it is probably impossible to deduce from his plays whether he was an Anglican or a Papist. The

---

[1] 'On Historical Scholarship and the Interpretation of Shakespeare', *Sewanee Review*, LXIV (Spring 1956), 186–206.

[2] *Language and Poetry in Shakespeare's Early Plays*. Annual Shakespeare Lecture of the British Academy, 1954 (Geoffrey Cumberlege, 1955).

[3] *Wise Fools in Shakespeare* (Michigan State University Press, 1955).

[4] *The Slave of Life* (Chatto and Windus, 1955).

quotations from St Thomas Aquinas do not prove that Shakespeare had Catholic sympathies; and the parallels with Plato and St Augustine seem weaker than those with Seneca and Montaigne, and much weaker than those with the *Homilies* or the *Declaration of Egregious Popish Impostures*. Of course Shakespeare may have read Harsnett without sympathising with his views and the equivocator in *Macbeth* may not be an allusion to Father Garnet, but recent work on *Measure for Measure* by Elizabeth Pope and Reimer suggests how cunningly Shakespeare evades denominational classification. But although we may be sceptical about the main thesis of this book, it does not stand or fall by its success or failure in that respect. It is well written, sensitive, and intelligent; it contains some good criticism on individual plays and some useful insights on the relation of one play to another. Most readers will agree with the author that Graham Greene was wrong when he complained that in Shakespeare

there is no profound and Christian grappling with the significant issues of being and conduct, the essential nature of knowledge and love.

Readers will be familiar with the articles on the Comedies which appeared in *Shakespeare Survey*, 8. They included J. R. Brown's retrospect,[1] Nevill Coghill on *Measure for Measure*,[2] Harold Jenkins on *As You Like It*,[3] Ludwig Borinski on 'Shakespeare's Comic Prose',[4] and Kenneth Muir on *Troilus and Cressida*.[5] On the last of these plays there has been an interesting chapter by I. A. Richards[6] who argues that the play is usually underestimated. He is particularly concerned with the plausible parallels with Plato, though the incidental comments contain the best criticism—on Ulysses as head of the intelligence service, on the debate in Act II, and on Troilus' speech after he has witnessed Cressida's unfaithfulness:

The opposites are all before him and are indistinguishable—as Ariadne's clue and Arachne's web are merged in Ariachne's broken woof.

Another problem play, *All's Well that Ends Well*, has been re-examined by John Arthos[7] and he concludes that "something about confusion at the very roots of love is the matter of Shakespeare's comedy" and that the ugliness of the plot may be overcome "if we are able to perceive the direction of the whole of the action and the emphasis on love and virtue". The parallel with Molière's *Amphitryon*, however, does not provide much illumination. Albert Howard Carter complains[8] that critical opinion

minimizes Bertram's virtues, lauds Helena, and ignores the ideas of the play.

Shakespeare depicts a Helena guilty of duplicity and a Bertram who matures during the play, and he shows the young asserting their youth. Norman Nathan defends[9] Isabella's marriage with Vincentio since they "love each other as they love virtue".

---

[1] 'The Interpretation of Shakespeare's Comedies', *Shakespeare Survey*, 8 (1955), 1–13.
[2] 'Comic Form in *Measure for Measure*', *ibid*. pp. 14–27.
[3] '*As You Like It*', *ibid*. pp. 40–51.
[4] 'Shakespeare's Comic Prose', *ibid*. pp. 57–68.
[5] '*Troilus and Cressida*', *ibid*. pp. 28–39.
[6] *Speculative Instruments* (Routledge and Kegan Paul, 1955), pp. 198–213.
[7] 'The Comedy of Generation', *Essays in Criticism*, v (April 1955), 97–117.
[8] 'In Defense of Bertram', *Shakespeare Quarterly*, VII (Winter 1956), 21–31.
[9] 'The Marriage of Duke Vincentio and Isabella', *ibid*. pp. 43–5.

Ernest Schanzer makes several useful points on *A Midsummer Night's Dream*.[1] He shows that Oberon and Titania, unlike Mustardseed, are nearly the size of adults, that they do not, as most critics pretend, behave irresponsibly, that "life among the faeries smacks more of Aldershot than of Cockaigne", and that Titania by her identification with Diana is to some extent merged with the moon.

Muriel C. Bradbrook is not primarily concerned in her book on Elizabethan comedy[2] with Shakespeare but her remarks about his comedies gain considerably from their place in the general survey. She is particularly good on pre-Shakespearian comedy and on stage-conventions. On some of the major dramatists she has not allowed herself enough space to develop her point of view. There are only two articles on the Histories. Wolfgang Clemen[3] analyses in great detail and from several points of view the scene in which Clarence is murdered, in order to demonstrate the degree to which in Shakespeare's dramatic art all the various aspects, stylistic as well as dramatic, are closely related. Peter Ure, who is editing *Richard II* in the Arden series, has an interesting article[4] on the significance of the looking-glass in the abdication scene. In previous literature the mirror had been a symbol both of truth-telling and of flattery, and Shakespeare makes use of both associations.

Herbert Weisinger's study of recent criticism of Shakespearian tragedy[5] convinces him that there is still something to be said for Bradley. He argues that one cannot interpret the plays by the means of imagery alone, and denies the contention that it is necessary to interpret them in the light of Elizabethan theories of psychology. Sylvan Barnet, however, believes[6] that modern critics can correct Coleridge in certain aspects. As he was a romantic, "reluctant to see evil in the universe", and as he believed that the poet should portray "the universal ideal through the particular", Coleridge was not at ease in discussing tragedy. He attempted

to force Shakespeare's plays into the mold of his own aesthetic theory.

The most substantial work on the Tragedies is Robert Speaight's *Nature in Shakespearian Tragedy*.[7] The title is a little misleading. Speaight purports to trace the ideas of Nature and Grace through five tragedies and *The Tempest*, though for long stretches the reader is allowed to forget the ostensible theme. The six essays, based on lectures and sometimes including matter which betrays their origin, contain many points of interest, including some that are new. Although Speaight writes as a Catholic, he is too good a critic to impose his own views on Shakespeare. He writes, for example, on the last act of *Antony and Cleopatra* in these terms:

Here is the end of contradiction and division; and the crucifying dialectic of human nature is resolved, not in terms of psychology or philosophy, but by the sheer superabundant power of the poetic image;

[1] 'The Moon and the Fairies in *A Midsummer Night's Dream*', *University of Toronto Quarterly*, XXIV (April 1955), 234–46.

[2] *The Growth and Structure of Elizabethan Comedy* (Chatto and Windus, 1955).

[3] 'Clarences Traum und Ermordung', *Sitzungsberichte der Bayerischen Akademie der Wissenschaften* (Jahrgang 1955, Heft 5).

[4] 'The Looking-Glass of Richard II', *Philological Quarterly*, XXXIV (April 1955), 219–24.

[5] 'The Study of Shakespearian Tragedy since Bradley', *Shakespeare Quarterly* VI (Autumn 1955), 387–96.

[6] 'Coleridge on Shakespeare's Villains', *Shakespeare Quarterly*, VII (Winter 1956), 9–20.

[7] *Nature in Shakespearian Tragedy* (Hollis and Carter, 1955).

not in terms of religious dogma, but in the triumph, beyond all reason or analysis, of a transcendent humanism....He asserts, without either moral censure or romantic compromise, his belief in the resurrection of the flesh.

Sometimes Speaight follows his characters off the stage to speculate about actions the dramatist does not show, and not all his views will meet acceptance—that there was an element of perversity in Desdemona, that the experience of the consummation of his marriage was so startling to Othello that it threw him off his balance, or that Gertrude never obtained erotic satisfaction from her first husband, as suggested by Barrault. But when he writes as an actor his views carry conviction, as when he urges that the Porter in *Macbeth* is dead sober.

Richard Laqueur expounds his conviction[1] that Shakespeare radically altered his first dramatic conception in all of his thirty-six plays and that, since he never revised or deleted anything in his first text, both conceptions are found side by side in the plays. In the chapters on *Othello, Lear, Macbeth* and *Hamlet*, which form the bulk of the book, we learn that in Shakespeare's later conception of these plays Desdemona, with Othello's connivance, had an affair with Cassio; that Cordelia was not the wife but the mistress of the King of France; that Lady Macduff was the mistress first of Ross and later of Macbeth, who murders her with his own hands; and that Gertrude was never married to Claudius. We also discover that in the later version of *Romeo and Juliet* Romeo is the lover not of Juliet but of the youthful Lady Capulet, whereas Juliet loves not Romeo but Tybalt whom she marries. Conservative scholars, it is to be feared, will not be entirely convinced by these shocking revelations of the depravity of Shakespeare's characters.

Clemen has written an interesting study[2] of the development of tragedy before Shakespeare by analysing the nature and function of the *Rede* in a number of plays from *Gorboduc* to *Edward II*. He suggests that the great tragedies of Shakespeare and his successors could not have been written without a marriage of academic drama, in which the set speeches are everything, with the popular drama in which action is all-important.

Of several articles on *Hamlet* that by Fredson Bowers is the most important.[3] It is a revealing commentary on the words "scourge and minister", often thought of as more or less synonymous. Hamlet could not be certain whether he was a scourge, a man already damned, who would avenge murder with murder, or a minister for whom God would provide an opportunity of executing his vengeance whilst keeping clear of crime. Heaven's intervention in the shape of the pirates made Hamlet realize that he was minister rather than scourge. The distinction is obviously of great significance, although it may be applied to the interpretation of *Hamlet* in more than one way. Wallace A. Bacon justly criticises[4] Harbage's *Shakespeare and the Rival Traditions*, particularly his interpretation of "quintessence of dust" as "the precious distillation of the spirit permeating all matter". Robert H. West takes[5] up Battenhouse's argument that the ghost is too vindictive to be a saved soul, and sensibly suggests that we "do not need to know the ghost's denomination". Shakespeare, as Dover Wilson implied, was deliberately ambiguous.

---

[1] *Shakespeares dramatische Konzeption* (Tübingen: Max Niemeyer Verlag, 1955).
[2] *Die Tragödie vor Shakespeare* (Heidelberg: Quelle and Meyer, 1955).
[3] 'Hamlet as Minister and Scourge', *PMLA*, LXX (September 1955), 740–7.
[4] 'A Footnote to Mr Harbage's "Hamlet", II, ii, 306–24', *Notes and Queries* (November 1955), pp. 475–7.
[5] 'King Hamlet's Ambiguous Ghost', *PMLA*, LXX (December 1955), 1107–17.

J. C. Maxwell points out[1] that Shakespeare is unique in introducing the notion of "the ghost from the grave" "at the point of highest tension and contrasting it with more theoretical conceptions". He refused "to sacrifice the imaginative potentialities of" popular ideas of the supernatural "at the dictates of contemporary sophisticated theory". Francis G. Schoff combines a warning[2] against "spatial" analysis with a description of Horatio as a nonentity "except in the degree that Hamlet's treatment of him makes us feel otherwise". J. Copley discusses[3] the significance of Ophelia's words on the owl and the baker's daughter in terms of symbolism, the owl representing Polonius, foreboding death, and suggesting St Valentine's Day.

S. A. Penasco regards[4] *Hamlet* as primarily a tragedy of ambition. The hero's delay in carrying out the commands of the Ghost is not due to weakness of character, but to the difficulties of the situation. His inner conflict arises from his subordination of revenge to his ambition. There are, of course, some lines in the play which may seem to support this interpretation, but there are others which do not.

Marvin Rosenberg, ably defending Iago,[5] claims that the ancient is not a devil, but merely a neurotic, the sort of man who suffers from gastric ulcers. His "aggressive drives", although magnified, are recognizably human. Paul N. Siegel adds a postscript[6] to his previous article on the damnation of Othello in answer to those critics who believe that the Moor was saved by his repentance. He shows that Christian repentance was distinguished from Judas' repentance. Othello has no faith in God's mercy, he suffers the punishments of hell in this life, and, like Judas, he kills himself. This may be theologically sound; but an audience would have less sympathy for an Othello who believed that he was forgiven; and even from a theological point of view it is possible to believe in the efficacy of Desdemona's prayers. N. K. Das Gupta's edition[7] of the play may be mentioned here for its long and informative introduction for Indian students. Robert B. Heilman, in what is apparently the introduction[8] to his forthcoming book on *Othello*, defines and defends imagistic criticism as used in his book on *King Lear*. Moody E. Prior, on the other hand, questions[9] whether imagery can be used as a test of authorship. He shows that in the additions to *The Spanish Tragedy*, as in Kyd's own scenes, there are frequent suggestions of night and darkness; he claims that iterative imagery is to be found in *Tamburlaine*; and he argues that there is an image-cluster in *A Woman Killed with Kindness* similar to one in *The Taming of the Shrew*. Prior, however, goes near to proving the opposite of what he intends. The suggestions of night and darkness do not constitute imagery; the iterative imagery in *Tamburlaine* is rudimentary, and although many poets use image-clusters, those analysed by Armstrong have not yet been discovered outside Shakespeare's acknowledged works, except in two apocryphal plays.

Siegel has another article[10] on the way in which Lear and Gloucester are refined by their

---

[1] 'Ghost from the Grave: A Note on Shakespeare's Apparitions', *Durham Univ. Journal*, XLVIII (March 1956), 55–9.
[2] 'Horatio: a Shakespearian Confidant', *Shakespeare Quarterly*, VII (Winter 1956), 53–7.
[3] '"They say the owle was a baker's daughter" (*Hamlet*, IV, v, 40)', *Notes and Queries* (Dec. 1955), pp. 512–13.
[4] 'El sentido de lo trágico en "Hamlet"', *Escritura*, III (December 1949), 104–22.
[5] 'In Defense of Iago', *Shakespeare Quarterly*, VI (Spring 1955), 145–58.
[6] 'The Damnation of Othello: An Addendum', *PMLA*, LXXI (March 1956), 279–80.
[7] *Othello* (Calcutta: H. Chatterji, 1955).
[8] 'Approach to *Othello*', *Sewanee Review*, LXIV (Winter 1956), 98–116.
[9] 'Imagery as a Test of Authorship', *Shakespeare Quarterly*, VI (Autumn 1955), 381–6.
[10] 'Adversity and the Miracle of Love in *King Lear*', *Shakespeare Quarterly*, VI (Summer 1955), 325–36.

sufferings, and he suggests that Lear's last words (in which he imagines that Cordelia is not dead) may be taken not as a pathetic delusion but as "an aspect of prophetic vision"—a vision of a future life. E. M. M. Taylor notes[1] that cynic philosophers scorned creature comforts and showed a preference for simple garments, and links this up with Edgar's blanket.

L. C. Knights has an impressive discussion[2] of the use of nature in *Macbeth*, more subtle and weighty than his earlier treatment of the same theme. He concludes that

it is only the man who recognizes his own humanity, and that of others, as something essentially other than a product of the natural world, who is really open to nature; neither fascinated nor afraid, he can respond creatively to its creativeness, and, paradoxically, find in nature a symbol for all that is natural in the other sense,—that is, most truly human.

Robert R. Boyle discusses[3] the imagery of a passage in *Macbeth* (I, vii, 21–8). He points out that when Shakespeare speaks of cherubs he thinks not of powerful beings but of "pink, chubby, winged infants" and that the "intent" for whose sides Macbeth has no spur is not his intent to kill Duncan but rather his intent to do good. This interpretation is difficult to square with the speech as a whole or with the subsequent scene with Lady Macbeth. Graham Martin applies the methods of the New Criticism to the same speech.[4] Jane H. Jack discusses[5] the influence of King James on the play particularly of his *Fruitful Meditation*, a commentary on some verses from Revelation. Certainly James touches on a number of themes which are to be found in *Macbeth* and he quotes some biblical passages which Shakespeare appears to have echoed, such as "wide is the waye that leadeth to destruction". Some of the passages about blood and babes may be coloured by memories of Revelation; there is one probable allusion to the story of Saul; and Jeremiah's denunciation of a man who listens to false prophets—"write this man destitute of children"—may, as well as Holinshed, underlie Macbeth's complaint of his barren sceptre. But, of course, Shakespeare did not have to read James to be reminded of the familiar stories of Herod and Saul, and there is other evidence that he knew Revelation directly.

Ernest Schanzer has followed up his article on Brutus with a more general interpretation of *Julius Caesar*,[6] in which he examines the psychological problem of the nature of the real Caesar and the ethical problem of his assassination, showing that Shakespeare avoided the simple medieval and renaissance views of Caesar as hero or tyrant, while indicating that Brutus was a blundering idealist. He regards it as one of Shakespeare's Problem Plays.

Daniel Stempel stresses[7] the references to witchcraft in *Antony and Cleopatra* and points out the association of lust and witchcraft in *Malleus Maleficarum*. It is difficult to agree that Octavius's words "Not so, adieu!" represent "a decisive refusal" of Cleopatra's "proffered dominion"; to suppose that Antony is indifferent to the objects of his passion; or to regard "lass unparalleled" as a reference to Cleopatra's inability to rise above the vices of her sex. To Stempel "the maid

[1] 'Lear's Philosopher', *Shakespeare Quarterly*, VI (Summer 1955), 364–5.
[2] 'On the Background of Shakespeare's Use of Nature in *Macbeth*', *Sewanee Review*, LXIV (Spring 1956), 207–17.
[3] 'The Imagery of *Macbeth*, I, vii, 21–8', *Modern Language Quarterly*, XVI (June 1955), 130–6.
[4] John Wain, *Interpretations* (Routledge and Kegan Paul, 1955), pp. 17–30.
[5] 'Macbeth, King James and the Bible', *ELH*, XXII (September 1955), 173–93.
[6] 'The Problem of *Julius Caesar*', *Shakespeare Quarterly*, VI (Summer 1955), 297–308.
[7] 'The Transmigration of the Crocodile', *Shakespeare Quarterly*, VII (Winter 1956), 59–72.

that milks" means that Cleopatra is "governed by no specifically noble passion" though, in a famous speech, Queen Elizabeth said

If I were a milkmaid with a pail on my arm, whereby my private person might be a little set by, I would not forsake that poor and single state to match with the greatest monarch.

Joseph Stull, commenting[1] on the dismissal of the messenger (III, v, 103–6) argues that Cleopatra magnanimously presents Antony's gifts to the messenger. W. M. Merchant has a valuable essay[2] on the significance of the painter-poet scenes in *Timon of Athens* and their relation to the contrast between appearance and reality throughout the play.

John H. Long argues convincingly[3] that the second dance in *Pericles*, II, 3, is performed by Pericles and Thaisa alone, and that it represents "the third test of Pericles in which his fitness in the art of love is examined". J. M. Nosworthy, in a by-product of his edition of *Cymbeline*, argues[4] for the authenticity of disputed passages. F. D. Hoeniger shows once more[5] that there is a re-enactment of Prospero's forgiveness in the three hours action of *The Tempest*, and that even the villains learn that miracles are possible. Walther Fischer briefly discusses[6] the theme of reconciliation and forgiveness in Shakespeare's last plays.

J. W. Lever's book on *The Elizabethan Love Sonnet*[7] has been undervalued by some reviewers. It is not profound, but modesty, scholarship and commonsense have combined to make it a valuable study of its subject. Lever is, perhaps, unnecessarily severe with some of the minor sonneteers. Constable may deserve his dismissal but Drayton is more often successful than Lever allows. But he has some illuminating comparisons of English sonnets with their French and Italian models and he shows that working within a tradition does not prevent the English poets from being individual and even original. Above all, Lever's hundred pages on Shakespeare's sonnets are remarkably sane and well-balanced. In contrast to Lever's literary study there is C. Van Emde Boas' psychological study[8] of the way in which the conflict between a boy and a woman for a man's love in the Sonnets is related to the dressing up of Viola and Rosalind. Boas opposes Wilde's Willie Hughes theory, suggests that any identification by Shakespeare of a boy-actor with the youth of the sonnets was subjective and "intrapsychic", and avers that Shakespeare cannot be shown to have been consciously homosexual or bi-sexual. He gives a case-history of the poet on what seems to be slender evidence. T. Walter Herbert explicates sonnet CXLII.[9] Muriel Bradbrook replies[10] to Ronald Bates on 'The Phoenix and the Turtle' and avers that the key-word of the poem is "simplicity" in the philosophic sense:

The marriage bed, the funeral pyre, the Phoenix' nest, and the kiss of the spouse, the ingression into the divine shadow are all subsumed under one image.

[1] 'Cleopatra's Magnanimity: the Dismissal of the Messenger', *ibid.* pp. 73–8.
[2] 'Timon and the Conceit of Art', *Shakespeare Quarterly*, VI (Summer 1955), 249–57.
[3] 'Laying the Ghosts in *Pericles*', *Shakespeare Quarterly*, VII (Winter 1956), 39–42.
[4] 'The Integrity of Shakespeare: Illustrated from *Cymbeline*', *Shakespeare Survey*, 8 (1955), 52–6.
[5] 'Prospero's Storm and Miracle', *Shakespeare Quarterly*, VII (Winter 1956), 33–8.
[6] 'Shakespeares Späte Romanzen', *Shakespeare Jahrbuch*, XCI (1955), 7–24.
[7] *The Elizabethan Love Sonnet* (Methuen, 1956).
[8] *Shakespeare's Sonnetten en hun Verband met de Travesti-Double Spelen* (Amsterdam-Antwerpen: Wereld-Bibliotheek, 1951).   [9] 'Shakespeare's Sonnet CXLII', *The Explicator*, XIII (April 1955).
[10] "'The Phoenix and the Turtle'", *Shakespeare Quarterly*, VI (Summer 1955), 356–8.

A. Alvarez gives us yet another interpretation of the poem[1] in which he, like J. V. Cunningham, finds scholastic terminology. The poem, he suggests, is

A way...of showing that the highest mysteries of Love demand their own metaphysic, religion and logic, and their own poetic ritual to give them at once grandeur and detachment.

The steps by which he arrives at this conclusion are not, perhaps, less difficult than the poem itself. Finally, it may be mentioned that T. K. Dutt gives[2] an elementary account of Shakespeare's poems, and Roberto Bula Piriz a short introductory study[3] for secondary schools.

T. W. Baldwin's survey[4] of the present state of Shakespeare studies is notable for his disclaiming the view, derived sometimes from his books, that Shakespeare was "learned". Borinski discusses[5] the juxtaposition of the opposed types of soldier and politician in English Renaissance literature, and especially in some of Shakespeare's plays. In another article[6] he argues that Shakespeare's plays written between 1600 and 1610, with their concern with evil, particularly infidelity and treachery, and their moral despair, reflect a new spiritual awareness which is also found in the other English literature of that decade. Theodor Spira looks[7] on Shakespeare's work in relation to the main political and spiritual problems of the age in an attempt to discover the poet's attitude towards them. Paul J. Aldus discusses[8] mirror scenes which do not advance the plot but add enormously to our understanding of the theme (e.g. *Julius Caesar*, I, i; *1 Henry IV*, I, ii; *Antony and Cleopatra*, II, vii). Paul A. Jorgensen comments[9] on the fact that in *1 Henry IV*, *1 Henry VI*, *Julius Caesar* and *Coriolanus* the command of an army is divided. Roy Walker, in a lively article,[10] analyses the importance of cosmic imagery in the plays.

J. Loiseau describes[11] the plans for a new edition of the plays with French translations and introductions by different scholars, sometimes adapted from books and articles. A. Koszul discusses[12] the eternal problem of translation in relation to a prose version of the sonnets by P. J. Jouve, which he compares with Legouis' fine verse translation. Koszul is himself responsible for an excellent translation[13] of *The Shoemaker's Holiday* and, in collaboration with F. Sauvage, of *Henry VI*.[14] Władysław Tarnawski has made an accurate Polish version of *Hamlet*,[15] Takeshi

---

[1] John Wain, *op. cit.* pp. 1–16.   [2] *Critical Studies of English Poets* (Allahabad, 1956), pp. 41–7.

[3] *William Shakespeare* (Montevideo: Eduardo Acevedo, 1952).

[4] 'On Atomizing Shakespeare', *Shakespeare Jahrbuch*, XCI (1955), 136–44.

[5] '"Soldat" und "Politiker" bei Shakespeare und seinen Zeitgenossen', *ibid.* pp. 87–120.

[6] 'Die tragische Periode der englischen Literatur', *Die Neueren Sprachen*, Heft 7 (Jahrgang 1955), 289–307.

[7] 'Shakespeares Dichtung und die Welt der Geschichte', *Shakespeare Jahrbuch*, XCI (1955), 65–86.

[8] 'Analogical Probability in Shakespeare's Plays', *Shakespeare Quarterly*, VI (Autumn 1955), 397–414.

[9] 'Divided Command in Shakespeare', *PMLA*, LXX (September 1955), 750–61.

[10] 'The Celestial Plane in Shakespeare', *Shakespeare Survey*, 8 (1955), 109–17.

[11] 'L'Éternel Problème de la Traduction: à propos d'une Nouvelle Édition avec Traduction de Shakespeare', *Études Anglaises*, IX (Janvier–Mars 1956), 10–13.

[12] 'L'Éternel Problème de la Traduction: à propos d'une Nouvelle Version des Sonnets de Shakespeare', *ibid.* pp. 1–9.

[13] *Fête chez le Cordonnier* (Paris: La Société d'Édition Les Belles Lettres, 1955).

[14] *Le Roi Henri VI* (Part I) (Paris: La Société d'Édition Les Belles Lettres, 1955).

[15] Stanisław Helsztyński (Editor) and Władysław Tarnawski (Translator), *Hamlet* (Breslau: Ossoliński, 1955).

Saito a Japanese version of *King Lear*,[1] Henrique Pongetti and Willy Keller a free adaptation of *The Comedy of Errors*,[2] C. Van Emde Boas a Dutch version of some of the *Sonnets*[3] and Eduardo Dieste a somewhat pedestrian version of others.[4] Rudolf Stamm provides a detailed discussion of Flatter's translation of *Hamlet*.[5]

2. SHAKESPEARE'S LIFE, TIMES AND STAGE

reviewed by R. A. FOAKES

In an article[6] castigating those modern critics who wish to interpret Shakespeare's tragedies in Christian terms and to see Othello and Lear in particular saved, Sylvan Barnet observes that to extend the lives of characters beyond the play into the next world is just as much an error as the old fault of reconstructing their career before the play begins; he continues:

> Shakespeare presents such full worlds that it is possible with a little ingenuity and effort to find in him almost any theory which the researcher wishes to discover.

If it is possible to discern a devout Shakespeare, it is also possible to shape out a pagan Shakespeare, or even, according to Paul Arnold, a Rosicrucian Shakespeare. He believes that in *Ésotérisme de Shakespeare*[7] he is revealing for the first time the true meaning of the last plays and several comedies, as expressions of a cabalistic philosophy, which, it seems, was the major preoccupation of the Elizabethan *élite*, and the sole genuine interest of all the poets and dramatists. A similar lack of restraint makes it impossible to take seriously Calvin Hoffman's *The Man who was Shakespeare*,[8] which claims that Marlowe did not die in 1593, but escaped to live in exile and despatch his manuscripts to Sir Thomas Walsingham, who paid an obscure actor named Shakespeare to lend his name to Marlowe's work; this, incidentally, included not only his known plays and Shakespeare's but *Locrine*, *The Spanish Tragedy* and *Edward III*. Fortunately the tone of the book will prevent the careful reader from being misled by a parade of "evidence" which is no more than conjecture, and of parallelisms which merely show that Shakespeare knew Marlowe's plays. If any doubt still lingers, he might turn to the equally ingenious and equally baseless argument of H. Amphlett's *Who was Shakespeare? A New Enquiry*,[9] which restates the theory that Edward de Vere, Earl of Oxford, wrote Shakespeare's plays. This is founded on assumptions such as that Shakespeare must have been an aristocrat in order to write about aristocrats, and must have had a university education in order to read Latin: this kind of reasoning, pursued very far, might lead to most strange conclusions, that a Moor wrote *Othello*, that a woman created Cleopatra.

[1] *King Lear* (Tokyo: Kaibunsha, 1955).

[2] *A Comédia dos Equívocos* (Rio de Janeiro: Depart. de Imprensa Nacional, 1955).

[3] *Keur Uit Shakespeare's Sonnetten* (Amsterdam-Antwerpen: Wereld-Bibliotheek, 1951?).

[4] *21 Sonetos* (Montevideo: Editorial Independencia, 1944).

[5] 'Hamlet in Richard Flatter's Translation', *English Studies*, XXXVI (October, December 1955), 228–38, 299–308.

[6] 'Some Limitations of a Christian Approach to Shakespeare', *ELH*, XXII (June 1955), 81–92.

[7] Paris: Mercure de France, 1955.

[8] Max Parrish, 1955; see the review and the author's reply in *Times Literary Supplement*, 27 January and 17 February 1956.   [9] Heinemann, 1955.

New insights into Shakespeare's life and career have been provided indirectly[1] this year in two important articles. In one[2] I. A. Shapiro shows that the date on the manuscript of Mundy's *John a Kent* is not 1596, as commonly believed, but 1590. This "reopens the whole problem of *Sir Thomas More*", has a bearing upon the chronology of plays by Marlowe, Green and Shakespeare, and may cause a revision of accepted ideas regarding the development of the history-play. Another contribution to the evidence that Shakespeare was active in the theatre much earlier than used to be supposed has been made by J. Isaacs,[3] who tracks a number of interesting connexions between his plays and "scenes and sounds in plays available to him in some form or other before the end of 1594", showing how he stored them in his memory and used them even in his last plays. Two other articles deal with allusions to Shakespeare. Warren B. Austin[4] has put forward a convincing argument that Sonnet IX of R. B.'s *Greene's Funerals* has no connexion with Shakespeare, and does not refer to the "upstart crow" passage in Greene's *Groatsworth of Wit*; he claims that, like the rest of the volume, it attacks Gabriel Harvey and Wolfe, the printer of Harvey's *Three Letters*, and alludes to Harvey's denigration of Greene's "borowed & filched plumes". Ernest Sirluck[5] has found sixteen new allusions to Shakespeare's work and that of Jonson in civil war pamphlets, chiefly puritan, and believes that during the Commonwealth period there may have been no decline in the frequency of allusions, as G. E. Bentley suggested in his *Shakespeare and Jonson*, but merely a change in their character "from the predominantly literary to the predominantly political".

This year has not yielded much in the way of additions to our knowledge of the sources of Shakespeare's plays. The most exciting work has again been indirect, illuminating the way in which he used source material, or dealing with influences upon him. The most important study is Wolfgang Clemen's *Die Tragödie vor Shakespeare*,[6] which analyses the development of pre-Shakespearian tragedy as revealed in dramatic speech. Clemen surveys the forms of speech derived from older drama, Seneca and the morality, and Elizabethan classifications of speech-forms, such as are found in Wilson's *Arte of Rhetorique*, and examines the way these are used in a wide range of plays, giving particular attention to the work of Peele, Greene, Kyd and Marlowe. The book concludes with a long section devoted to the complaint, showing how topics and modes of address and apostrophe were carried over from the early drama and used again and again. So, for instance, the author traces, from *Hercules Oetaeus* through the complaints of

[1] The nearest thing to a direct contribution is Alan Keen's further investigation of what he calls 'Shakespeare's Northern Apprenticeship' (*Times Literary Supplement*, 18 November 1955 and 30 March 1956); he has identified the "ffoke Gyllome" of Alexander Houghton's will as the son of a Chester embroiderer, and thinks father and son were guild players. It would seem simpler to think that the Shakeshafte associated with them was also a local man from Cheshire, and not Shakespeare, as Keen maintains.

[2] 'The Significance of a Date', *Shakespeare Survey*, 8 (1955), 100–5.

[3] 'Shakespeare's Earliest Years in the Theatre', *Proceedings of the British Academy*, XXXIX (1955), 119–38. This formed the Annual Shakespeare Lecture of 1953.

[4] 'A Supposed Contemporary Allusion to Shakespeare as a Plagiarist', *Shakespeare Quarterly*, VI (Autumn 1955), 373–80.

[5] 'Shakespeare and Jonson among the Pamphleteers of the First Civil War: Some Unreported Seventeenth-Century Allusions', *Modern Philology*, LIII (November 1955), 88–99. Raymond S. Biswanger Jr. has found a few 'More Seventeenth-Century Allusions to Shakespeare' in D'Urfey's *Richmond Heiress* (1693), and reports them in *Notes and Queries* (July 1955), pp. 301–2.

[6] Subtitled *Ihre Entwicklung im Spiegel der dramatischen Rede* (Heidelberg: Quelle & Meyer, 1955).

Bajazeth in *Tamburlaine*, Clifford in *2 Henry VI*, and passages in a variety of other plays, Cleopatra's lament over Antony,

> O sun,
> Burn the great sphere thou movest in! darkling stand
> The varying shore o' the world....

Shakespeare's tragedies are seen as the high point of this development, displaying a rich diversity of means working towards a single end, as the individual elements of earlier plays were integrated into a new art-form.

Some shorter studies throw light on the way Shakespeare's mind worked. A. S. Cairncross[1] ingeniously explains an inconsistency in *3 Henry VI*, where Montague appears first as York's nephew, then in place of the Salisbury of the chronicles: it seems that he replaces Falconbridge, who had replaced Salisbury, the clue to the latter identification being provided by *The True Tragedy*. This gives his relationship to York as "cousin", which fits Salisbury, whereas Shakespeare's "brother" fits Falconbridge. Also ingenious, but less convincing, is Rudolf Fiehler's account[2] of the transmutation of Oldcastle into Falstaff; he believes that in *The Famous Victories of Henry the Fifth* one actor doubled the parts of the clown Dericke and the highwayman Oldcastle, which Shakespeare combined into Falstaff. Ernst Künstler[3] shows that Shakespeare's geography in *The Winter's Tale* is not, after all, so strange, for Aeneas Sylvius had described Bohemia as situated on the Baltic, an inland sea stretching from the Danube to the Adriatic, and this notion, transmitted into England by the humanists of the sixteenth century, could well have led Greene and Shakespeare to think of that country as located not on one but two seas. The riddle of Antiochus in *Pericles* has been traced back to the Latin by P. Goolden,[4] who claims that it was correctly but obscurely translated by Gower, and explains the difficult clues of "son" and "mother" in

> He's father, son and husband mild;
> I mother, wife and yet his child

as in-law relationships resulting from a daughter's incest with her father.

A useful study of sources is the comprehensive survey by Laurence Michel and Cecil C. Seronsky[5] of the relationship between Shakespeare's history plays and the work of Samuel Daniel; they conclude that Shakespeare was influenced by the latter's *Complaint of Rosamond*, *Civil Wars* and possibly his *Cleopatra*. Holger Nørgaard[6] finds a source in the 1606 text of this play for the image of the "spent swimmers" in *Macbeth*, but the borrowing might have been in the other direction. Other articles on *Macbeth* include an attempt by Jane H. Jack[7] to show that Shakespeare was influenced by a number of the works of King James, including the *Basilikon Doron*. The biblical analogies she finds, with the death of Saul and the unleashing of Satan in

---

[1] 'An "Inconsistency" in "3 Henry VI"', *Modern Language Review*, L (October 1955), 492–4.

[2] 'How Oldcastle Became Falstaff', *Modern Language Quarterly*, XVI (March 1955), 16–28.

[3] 'Böhmen am Meer', *Shakespeare Jahrbuch*, XCI (1955), 212–16.

[4] 'Antiochus's Riddle in Gower and Shakespeare', *Review of English Studies*, n.s. VI (July 1955), 245–51.

[5] 'Shakespeare's History Plays and Daniel: An Assessment', *Studies in Philology*, LII (October 1955), 549–77.

[6] 'The Bleeding Captain Scene in *Macbeth* and Daniel's *Cleopatra*', *Review of English Studies*, n.s. VI (October 1955), 395–6.

[7] '*Macbeth*, King James and the Bible', *Journal of English Literary History*, XXII (September 1955), 173–93.

Revelation, are more interesting, if not more convincing than the favourite identifications of Duncan with Christ, Macbeth with Judas, which Paul N. Siegel[1] seeks to bolster. William B. Bache comments[2] further on Shakespeare's possible indebtedness to Deloney's *Thomas of Reading*.

The usual notes reporting analogues or parallels for passages in the plays include an account of the development of the idea of the noble savage before Shakespeare's time,[3] indications of the influence of Erasmus, who formulated the image of the mind as a troubled fountain,[4] and of Aphthonius,[5] who seems to have provided hints for Gaunt's speech on England in *Richard II*. The juxtaposition of "Massiliensis, Hilurios" in *Menaechmi*, observed by L. G. Salingar,[6] serves to explain why Sebastian and Viola in *Twelfth Night* come to Illyria from Messaline. The early analogue found by P. J. Frankis[7] for a famous speech in *King John* in Andrew Borde's *Introduction of Knowledge* (1548) may affect the dating of the play. In another note which affects a dating Charles S. Felver[8] argues that Robert Armin's *Two Maids of Moreclacke* was written prior to *As You Like It*, in which Shakespeare compliments the goldsmith turned clown by calling him Touchstone, an allusion to the clown Tutch in his own play. Attention has also been drawn to parallels between various plays and works by Horace, Greene and Ben Jonson,[9] and Arthur M. Z. Norman surveys Shakespeare's debt to Plutarch in *Antony and Cleopatra*.[10] Of more general interest is Ralph Graham Palmer's edition of Seneca's *De Remediis Fortuitorum*,[11] a work in which Jonson, Marston and possibly other dramatists seem to have delved. One further peripheral study is Rudolf Stamm's *Englischer Literaturbarock*,[12] which seeks to define the baroque in English literature in terms of the intrusion of a subjective element into the objective world of early seventeenth-century poetry, and to explain why there was no great baroque drama.

A fresh survey of the Elizabethan drama for the general reader has been made by Romain Sanvic in *Le Théâtre Élisabéthain*;[13] having not only read but seen the major and many of the

[1] 'Echoes of the Bible Story in "Macbeth"', *Notes and Queries* (April 1955), pp. 142–3.

[2] '"The Murder of Old Cole": A Possible Source for *Macbeth*', *Shakespeare Quarterly*, VI (Summer 1955), 358–9. J. C. Maxwell has a brief note on 'The Relation of "Macbeth" to "Sophonisba"', *Notes and Queries* (September 1955), pp. 373–4.

[3] Gosta Langenfelt, '"The Noble Savage" until Shakespeare', *English Studies*, XXXVI (October 1955), 222–7.

[4] Rolf Soellner, 'The Troubled Fountain: Erasmus formulates a Shakespearian Simile', *Journal of English and Germanic Philology*, LV (January 1956), 70–4.

[5] William C. McAvoy, 'Form in *Richard II*, II, i, 40–66', *Journal of English and Germanic Philology*, LIV (July 1955), 355–61.

[6] 'Messaline in "Twelfth Night"', *Times Literary Supplement*, 3 June 1955.

[7] 'Shakespeare's "King John" and a Patriotic Slogan', *Notes and Queries* (October 1955), pp. 424–5.

[8] 'Robert Armin, Shakespeare's Source for Touchstone', *Shakespeare Quarterly*, VII (Winter 1956), 135–7.

[9] L. P. Wilkinson, 'Shakespeare and Horace', *Times Literary Supplement*, 6 May 1955; Kenneth Muir, 'Greene and "Troilus and Cressida"', *Notes and Queries* (April 1955), pp. 141–2; Claire McGlinchee, '"Still Harping..."', *Shakespeare Quarterly*, VI (Summer 1955), 362–4.

[10] 'Source Material in "Antony and Cleopatra"', *Notes and Queries* (February 1956), pp. 59–61. Paul E. Bennett's argument in *Notes and Queries* (October and November 1955), pp. 422–4, 462–3, that the allusion in *A Knack to Know a Knave* to *Titus Andronicus* cannot be taken seriously is based on some rash assumptions and an improbable emendation.

[11] Chicago: Institute of Elizabethan Studies, 1953.

[12] Reprinted from *Die Kunstformen des Barockzeitalters* (Berne: Francke Verlag, 1955), pp. 383–412.

[13] Brussels: Collections Lebègue et Nationale, 1955.

lesser plays, he has a fine sense of their relative qualities, and writes with balance and urbanity. The current presentation of Shakespeare has received more attention than his own stage this year, but there have been a number of attempts to probe further into methods of staging and acting in the Elizabethan theatre. The most specific is Robert James Fusillo's examination of the Bosworth Field scenes in *Richard III*,[1] which he claims are unique in the drama of the time in presenting "two wholly distinct groups—each represented in a different locale—sharing the stage"; he thinks the stage-doors indicated the two locations, and were perhaps adorned to suggest tents. Several other comments stem directly from two of the most provocative books of recent years, Alfred Harbage's *Shakespeare and the Rival Traditions* and Leslie Hotson's *The First Night of Twelfth Night*.[2] Wallace A. Bacon enters an objection against the former as making what he sees as over-simple generalization based on a doubtful interpretation of the speech on man in *Hamlet*.[3] The most important reply to Hotson's book is that of A. M. Nagler,[4] who has found, in a description of the way in which a hall in Florence was arranged for the performance of a play in 1585, the phrase "intorno intorno" used of tiers of seats which clearly occupied three sides, the stage taking up the fourth. He claims that Don Virginio Orsino meant the same by his "atorno atorno", and was not trying to indicate an arena stage, as Hotson supposed. J. W. Saunders[5] also quarrels with Hotson's interpretation of this phrase, and his assertion that 'mansions' were used generally on the stage. Madeleine Hope Dodds[6] has re-examined the manuscript describing the reception of Don Virginio, confirming that it is dated 1601/2, which remains its most puzzling feature, since it refers to a visit made in 1600/1.

The 1955 *Shakespeare Jahrbuch* takes as its main theme Shakespeare in the theatre. In a general discussion of recent research, Rudolf Stamm[7] deplores what he sees as a tendency for the plays to be treated either as literature or as theatre: he would like to see both approaches integrated into one. Anton Müller-Bellinghausen[8] considers the way in which Shakespeare paints scenes in words, observing a development from the early plays, which tend to convey a precise sense of place and time, to the later plays, in which the scene-painting is atmospheric and intimately linked with action and imagery. The idea of a "syntax of gestures" in a play by Shakespeare, of finding a balance of scenes with many gestures against scenes with few, and perhaps a dominant gesture, might prove fruitful, but Arthur Gerstner-Hirzel's essay[9] seems mechanical, includes pointless statistics, and reveals nothing new. Bertram Joseph cautions against thinking of an Elizabethan play in terms of the modern stage,[10] referring again to Bulwer's *Chirologia* and *Chironomia*, and claiming that the rhetorical gestures he describes arise naturally and help an audience to respond to the poetry as vividly in the theatre as in the study. Thus "when the words

---

[1] 'Tents on Bosworth Field', *Shakespeare Quarterly*, VI (Spring 1955), 193–4.

[2] Reviewed respectively in *Shakespeare Survey*, 7 and *Shakespeare Survey*, 8.

[3] 'A Footnote to Mr Harbage's "Hamlet", II, ii, 306–24', *Notes and Queries* (November 1955), pp. 475–7.

[4] 'Shakespeare's Arena Demolished', *Shakespeare Newsletter*, VI (February 1956), 7.

[5] 'The Elizabethan Theatre', *Times Literary Supplement*, 11 November 1955.

[6] 'The First Night of Twelfth Night', *Notes and Queries* (February 1956), pp. 57–9. The comments by W. G. Hiscock (*Times Literary Supplement*, 29 July 1955) and Sara Ruth Watson (*Notes and Queries*, November 1955) seem pointless.   [7] 'Dramenforschung', *Shakespeare Jahrbuch*, XCI (1955), 121–35.

[8] 'Die Wortkulisse bei Shakespeare', *ibid.* pp. 182–95.

[9] 'Stagecraft and Poetry', *ibid.* pp. 196–211.

[10] 'The Elizabethan Stage and the Art of Elizabethan Drama', *ibid.* pp. 145–60.

are performed properly in the theatre, the audience responds to what is a literary experience". This seems a fine ideal, but presupposes an ideal audience; in any case Bulwer's precepts have no reference to acting, and one wonders whether it is justifiable to identify the art of the orator with that of the actor simply on the grounds that a similar vocabulary had to serve to describe both.

Other essays are concerned with modern producing. Ronald Watkins[1] pleads for a return to an Elizabethan simplicity of staging, and demands actors who can sing, dance, fence, mime, and possess true poetic sensibility, in fact a company of virtuosi. Hannes Razum[2] desires a full integration of colours, costumes, music, lighting, the bearing and gait of the actors. The most severe requirements are those of Alfred Harbage,[3] who puts the responsibility for the disappointment he feels with recent major productions upon the shoulders of the directors or producers: he claims that at the Globe "no agency intervened" between the script and the actors, and he attacks directors who rearrange or distort a play in order to "vitalize" it. He believes we need a new kind of director, who will be reverent, learned, able to train his actors, and knowing "more about Shakespeare's language and frame of reference than the professors, and more about Shakespeare's theatre than the builders of model Globes". This essay is reprinted with slight alterations in the author's book *Theatre for Shakespeare*,[4] which develops the argument further. He castigates particularly modern productions employing 'star' actors, such as those at Stratford-upon-Avon and the Old Vic, seeing danger in "over-direction and sophistication", but his main complaint is the "inadequacy of the actors". The chief need, he thinks, is for a company working in a permanent repertory of three or so plays a season, and able, by paying enough, to attract good actors for small parts.

Many will think Harbage's strictures are harsh on, for instance, the Old Vic, and will wonder whether Shakespeare's plays would lend themselves to a uniformity of acting style as easily as the French classical drama. Some points in the argument seem contradictory, and the reader may experience surprise when he finds the best film versions praised for "respectful adaptation" ("There is nothing wicked about adaptation"), while the stage-directors are chastized for their egotism in "getting between us and Shakespeare". But though one may quarrel with many of Harbage's views and all of his practical proposals, it is to be hoped that his righteous anger will make actors and directors everywhere look to their laurels. Harbage speaks of Granville-Barker's work as the beginning of a "golden age". It is difficult to realize now how revolutionary his 1912 production of *The Winter's Tale* was, and C. B. Purdom's biography of him[5] does not attempt that most difficult task of recreating the effect it made, though the photographs reproduced serve to show how much modern producers have learned from him in simplifying settings. What this book shows is how small a part of Granville-Barker's activities as actor, director and writer was devoted to Shakespeare; nevertheless, it is questionable whether it does justice to this part of his work. His productions are merely reported with much detailed and irrelevant information; his Shakespearian criticism provides an occasion for the expression of the author's

[1] 'The Actor's Task in Interpreting Shakespeare', *ibid.* pp. 174–81.
[2] 'Probleme der Shakespeare-Regie', *ibid.* pp. 225–32.
[3] 'The Role of the Shakespearean Producer', *ibid.* pp. 161–73.
[4] The Alexander Lectures, 1954–5 (University of Toronto Press, 1955). The book also reprints an article on 'Elizabethan Acting' which first appeared in *Publications of the Modern Language Association of America* of 1933.
[5] *Harley Granville-Barker. Man of the Theatre, Dramatist and Scholar* (Rockliff, 1955).

own rather naive views, for attacks on scholars in general, and on Granville-Barker for becoming a scholar; so the valuable *Preface to Coriolanus* is dismissed as "an academic work; on that level excellent, but below the level of such a man of the theatre". Altogether this is a pedestrian narrative, full of strange asides and undigested notes; its greatest value lies in the many, and often entertaining, letters of Granville-Barker, G. B. Shaw and Gilbert Murray which are printed in full or in part.

Commentary on current productions grows apace, as the number of Shakespeare theatres and festivals grows. Of especial interest are reports on the recently established theatres at Stratford, Ontario, and Stratford, Connecticut. The former, built in a small town in an area which had been, according to Arnold Edinborough,[1] a cultural desert, has employed well-known actors and producers, such as Alec Guinness and Tyrone Guthrie, and seems to have been a huge success. Guthrie himself[2] recounts the origin and development of the festival theatre.[2] The new festival in Connecticut seems to have been disappointing, and Alice Griffin[3] complains of "uninspired, old-fashioned and plodding presentations", feeling that the importing of 'stars' from Hollywood was a mistake. One feature of recent Shakespeare festivals has been the successful staging of unfashionable plays, and perhaps the adjective no longer applies to *All's Well*, performed in Canada, at the Old Vic and at Ashland, Oregon, where an enterprising repertory also included *Timon* and *3 Henry VI*.[4] The Antioch College festival is emulating the Old Vic in producing all the plays in six seasons,[5] and it seems that altogether thirty-one of the plays and *The Two Noble Kinsmen* have been presented in the past year.[6] If the performance of some rarely acted early plays, especially *Titus Andronicus* at Stratford-upon-Avon and Cambridge, has proved for M. St Clare Byrne[7] that they are still "the exciting and viable plays they were written to be", and not "unstageable literary curiosities", the major companies have also provoked some hostile criticism, which would lend support to Alfred Harbage's dissatisfaction with modern staging of Shakespeare. For though Richard David[8] found much that was exciting in the season at Stratford-upon-Avon and London, he has many complaints, and Alan S. Downer,[9] reviewing the same season, feels that

The modern producer nods respectfully in the direction of William Poel and Adolf Appia, but he sits at the feet of Henry Irving and Beerbohn Tree.

A. C. Sprague is equally severe upon the New York productions, especially the Old Vic's *A Midsummer Night's Dream*,[10] and it may be that the best Shakespeare is to be seen on provincial

[1] 'Shakespeare Confirmed: At Canadian Stratford', *Shakespeare Quarterly*, VI (Autumn 1955), 435–40.

[2] 'Shakespeare at Stratford, Ontario', *Shakespeare Survey*, 8 (1955), 127–31.

[3] 'The American Shakespeare Festival', *Shakespeare Quarterly*, VI (Autumn 1955), 441–6.

[4] Horace W. Robinson, 'Shakespeare, Ashland, Oregon', *Shakespeare Quarterly*, VI (Autumn 1955), 447–51.

[5] Omar Ranney, 'Antioch Shakespeare Festival', *Shakespeare Quarterly*, VI (Autumn 1955), 453–4.

[6] Alice Griffin, 'Current Theatre Notes', *Shakespeare Quarterly*, VII (Winter 1956), 79–96.

[7] 'Two *Titus* Productions', *Theatre Notebook*, X (January–March 1956), 44–8.

[8] 'Plays Pleasant and Plays Unpleasant', *Shakespeare Survey*, 8 (1955), 132–8.

[9] 'A Comparison of Two Stagings: Stratford-on-Avon and London', *Shakespeare Quarterly*, VI (Autumn 1955), 429–33. In view of these comments it is valuable to have on record a description by a director of her problems and attempts to return to a simpler staging, in Ngaio Marsh's 'A Note on a Production of *Twelfth Night*', *Shakespeare Survey*, 8 (1955), 69–73.

[10] 'Shakespeare on the New York Stage', *Shakespeare Quarterly*, VI (Autumn 1955), 423–7.

stages. Kurt Dörnemann[1] feels this to be true in Germany, in his report on post-war performances in the Rhine valley and the Ruhr. *Shakespeare Jahrbuch* also contains accounts of productions on the Berlin and Vienna stages in recent years[2] in southern Germany[3] and in provincial German theatres.[4]

A work which may be of use to modern producers is John H. Long's *Shakespeare's Use of Music*,[5] which discusses the music in seven comedies ranging from *Two Gentlemen* to *Twelfth Night*, and provides many settings of songs from music by Elizabethan composers, as well as a description of musical instruments then in use. The author argues that music should be played on three occasions in *A Midsummer Night's Dream* when there are no stage directions calling for it, supports Richmond Noble's division of the last song in this play, thinks II, vi in *As You Like It* should precede II, v, and believes Balthasar was introduced into *Much Ado* to give employment to the singing talents of Robert Armin, who also had the parts of Amiens and Feste, and began his connexion with the Chamberlain's Men "about two years earlier than has been believed heretofore". There are one or two contradictions in the book, and it is a pity that Long thinks both "Who is Sylvia?" and Feste's final song to be extraneous to the drama: the bibliography contains a few strange errors, and omits W. R. Bowden's *The English Dramatic Lyric, 1603–42*. Macdonald Emslie has found a setting of Hamlet's "To be or not to be" soliloquy,[6] apparently selected by Pepys, which may afford a clue to the "way in which Betterton delivered this familiar passage".

A piece of acute detective-work has enabled Allan Stevens[7] to track down the names of a cast-list decapitated by a binder of Fletcher's *Night-Walker*, and to throw light on the dating of cast-lists in a copy of the Third Folio in the Folger Library, which seem to belong to a period prior to 1682. George Winchester Stone Jr. shows that Garrick did not maltreat *The Tempest*[8] in his later productions of it. Wilhelm Dobbek claims[9] that Herder's interpretation of Shakespeare gave inspiration to the young poets of the 'Sturm und Drang' period in Germany, and Hans Heinrich Borcherdt[10] discusses the relationship of Schiller's stage-adaptions of Shakespeare's plays to his own original plays. Finally, E. J. West[11] considers contemporary criticism of Sir Henry Irving's Shakespearian roles, and, in an attack on the actor for distorting his parts, says that "he could not or would not even attempt real interpretation"; but these strictures should not be taken too seriously—Irving, it seems, turned his roles into vehicles for his own character, rather than making himself a vehicle for the part, and many of the best actors have done this.

[1] 'Shakespeare an Ruhr und Rhein', *Shakespeare Jahrbuch*, XCI (1955), 238–50; this should be read in conjunction with Gerhard Schön's 'Vorwärts zu Shakespeare', *ibid.* pp. 233–7.

[2] Hans Knudsen, 'Shakespeare auf Berliner Bühnen 1945–55', and Harald Kunz, 'Wiener Shakespeare-Aufführungen 1952/54', *ibid.* pp. 251–9, 268–77.

[3] Hanns Braun, 'Shakespeare auf süddeutschen Bühnen nach dem Kriege', *ibid.* pp. 260–7.

[4] Wolfgang Stroedel, 'Bühnenbericht', *ibid.* pp. 217–24.

[5] Sub-titled *A Study of the Music and its Performance in the Original Productions of Seven Comedies* (University of Florida Press, 1955). [6] 'Pepys' Shakespeare Song', *Shakespeare Quarterly*, VI (Spring 1955), 159–70.

[7] 'The Case of the Decapitated Cast or *The Night-Walker* at Smock Alley', *Shakespeare Quarterly*, VI (Summer 1955), 275–96.

[8] 'Shakespeare's *Tempest* at Drury Lane During Garrick's Management', *Shakespeare Quarterly*, VII (Winter 1956), 1–7. [9] 'Herder und Shakespeare', *Shakespeare Jahrbuch*, XCI (1955), 25–51.

[10] 'Schillers Bühnenbearbeitungen Shakespearescher Werke', *ibid.* pp. 52–64.

[11] 'Irving in Shakespeare: Interpretation or Creation?', *Shakespeare Quarterly*, VI (Autumn 1955), 415–22.

3. TEXTUAL STUDIES

reviewed by JAMES G. MCMANAWAY

Working full time, Dr Henry Howard Furness, the founder of the New Variorum Shakespeare, could at the top of his powers edit a play in three years. His current successors must not only fit their editorial labours into full-time professional schedules but must grapple with a much more formidable volume of commentary and with textual problems of a complexity undreamed of in the leisurely days of Furness. In consequence, they live for many years with their plays and, as in the case of Matthew W. Black with *Richard II*,[1] achieve an admirable mastery of material and ripeness of scholarship. These qualities are the more desirable because of the editorial necessity to exclude all that is doubtful and to present the rest with severe compression. The only serious loss in the present volume is the skimping of textual and bibliographical material.

As Miss Alice Walker points out in her review,[2] it would have been wiser to base the text on Q1 (except for the deposition scene) than on F, and it was a mistake to omit the formal tabulation of variants in Q1 and the discussion of these readings. Black is to be commended for his zeal in collating multiple copies of the quartos of *Richard* and in particular for securing photostats of the Petworth copy of Q1 that had not previously been examined by scholars. As the editor notes, the Petworth copy is unique, for example, in having forme D (i) in the uncorrected state, with four readings that are corrected in the other three extant copies. Two of these readings (II, i, 194–6; ii, 35–6) are omissions of more than a line, the insertion of which by stop-press correction implies strongly that at least some of the proofs were read with reference to copy. Unfortunately, the editor overlooked four other variants in Petworth D (i). Its "At nothing" (II, ii, 14) is corrected to "With nothing"; "Shews" (II, ii, 21), to "Shew"; "in the" (II, ii, 82), to "on the"; and "his owne" (II, i, 176), to "my owne". This last alteration is a patent error:

Petworth (uncorrected)   About his mariadge, nor his owne disgrace,

Devonshire, Capell (corrected)   About his mariadge, nor my owne disgrace,

First Folio   About his marriage, nor my own disgrace

Failing to note it deprived the editor of restoring the true reading in a passage that has baffled all commentators.[3]

The two volumes of the New Arden Edition that have appeared this year illustrate the liberty now allowed the editors in their methods of handling the text. J. R. Brown, who bases his text of *The Merchant of Venice*[4] on Q1, has examined (he does not say collated) the six British copies and found only one press correction, that on G4.[5] He also collated thoroughly the copy of the

---

[1] *The Life and Death of King Richard the Second*, A New Variorum Edition (Philadelphia, 1955).

[2] *Shakespeare Quarterly*, VII (Spring 1956), 243–6.

[3] The four variants overlooked by Black in the Petworth copy were first noted by John Crow, who pointed them out to me.

[4] *The Merchant of Venice* (Methuen, 1955).

[5] Unfortunately he did not collate the Kemble-Devonshire-Huntington copy, which contains a variant on K2, as Furnivall pointed out in his Old-Spelling edition in 1909 and I noted in *Modern Language Notes*, LV, 634. The curious reading, "intergory" (for "intergotory" of other copies), may in the present state of knowledge represent either the uncorrected or the corrected state of the forme. And there may be other variants.

First Folio in the Shakespeare Birthplace Library and used copies of Qq2–3 and Ff2–4 in the same collection. There is reference to the compositors, about whom Brown had published earlier, and whose conservative workmanship warrants his reprinting of the Q text with a minimum of emendation. The copy for Q was, he cautiously hopes, very close to Shakespeare's manuscript. He is also cautious about the date of composition. Skirting the possibility that Shakespeare may have touched up an earlier version of his play, he is content to date *The Merchant* "after 30 July 1596 and before 22 July 1598". Nothing is said about the date of the additions from the prompt book that find their way into F, but it might be remembered that according to the late W. J. Lawrence the F stage direction at II, i, 'Flo[urish] Cornets', could not have been written before 1609.

In his edition of *Julius Caesar*,[1] T. S. Dorsch concerns himself primarily with annotation and commentary. He believes that a scribal transcript of Shakespeare's foul sheets was marked for prompt use and that this playhouse document was supplied to Jaggard as copy for F. He assumes that the two contradictory accounts of Portia's death represent an insertion by Shakespeare and the cancellation of the first version. His doubt whether the revision was made in the foul papers or the prompt book seems unnecessary. Greg (*The Shakespeare First Folio*, p. 291) is much nearer the truth when in discussing the anomalous speech heading "Boy" at IV, iii, 158, he suggests the possibility "that the insertion was more extensive than has been supposed, and if it was made in the prompt-book and not in the foul papers—as is likely in view of the retention of the deleted passage later—the whole episode may have escaped revision by the book-keeper". Since the text of *Caesar* is unusually clean, the edition suffers little by the editor's avoidance of bibliographical and textual problems, but it is disheartening to read (p. xxvi) that the text is based on a facsimile which the editor "assumes" is perfect but which was produced he knows not how (a letter to the editor or to the publisher would have elicited the information), and that there was no examination of an original Folio even to remove doubts about blurred or broken types (these were, however, checked in a different facsimile).

In a recent review,[2] Sir Walter Greg confessed to a feeling of depression because the book under discussion suggested "that the essential foundations for a critical edition of Shakespeare are more remote than one had allowed oneself to hope". Greg had in mind the tendency to hypothecate many sorts of dramatic manuscripts (including transcripts). Probably the textual and bibliographical situation will grow even more complicated until all the facts shall have been discovered and fitted into place.

Meanwhile, there is also dissatisfaction with what may be called semi-popular texts of Shakespeare. In a paper[3] read at the English Institute, Arthur Brown states some of the problems to be solved by the editor of a play in such editions as the New Cambridge, the New Arden, or the Yale. Everyone who uses a semi-popular edition will profit by Brown's essay. It should be required reading for every prospective editor—and reviewer. Brown advocates modernized spelling and light, modernized punctuation. Even if he accepts these principles, however, the

---

[1] *Julius Caesar* (Methuen, 1955).

[2] Of Fredson Bowers' *On Editing Shakespeare and the Elizabethan Dramatists*, *Shakespeare Quarterly*, VII (Winter 1956), 101–4.

[3] 'Editorial Problems in Shakespeare: Semi-Popular Editions', *Studies in Bibliography* (Charlottesville, Virginia, 1956), VIII, 15–26.

editor's path will not be roses all the way. There is nothing simple or easy in editing Shakespeare. As for textual apparatus, bibliographical technicalities, and annotation, most people will agree with Brown that, in the past, editors have been working "not with any class of reader clearly in mind, but in order to give expression to their own particular interests, their own private line of business in the great Shakespeare industry". "The result is editing for the sake of the editor, not the reader", and Brown adjures future editors to "reform it altogether".

The eighth title in the Shakespeare Problems Series is a two-volume discussion[1] by C. J. Sisson of the cruces in Shakespeare's text. Incidentally it provides an explanation and defence of the readings adopted in his recent edition of Shakespeare's *Works*. After a lifetime of reading documents in the Public Record Office, Sisson has a knowledge of Elizabethan idiom and a familiarity with Elizabethan handwriting that are perhaps unequalled by any previous editor. In consequence, his Introduction and his conjectures and emendations command the most respectful consideration. Many of the readings proposed or defended will, of course, occasion controversy, but that will hardly dismay the author, for though he quails before the decision between *Innogen* and *Imogen* (p. 16) he has not hesitated to challenge received opinions. He rejects, for instance, the transliterations by Maunde Thompson (*Willm̃ Shakp*) and Chambers (*Willm̃ Shaksp*) of Shakespeare's signature to his deposition in the Mountjoy case and produces evidence that the character following *k* is a generic mark of abbreviation, so that the signature is really *Willm̃ Shak̃* (pp. 4–5). The book should be read with Sisson's edition open on the table, but the Introduction is filled with the author's wit and wisdom, valuable alike to layman, scholar, and Shakespearian director.

In commenting upon the text of *Julius Caesar*, T. S. Dorsch (p. xxv) noted the inaccuracy of speaking of *the* Folio text of a play before the completion of C. K. Hinman's project of collating all the Folger Shakespeare Library copies. This work goes on apace, but in terms of the number of plays completed the progress may seem to the uninitiated to be like that of Hamlet's crab. Hinman's latest interim report[2] discloses that the finding of hitherto unnoticed typographical evidence has necessitated re-examination of many plays previously collated. This has not been a mere duplication of labour. Its first result—and others will be reported later—is the revolutionary discovery that the compositors of the First Folio did not begin at p. 1 and proceed to p. 2 and so on through the twelve pages of the six-leaf quires.

The fact is that no play in the First Folio was set in this way. Independently of both the number of compositors and the number of skeletons employed, the First Folio was set throughout, not by successive pages, but *by formes*. When the compositor had set what was to be page 1 of a given quire, that is, he then set page 12; then page 2 and page 11, then 3 and 10, and so on. Or, and in fact far more often, he first set what were to become pages 6 and 7, then set 5 and 8, then 4 and 9, and so on until he had done 1 and 12—and then proceeded to pages 6 and 7 of the following quire. Or, if two compositors were working, A set page 6 while B set page 7, then A set 5 while B set 8, and so on until A had set page 1 and B page 12, at which point B set page 6 of the next quire while A set page 7—and so on again, but with B now setting the pages, in reverse of their "normal" order, of the first half of the quire, ending with page 1, while A set the others, ending with page 12. The sequence of formes that was followed from

[1] *New Readings in Shakespeare* (Cambridge University Press, 1956).
[2] 'Cast-off Copy for the First Folio of Shakespeare', *Shakespeare Quarterly*, VI (Summer 1955), 259–73.

quire to quire was not always the same; nor, in quires set by two compositors, did each invariably set exactly the same number of pages as the other. On the contrary, there were many departures from what may be regarded as the usual—or perhaps we should say the ideal—method of working. But setting was nevertheless always by formes rather than by successive pages of text (p. 261).

This means that before the compositors began work on a play, someone had to cast off the copy, marking the exact word which would appear first on each page of each quire. The casting-off might be relatively easy if the copy were an unmarked quarto or a clean manuscript; it would be less easy if, as in the case of *Lear*, a quarto had been collated with a theatrical manuscript and were filled with interlineations and marginal corrections. It might be equally difficult if the copy were the author's foul sheets. But easy or difficult, someone did count off the copy, as the photographic illustrations of Hinman's lucid article prove conclusively. Sometimes there were miscalculations, which the compositors learned to deal with by spacing out or compressing their text. Such mechanical adjustments were not necessarily momentous. The changes, how-ever, were not always innocent—see for example the passage from *Antony* about which Hinman is certain "that the copy is not accurately reproduced in this speech" (p. 268).

Whether compositors, when much pressed for space, often solved their problems by tampering with the text in these or other "more drastic" ways I do not know. But there is abundant evidence that the amount of text that could be got comfortably into a page was frequently misjudged; and it would hardly be surprising if, in an already crowded page, something not considered essential were left out. Is this, rather than either imperfect copy or mere careless error on the part of the compositor, the real reason why Folio *Othello* lacks after its fifteenth line (ss3ᵛ a 37, page 310), to the prejudice of both sense and grammar, the part-line "And in conclusion" that appears in Q1? And can it be that some of the verse that is printed as prose in the Folio also represents, not difficult marginal scribblings in the copy, but only another way of dealing with a space problem—of "justifying", as it were, a page rather than a line? And were there still more serious tamperings with the text of the copy—some of them, perhaps, undertaken during the casting-off process itself and so also by other persons than compositors? (p. 269).

The crowding and spacing-out of text constitute what Hinman calls presumptive evidence that copy was cast-off. His absolute proof rests upon the identification of some hundreds of individual types that appear throughout the Folio. A sample of this evidence is also given in photographic reproduction.

The goal towards which Hinman is pushing is an exact account of how each page (each column of each page, perhaps) of each play in the First Folio was put in type, the identity of the com-positor, and the order of the printing. The immediate results of the investigations thus far are, first, to prove triumphantly the validity and utility of this kind of study; second, to focus atten-tion on the collating machine, without which such research is impossible;[1] third, to demonstrate, once and for all it may be hoped, the wisdom and uncanny foresight of Henry Clay Folger in assembling so many copies of the First Folio in one place; fourth, to stimulate a quantity of

[1] With machines now in the British Museum, the Bodleian, the Houghton Library, the library of the University of Virginia, and the library of the University of Minnesota, it may be hoped that cognate studies of the First Folio and of other books will be undertaken.

studies of printing methods in Shakespeare's day, especially of compositorial habits; and fifth, to force a reappraisal of the now shaky editorial position about the nature of the copy used in printing each play in the First Folio.

Not long before his untimely death, Philip Williams read at the English Institute a survey[1] of current work on Shakespeare's text that is notable for its flashes of insight and for the questions it asks. What does it mean, for instance, that the compositors of the First Folio perpetuated the seemingly indiscriminate variations between the *oh* and *o* spellings of the quarto of *Troilus* but agreed to *o* in *Julius Caesar* and *oh* in *The Comedy of Errors*? Is it permissible to draw inferences about composite authorship of *1 Henry VI* from the fact that in Acts I and II compositor *A*, who is conservative in treatment of his copy, spells *Burgundy* but in Act III (coinciding with the introduction of scene division) always sets *Burgonie*? Or is it dangerous to go further than the supposition that the copy was (for whatever reason) in two or more hands? As for *Henry VIII*, which is often parcelled out between Shakespeare and Fletcher on the basis of *'em* and *them* spellings, how heavily must the statistics be discounted because compositor *B* appears to have felt no compunction about normalizing the spellings of the pronoun in the seven pages he set? Williams gives several other examples to drive home his point about the indispensability of compositor analysis in textual studies.

Another kind of bibliographical evidence that Williams alludes to is a remarkable anticipation of Hinman's discovery about the counting off of copy in the printing of the First Folio (p. 13). What a pity he did not live to follow up some of the clues so lavishly sprinkled throughout the essay!

Continuing the work of J. R. Brown (see above, p. 152) on the compositors who set *The Merchant* (1600) for James Roberts, Paul L. Cantrell and George W. Williams have made a study[2] of the 1600 quarto of *Titus Andronicus* that they also set. As might be expected, Q 1594 of *Titus*, of which Q 1600 is a reprint, exerted an influence on the compositors that is markedly different from that of the manuscript copy for *Merchant*, so that Cantrell and Williams had to devise new tests for the identification of each man's stint. Though their results are incomplete because of the tenuous nature of some of the evidence, others will profit from their findings and by knowledge of the new varieties of evidence they have employed. They conclude with a plea for "the accumulation of additional knowledge of the compositorial habits of *X* and *Y* by examination of other works, preferably plays, set by these two men, either together or singly", and for further research upon *Titus*, *Merchant*, and *Hamlet* (Q2).

Other *Hamlet* studies are even now in progress. In the first of two instalments,[3] Fredson Bowers essays to discover the precise relation between the 'Bad' and 'Good' Quartos. Building upon his earlier work on the printing of *Hamlet*, Q2, Bowers attempts to prove that bibliographical links between the two quartos are so close and continuous in sheets B, C, and D of Q2 as to require belief that Q1 was consulted constantly or that an annotated copy may actually have been used as printer's copy. This section of the text, constituting Act I, was put into type by compositor *X*, many of whose characteristics are now a matter of record. Bowers observes that a number of words that are spelled in Q1 in a form characteristic of *X* appear in Q2 with

[1] 'New Approaches to Textual Problems in Shakespeare', *Studies in Bibliography*, VIII, 3–14.
[2] 'Roberts' Compositors in *Titus Andronicus* Q2', *Studies in Bibliography*, VIII, 27–38.
[3] 'The Textual Relation of Q2 to Q1 *Hamlet* (1)', *Studies in Bibliography*, VIII, 39–66.

different spelling, and he attributes the change to the influence of MS. copy. Even stronger proof of MS. influence is supplied by such a passage as I, v, 55–7. Q2 reads:

> So but though to a radiant Angle linckt,
> Will sort it selfe in a celestiall bed
> And pray on garbage.

Angle linckt (for *Angel linked*) shows that Q1 was presumably consulted:

> So Lust, though to a radiant angle linckt,
> Would fate it selfe from a celestiall bedde,
> And prey on garbage:

The Folio supports *Lust* and *sate* (misprinted *fate* in Q1) and corrects *from* to *in*. Here it is almost impossible to believe that the compositor was using other than manuscript copy. The conclusion of Bowers' case will be awaited eagerly.[1]

Encouraged, perhaps, by Miss Walker's advocacy of annotated quartos as copy for the First Folio, Andrew S. Cairncross examines the printing of *Henry V*.[2] He argues "that the First Folio Text of *Henry V* was set up, so far as that was found feasible, from one or more corrected exemplars of the bad quarto". Actually, he believes that a heavily annotated copy of Q3 served as copy but that in emergencies leaves were abstracted from a copy of Q2 to facilitate type setting. He cites bibliographical links (p. 71) and particularly the spelling of speech prefixes (p. 72) to show that the introduction of passages from the playhouse manuscript is accompanied by changes in the spelling that persist only until Q copy is resumed. The facsimiles that Cairncross reproduces to show how annotation might have been effected and how it may explain certain redundancies in the text and other anomalies are impressive. Upon one thing he is insistent: that the quartos were annotated by Jaggard in the printing house. If this be true, what manuscript supplied the new passages of text? Not the prompt book, surely; on occasion the prompt book was taken to Stationers' Hall to permit entry of a play for publication, but there is no evidence that the King's Men permitted any of their prompt books to go to a printer. If it was a transcript that Jaggard used to annotate the quartos, why did his compositors not use it as copy?

Miss Walker has suggested that Jaggard's shop had a strong preference for printed copy, and Cairncross agrees. He has gone through several of the Bad Quartos in search of their possible influence on the First Folio. He is confident that earlier theories, such as those about the use of marked quartos as prompt books, the replacement of lost or worn leaves of a prompt book or other theatrical manuscript with marked pages abstracted from a quarto, and the annotation of quartos by Heminges and Condell (or their agents) for Jaggard's use, are based on misreading of the evidence. The substitution of quartos for manuscript copy was the act of Jaggard. The implication is that Heminges and Condell provided manuscript copy and were unaware of Jaggard's substitution. But in some cases, *Richard III* and *Lear* for example, one copy of a quarto seems not to have sufficed. Cairncross attacks the idea of the use of *one* physical copy of

---

[1] Elsewhere ('Hamlet's "Sallied" or "Solid" Flesh: A Bibliographical Case-History', *Shakespeare Survey*, 9 (1956), 44–8), Bowers establishes that the correct reading at *Hamlet* I, ii, 129 is 'sallied', a rare variant of 'sullied'.

[2] 'Quarto Copy for Folio *Henry V*', *Studies in Bibliography*, VIII, 67–93.

a quarto. In the case of *Lear*,[1] P. A. Daniel erred in thinking that Q1 was the only printed text used in setting Folio *Lear*, as Miss Doran pointed out several years ago; the agreements of F with Q1 and Q2 "run in sequences, which are mutually exclusive, and coincide, as we should expect, with the pages of one quarto or the other". The use of more than one copy of a quarto of *Lear* would have been extremely difficult to prove, had not chance provided (we may suppose) a copy each of Q1 and Q2 instead of two copies of either quarto. We still need to discover what manuscript was collated with Qq and exactly where the scribal work took place (whether in the playhouse or at the printer's). It seems not unlikely that printed copy may have been preferred above manuscript, not only because composition would be swifter, but also because casting off copy would be easier.[2]

Some years ago J. S. G. Bolton explained some curious readings in the second quarto of *Titus Andronicus* by showing that they were anonymous reconstructions of passages in the worn or otherwise mutilated copy of Q1 that was used in setting Q2. The same kind of physical defect in copy may well, in his opinion,[3] be the reason for the omission or corruption of a number of passages in the quartos of six plays, *Hamlet, Othello, Lear, Troilus, Richard III*, and *2 Henry IV*. Bolton's assumption is that if a leaf of manuscript copy is seriously defective at top or bottom, one or more words or lines on each side may be lost or rendered illegible, and that in consequence there are likely to be omissions or corruptions in the quarto at intervals of forty to fifty lines. This condition is precisely what one finds more frequently than would be expected. Some of the omissions occur, not in pairs, but in three's or five's, as if two or more consecutive leaves had been defective. Bolton avoids dogmatism by admitting that any given passage may have been corrupted in some other fashion, as by memorial reconstruction, and he gives warning that more than half of the omitted passages do not occur in pairs. Even so, his table of omissions that occur at intervals of forty to fifty lines is long enough to command serious attention.

A new factor in the making or marring of the First Folio text is introduced by J. K. Walton,[4] namely the collator, whose variable conscientiousness and accuracy in collating the quartos of *Richard III*[5] and *Lear* with playhouse manuscripts account for many of the textual puzzles. That the collator was a frail human will be readily conceded, and it may be that his efficiency varied from hour to hour and also that he trusted his memory unduly; but Walton's hypothesis is by its nature very difficult to prove conclusively. There should be collateral studies to discover if possible whether the same collator worked on other plays, and how.

Ever since Heminges and Condell warned purchasers of the First Folio against "stolne, and surreptitious copies" of some of the quartos, there has been controversy about their precise meaning. Most people now agree that some of the pre-Folio quartos are 'Bad', and there is general agreement about the source and nature of the badness. But many points are still in dispute; so Leo Kirschbaum's treatise,[6] the result of his first-hand examination of the records of

---

[1] 'The Quartos and the Folio Text of *King Lear*', *Review of English Studies*, n.s. VI (July 1955), 252–8.

[2] Cairncross assumes that compositor B worked alone on *Lear*, but it has been suggested that another man also had a hand. Proof of F's dependence on both Q1 and Q2 predisposes me to think there were two compositors, and I should like to know whether the compositorial pattern matches the Qq pattern.

[3] 'Worn Pages in Shakespearian Manuscripts', *Shakespeare Quarterly*, VII (Spring 1956), 176–82.

[4] *The Copy for the Folio Text of Richard III with a Note on the Copy for the Folio Text of King Lear* (Auckland, New Zealand: The Pilgrim Press, 1955).   [5] Walton maintains that only Q3 was used in printing F.

[6] *Shakespeare and the Stationers* (Columbus, Ohio, 1955).

the Stationers' Company, is a welcome addition to the literature of the subject. He is certainly right that there is no necessary connexion between the Goodness or Badness of a play text and the validity of the publisher's copyright—the Stationers had little if any concern for the quality of a text that was to be entered for publication. There is grave doubt, on the other hand, about Kirschbaum's belief that publication, and only publication, established copyright. The book must be read for the wealth of detail it contains about the publication of Shakespeare's plays and of all the other plays of the King's Men that got into print. Some of the details are subject to different interpretations than those given by Kirschbaum, but he makes provocative suggestions about the plays that cannot be ignored.

The third section of Dover Wilson's 'The New Way with Shakespeare's Texts'[1] tells how and why three pages of the manuscript play of *Sir Thomas More* are so important for the study of Shakespeare. The story, familiar enough to specialists, deserves to be known by all readers of Shakespeare, and it is told with zest by one of the men whose good fortune it was to establish the probability that Hand *D* is that of William Shakespeare. It is entertaining and instructive for the layman, because of the personal charm of the author and his manner of presentation, and is important to scholars for the anecdotes it preserves.

[1] 'In Sight of Shakespeare's Manuscripts', *Shakespeare Survey*, 9 (1956), 69–80.

BOOKS RECEIVED

[Inclusion of a book in this list does not preclude its review in a subsequent volume]

AMPHLETT, H. *Who was Shakespeare? A New Enquiry* (London: Heinemann, 1955).

ARNOLD, PAUL. *Ésotérisme de Shakespeare* (Paris: Mercure de France, 1955).

BRADBROOK, M. C. *The Growth and Structure of Elizabethan Comedy* (London: Chatto & Windus, 1955).

DÍESTE, EDUARDO and CACERES, ESTHER DE. *21 Sonetos de William Shakespeare*. Translation and Commentary (Montevideo: Editorial Independencia, 1944).

Escritura, vol. 8, December 1949 (Montevideo: Gaceta Comercial, 1950).

GOLDSMITH, ROBERT HILLIS. *Wise Fools in Shakespeare* (Michigan State University Press, 1955).

HARBAGE, ALFRED. *Theatre for Shakespeare*. The Alexander Lectures, 1955 (Toronto University Press; London: Geoffrey Cumberlege, 1956).

HELSZTYŃSKI, STANISŁAW (Editor) and TARNAWSKI, WŁADYSŁAW (Translator). *Hamlet*. Biblioteka Narodowa, no. 20, Series II (Wrocław: Ossoliński, 1955).

HOFFMAN, CALVIN. *The Man who was Shakespeare*. (London: Max Parrish, 1955).

KITTO, H. D. F. *Form and Meaning in Drama* (London: Methuen, 1956).

LAQUEUR, RICHARD. *Shakespeares Dramatische Konzeption* (Tübingen: Max Niemeyer Verlag, 1955).

LEVER, J. W. *The Elizabethan Love Sonnet* (London: Methuen, 1956).

MEADER, WILLIAM G. *Courtship in Shakespeare. Its Relation to the Tradition of Courtly Love* (Columbia University Press; London: Geoffrey Cumberlege, 1954).

PALMER, RALPH GRAHAM. *Seneca's De Remediis Fortuitorum and the Elizabethans* (Chicago: Institute of Elizabethan Studies; Kendal: Titus Wilson and Son Ltd, 1953).

PARKER, M. D. H. *The Slave of Life* (London: Chatto & Windus, 1955).

PIRIZ, ROBERTO BULA. *William Shakespeare 1564–1616* (Montevideo: La Casa del Estudiante, 1952).

PURDOM, C. B. *Harley Granville Barker* (London: Rockliff, 1955).

SALTER, F. M. *Mediaeval Drama in Chester*. The Alexander Lectures, 1953–4 (Toronto University Press; London: Geoffrey Cumberlege, 1955).

SANVIC, ROMAIN. *Le Théâtre Élisabéthain*. Collections Lebègue et Nationale (Bruxelles: Office de Publicité, S.A., 1955).

Shakespeare Jahrbuch, Band 91 (Heidelberg: Quelle & Meyer, 1955).

Shakespeare Newsletter, vol. v (Pembroke, North Carolina, 1955).

Shakespeare Quarterly, vols. VI and VII (New York: Shakespeare Association of America, 1955–6).

SHAKESPEARE, WILLIAM. *Julius Caesar*. New Arden Shakespeare. Edited by T. S. Dorsch (London: Methuen, 1955).

SHAKESPEARE, WILLIAM. *The Life and Death of King Richard the Second*. New Variorum Shakespeare. Edited by M. W. Black (Philadelphia, 1955).

SISSON, C. J. *New Readings in Shakespeare*, 2 vols. Shakespeare Problems Series, General Editor, J. Dover Wilson (Cambridge University Press, 1956).

TINLING, CRISTINE I. *Perfiles de Algunos Personajes de Shakespeare*. Publicado por la Liga Nacional contra el Alcoholismo (Montevideo: Impresora Uruguay, S.A., 1937).

WALTON, J. K. *The Copy for the Folio Text of Richard III with a Note on the Copy for the Folio Text of King Lear*. Auckland University College Monograph Series, no. 1 (Auckland: The Pilgrim Press, 1955).

WILLCOCK, GLADYS D. *Language and Poetry in Shakespeare's Early Plays*. Annual Shakespeare Lecture of the British Academy, 1954 (London: Geoffrey Cumberlege, 1955).

INDEX

INDEX

INDEX

INDEX

INDEX

INDEX

INDEX

Skoda, Albin, 119
Skoumal, Aloys, 117
Smart, J. S., 14, 15, 24 n.
Smith, D. Nichol, 38 n.
Smith, William ("Gentleman" Smith), 72–3
Smith, W. D., 3
Smyth, Paul, 75
Söderwall, Margreta, 121
Soellner, Rolf, 146 n.
Somersalmi, Urho, 117
Sophocles, 36
Southern, Richard, 85, 89 n.
Speaight, Robert, 59 n.
   Nature in Shakespearian Tragedy reviewed, 137–8
Speed, John, *History of Great Britain*, 29
Spence, Joseph, 20
Spencer, Terence, 1
Spenser, Edmund, 17, 60
   Complaints, 25 n.
   Faerie Queene, 20
   Shepherd's Calendar, 20
Spira, Theodor, 142
Sprague, A. C., 149
Sprenger, James, *see* Kramer, Heinrich
Spurgeon, Caroline, 8
Stamm, Rudolf, 143, 146, 147
Stanyhurst, Richard, translation of Virgil's *Aeneid*, 30
Statius, 48
Steiger, André, 118
Stempel, Daniel, 10, 140–1
Stevens, Allan, 150
Stewart, J. I. M., 8, 98, 106 n.
Stirling, Brents, 8, 9
Stoedler, E., 5
Stoker, Willard, 125
Stoll, E. E., 6–7, 98, 99, 106 n.
Stone, George Winchester Jr., 150
Strachan, Bishop John, 111
Stratford Theatre, Connecticut, 149
Stratford Theatre, Ontario, Canada, 85, 89 n., 111–14, 149
Stringer, Michael, 85
Stroedel, Wolfgang, 119, 150 n.
Stroux, Karlheinz, 119
Stull, J. S., 10, 141
Suckling, Sir John, 14
Suetonius, 31, 35, 38
Summers, Montague, 88 n.
Sussex's Men, *see under* Theatre, Elizabethan
Swan Theatre, *see under* Theatre, Elizabethan
Swinburne, Algernon Charles, 50
Sylvius, Aeneas, 145

Tacitus, 29, 31, 35, 38 n.
Tadema, Sir Lawrence Alma-, 75
Tagg, Alan, 131
Talma, F. J., 74

Tamberlani, Carlo, 120
Taming of a Shrew, The, 80, 83, 87 n.
Tarnawski, Władysław, 120, 142
Tate, Nahum, 27
Taylor, E. M. M., 140
Taylor, Ray, 125
Tennyson, Alfred Lord, 15–16, 17
Theatre, Elizabethan:
  recent work on reviewed, 146–8
  Companies
    Chamberlain's men, 150
    Derby's men, 69
    Pembroke's men, 69
    Sussex's men, 69, 72
  Theatres
    Blackfriars, 87 n.
    Curtain, 87 n.
    Fortune, 80
    Globe, 75, 77, 84, 87 n., 88 n., 89 n., 114, 148
    Red Bull, 77, 87 n.
    Rose, 77
    Swan, 77, 80, 84, 86 n., 87 n.
Theatres
  Birmingham Repertory Theatre, 124
  Covent Garden Theatre, 72, 73, 74
  Drury Lane Theatre, 72, 73, 75, 76, 88 n., 150
  Her Majesty's Theatre, 75
  Mermaid Theatre, 85, 89 n.
  Old Vic Theatre, 123–5, 130, 133, 148, 149
  Shakespeare Memorial Theatre, Stratford-upon-Avon, 123–4, 126, 133, 148, 149
  Stratford Theatre, Connecticut, 149
  Stratford Theatre, Ontario, Canada, 85, 89 n., 111–14, 149
  See also under Productions of Shakespeare's plays
Theobald, Lewis, 28
Theotokas, George, 119
Thesiger, Ernest, 129
Thompson, Sir Edward Maunde, 153
Thomson, J. A. K., 6, 15, 16, 18, 25 n., 59 n.
Thomson, James (1700–48), version of *Coriolanus*, 72
Thurston, John, 73
Tieck, L., 119
Tiepolo, Giovanni Battista, 75
Tillyard, E. M. W., 3, 40, 44, 49 n.
Titian, Vecellio, 71, 76 n.
Titus and Vespasian, 2
Tolman, A. H., 7
Tonson, J., 72, 76 n.
Tooke, Andrew, 20
Torelli, Giacomo, 72, 76 n.
Tournier, Jacques, 118
Trajan, Emperor, 31
Traversi, D. A., 11
Tree, Sir Herbert Beerbohm, 75, 149, 150
Trollope, Anthony, 33

INDEX